T0347374

A Global Security Triangle

This book considers the interactions between Africa, Asia and Europe, analysing the short and long-term strategies various states have adopted in their external relations.

The urgency attached to the agenda of international terrorism and human and drug trafficking has forced the European Union into new co-operation with Africa and Asia. These inter-regional relations have taken on new dimensions in the context of contemporary international politics framed by new security challenges, and new competitive forces, particularly from Asia. This book provides both conceptual and empirical arguments to offer an innovative perspective on the EU as a global actor. It demonstrates how these three regions interact politically and economically to address global challenges as well as global opportunities, and thus provides an assessment of the multilateralism which the EU clearly stated in its Security Strategy paper. Addressing a broad range of topical issues, the book features chapters on European security; European migration policy; the African Union and its peace and security policy; terrorism and international security; China and its fast-growing global role; India, the biggest democracy in the world; and the impact of Asian economic growth on the global economy. Further it compares the different backgrounds, forms and priorities of regional integrations.

A Global Security Triangle will be of interest to all scholars of European politics, security studies, African and Asian studies, and International Relations.

Valeria Bello is a Marie Curie Fellow at the IBEI – Institut Barcelona d'Estudis Internacionals. **Belachew Gebrewold** is Lecturer in International Relations at Helmut Schmidt University, University of the Federal Armed Forces Hamburg, Germany.

Routledge/GARNET series: Europe in the World

Edited by David Armstrong
University of Exeter, UK
and
Karoline Postel-Vinay
Centre for International Studies and Research (CERI), France

The Routledge GARNET series, *Europe in the World*, provides a forum for innovative research and current debates emanating from the research community within the GARNET Network of Excellence. GARNET is a Europe-wide network of forty-three research institutions and scholars working collectively on questions around the theme of 'Global Governance, Regionalisation and Regulation: the Role of the EU', and funded by the European Commission under the sixth Framework Programme for Research.

A Global Security Triangle

European, African and Asian interaction

Edited by Valeria Bello and
Belachew Gebrewold

LONDON AND NEW YORK

First published 2010
by Routledge
2 Park Square, Milton Park, Abingdon, Oxon OX14 4RN

Simultaneously published in the USA and Canada
by Routledge
711 Third Ave, New York, NY 10017

Routledge is an imprint of the Taylor & Francis Group, an informa business

First issued in paperback 2013

Typeset in Garamond by Wearset Ltd, Boldon, Tyne and Wear

British Library Cataloguing in Publication Data
A catalogue record for this book is available from the British Library

Library of Congress Cataloging in Publication Data
A global security triangle : European, African and Asian interaction /
edited by Valeria Bello and Belachew Gebrewold.
p. cm. – (Routledge/Garnet series)
Includes bibliographical references and index.
1. Security, International. 2. Regionalism (International
organization) I. Bello, Valeria. II. Gebrewold-Tochalo, Belachew,
1968–JZ5588.G586 2009
355′.033–dc22
2009017567

ISBN13: 978-0-415-49657-5 (hbk)
ISBN13: 978-0-203-86687-0 (ebk)
ISBN13: 978-0-415-84799-5 (pbk)

Contents

Illustrations

Figures

Tables

Contributors

Valeria Bello has a Ph.D. in sociology and political sociology, and is currently a Marie Curie Fellow at the IBEI – Institut Barcelona d'Estudis Internacionals. She has also been a researcher at the Jean Monnet European Centre of the University of Trento (Italy) since October 2003. At the University of Trento she has assisted courses in the Sociology of International Relations and the Sociology of European Integration at both Bachelor and Master levels. Her research interests include: European identity, interethnic relations, the international relations of the EU, European civil society and regional governance. Her main publications include: 'A European model of public sphere: towards a networked governance model', (in collaboration with C. Bee) in J. Harrison and B. Wessels (eds) *Mediating Europe: New media, Mass Communications and the European public sphere*, Oxford: Berghahn Books, 2009; 'Dinamiche di costruzione dell'identità: un' indagine sul Comitato Economico e Sociale Europeo', in C. Bee and R. Scartezzini (eds) *La costruzione sociale dell'Europa: europeizzazione, identità e società civile*, Soveria Mannelli: Rubettino, 2010; 'Europeanisation and social identity: an interpretative analysis carried out on Italian civil society representatives', Paper presented at the 38th World Congress of the International Institute of Sociology, 26–30 June 2008, Budapest, Hungary, 2008, Online Working Papers Jean Monnet European Centre – Università degli Studi di Trento, 2008.

Stefan Brüne is a Professor of International Relations and Social Geography working with the Intergovernmental Authority on Development in Djibouti. Specialising in foreign policy and development-related issues studies, he has taught in universities in Addis Ababa, Osnabrück, Hamburg, Paris (Sciences – Po), Nancy, Eichstätt and Prague. Having teaching and research experience in African, Asian and Latin American countries, as a former series editor of *Jahrbuch Dritte Welt* and *Nord-Süd aktuell*, his main Africa-related publications include *Africa and Europe: Relations of Two Continents in Transition* (with Winrich Kühne and Joachim Betz, 1994), *Die französische Afrikapolitik* (1996), 'Europas Außenbeziehungen und die Zukunft der Entwicklungspolitik' (2005), 'Die autonomen Militärmission der EU in Afrika. Eine erste Bilanz' in H. G. Justenhoven and H. G. Ehrhart (eds) *Intervention im Kongo. Eine kritische Analyse der Befriedungspolitik von UN und EU* (2008).

Mary Farrell teaches courses in European integration and international politics at the University of Greenwich, London, is associate Senior Research Fellow at the Centre d'Etudes et de Recherches Internationales, Paris, and editor of the Routledge GARNET series 'Europe in the World'. Her research interests include the international relations of the EU, EU–Africa co-operation, regional integration, and regional and global governance.

Paolo Foradori is Adjunct Professor of the Sociology of European Integration and International Relations at the University of Trento, where he is also Executive Director of the MA Programme in Peace-building and Conflict Resolution. His research interests include conflict analysis, European foreign and security policy, and international relations theory. His most recent publications are *Managing a Multilevel Foreign Policy: the EU in International Affairs* (ed. with P. Rosa and R. Scartezzini, 2007) and *Caschi blu e processi di democratizzazione* (2007).

Belachew Gebrewold is Assistant Professor of African Politics at the University of Innsbruck, Austria. His key research areas are peace, conflict and violence and the contemporary Euro-African relations. His publications include *Africa and Fortress Europe: Threats and Opportunities* (ed., 2007); 'Defining genocide as epistemological violence', *Journal of Peace Review* (2008), 'The civilizing process of globalization and African integration' in A. Exenberger and A. Eberharter (eds) *Globalisierung und Gerechtigkeit* (2007), 'European migration policy towards Africa: a balancing act between humanitarianism and fortress Europe' in A. Pelinka and F. Plasser (eds) *Festschrift für Heinrich Neisser* (2007), 'Civil militias and the militarization of society in the Horn of Africa' in D. Francis (ed.) *Civil Militias: Africa's Intractable Security Menace?* (2005).

Emil J. Kirchner is Professor of European Studies and Jean Monnet Chair at the University of Essex, Colchester. His main interests include European security policy, regional and global governance and cross-border co-operation. His publications include *EU Security Governance* (co-authored, 2007), *Global Security Governance* (co-edited, 2007), *Studies on Policies and Policy Processes of the European Union* (co-authored, 2003) and 'The new security threats in Europe: theory and evidence' (co-authored), *European Foreign Affairs Review* (2002).

Dirk Kohnert, economist, is Deputy Director of the Institute of African Affairs at the German Institute of Global and Area Studies, Hamburg, and since 1991 managing editor of the scholarly journal *Afrika Spectrum*. Previously he was lecturer in development planning and senior development expert in several African countries. He has published numerous books and articles in learned journals on economic, social and cultural development, planning and evaluation.

Ludger Kühnhardt is Managing Director of the Centre for European Integration Studies (ZEI) at Friedrich Wilhelm University, Bonn. Between 1991 and 1997 he was Professor of Political Science at Freiburg University, where he also served as dean of his faculty. He was speechwriter for Germany's Federal President Richard von Weizsäcker and visiting professor at various universities around the world. His publications include *Beyond Divisions and After: Essays on Democracy, the Germans and Europe* (1996), *Kontinent Europa* (with Hans-Gert Pöttering, 1998; Czech edition 2000), *Constituting Europe: Identity, Institution-building and the Search for a Global Role* (2003) and *European Union: the Second Founding. The Changing Rationale of European Integration* (2008).

Martin Malek obtained a Ph.D. in Political Science at Vienna State University in 1991. Since 1997 he has been a civilian researcher at the Institute of Peace Support and Conflict Management at the National Defence Academy, Vienna. He has occupied several internships in research institutes in Germany, Russia, Ukraine and the US. His main areas of expertise are state failure theory, theories of ethnic conflict, security and military policy in the Commonwealth of Independent States (especially Russia, Ukraine, South Caucasus) and energy policy in Eurasia. He is the author or editor of several books and some 250 articles published in thirteen countries.

Philomena Murray is Associate Professor in the School of Social and Political Sciences and Director of the Contemporary Europe Research Centre at the University of Melbourne, Australia. She holds a personal Jean Monnet Chair (*ad personam*). Her research interests are in European integration analysis, EU–Australia relations, EU–Asia relations, EU governance and comparative regional integration. She was joint editor of the *Australian Journal of Political Science* 1996–98 and is a member of the editorial and international advisory boards of several international journals. Her book *Australia and the European Superpower* (2005) was the first to examine Australia's relationship with the EU in twenty-five years. Her edited volumes include *Europe and Asia: Regions in Flux* (2008) and, with L. Holmes, *Citizenship and Identity in Europe* (1999) and *Europe: Rethinking the Boundaries* (1998).

Heinrich Neisser is Professor of the Politics of European Integration in the Department of Political Science at the University of Innsbruck. He was the second President of the Austrian National Assembly. His key research areas are the political system of the EU and the European Constitution.

Liselotte Odgaard is an associate professor at the Institute of Strategy, Royal Danish Defence College, and was a residential fellow at the Woodrow Wilson International Center for Scholars in Washington DC from September 2008 to May 2009. Her research includes numerous contributions to the field of Asia-Pacific security, including *The Balance of*

Power in Asia-Pacific Security: US–China Policies on Regional Order (2007) and *Maritime Security between China and South East Asia: Conflict and Co-operation in the Making of Regional Order* (2002).

Anton Pelinka has been Professor of Political Science and National-ism Studies at the Central European University, Budapest, since 2006. Between 1975 and 2006 he was Professor of Political Science at the University of Innsbruck. His key research focus is comparative politics, theory of democracy. He has published extensively, including *Austria: Out of the Shadows of the Past* (1998), *Politics of the Lesser Evil: Leadership, Democracy and Jaruzelski's Poland* (1999), *The Haider Phenomenon in Austria* (ed. with Ruth Wodak, 2002) and *Democracy Indian Style: Subhas Chandra Bose and the Creation of India's Political Culture* (2003).

Maximilian B. Rasch obtained his Ph.D. in government from the University of Essex. He was a researcher at the Jean Monnet European Centre of Excellence there and at the United Nations University Programme for Comparative Regional Integration Studies, Bruges. He now works at NATO headquarters as a fellow of the postgraduate programme in international affairs.

Michael Schulz is Senior Lecturer in Peace and Development Research, Head of the Regional Studies Section and Director of the Centre for Middle East Studies in the School of Global Studies at Göteborg University. He has published extensively on the Israeli–Palestinian conflict and the Middle East. His publications include 'Reconciliation through education: experiences from the Israeli–Palestinian conflict', *Journal of Peace Education* (2008), 'Hamas between Sharia rule and democracy' in R. Amer, A. Swain and J. Öjendal (eds) *Peace Building and Globalization* (2007), 'The intervention of regional organizations in peace building' (with Rodrigo Tavares) in Philippe De Lombaerde (ed.) *Indicators of Regional Integration* (2006) and *Democratization and Civil Society in the Middle East: Case Studies of Palestinian Self-rule Areas and Iraqi Kurdistan* (2006).

Acknowledgements

This book is the result of discussions that took place between its authors, first during meetings of the Garnet Network of Excellence, and then at the Jean Monnet International Summer School, held in September 2007 in Trento (Italy) and Innsbruck (Austria). The Summer School, on 'European External Relations with Africa and Asian Areas', was jointly organised by the Jean Monnet European Centre of the University of Trento and the Institute of Political Science of the University of Innsbruck.

First, we would like to thank the European Commission, DG Education and Culture, which has made these exchanges of knowledge possible through its support. Second, we must thank Professor Riccardo Scartezzini, Director of the Jean Monnet Centre of Excellence of the University of Trento, which has put considerable financial and human resources into the realisation of this book. His comments on the whole text have been enormously helpful.

Special thanks go to Heinrich Neisser and Günther Pallaver of the University of Innsbruck for their collaboration on the organisation of the Jean Monnet International Summer School, to Henriette Lundblad Andersen for commenting on Liselotte Odgaard's chapter, to Andrew Hunt for language revision of non-English authors' chapters and to Ulrich Sandner for style editing.

V.B.
B.G.

Abbreviations

ACP	Africa, the Caribbean and the Pacific
AEC	African Economic Community
AI	Amnesty International
AMU	Arab Maghreb Union
APRM	African Peer Review Mechanism
ASEAN	Association of South East Asian Nations
ASEM	Asia–Europe Meeting
AU	African Union
BJP	Bharatiya Janata Party (Indian People's Party)
BTC	Baku–Tbilisi–Ceyhan
BTE	Baku–Tbilisi–Erzurum
CACR	Central Asia and the Caspian Region
CAERT	African Centre for Study and Research on Terrorism
CARICOM	Caribbean Community
CARIFORUM	Caribbean Forum of African, Caribbean and Pacific States
CEMAC	Commission de la Communauté Economique et Monétaire de l'Afrique Centrale (Economic and Monetary Community of Central Africa)
CEN-SAD	Community of Sahelo-Saharan States
CFSP	Common Foreign and Security Policy
CIS	Commonwealth of Independent States
CNP	Congolese National Police
COMESA	Common Market for East and Southern Africa
COPPS	Co-ordinating Office for Palestinian Policing Support
COREPER	Committee of Permanent Representatives
CTBT	Comprehensive Test Ban Treaty
CTR	Co-operative Threat Reduction
CUD	Coalition for Unity and Democracy
DDRR	disarmament, demobilisation, reintegration and reinsertion
DDRRR	disarmament, demobilisation, repatriation, reintegration and resettlement
DM	Deutsche Mark (Deutschmark)
DPRK	Democratic People's Republic of Korea

DRC	Democratic Republic of Congo
E3/EU	EU3 Ministers: France/Germany/Great Britain/High Representative of the CFSP
EAC	East African Community
EBA	everything but arms
EC	European Community
ECA	Economic Commission for Africa
ECCAS	Economic Community of Central African States
ECOWAS	Economic Community of West African States
ECSC	European Coal and Steel Community
EDF	European Development Fund
EEC	European Economic Community
EMCCA	Economic and Monetary Community of Francophone Central Africa
ENP	European Neighbourhood Policy
EPA	Economic Partnership Agreement
EPG	Eminent Persons' Group
EPRDF	Ethiopian People's Revolutionary Democratic Front
ESDP	European Security and Defence Policy
ESS	European Strategic Security
ETC	Ethiopian Calendar
EU	European Union
EUC	Council of the European Union
EUEOM	EU Election Observation Mission
EUFOR RD Congo	EU Force in the Democratic Republic of Congo
EUPOL Kinshasa	EU Police Mission in Kinshasa
EUPOL RD Congo	EU Police Mission in the Democratic Republic of Congo
EURODAC	European Dactyloscopie
EUSEC DRC	EU security sector reform mission in the Democratic Republic of the Congo
EUSR	European Union Special Representative
FAO	Food and Agriculture Organisation
FDI	foreign direct investment
FOCAC	Forum on China–Africa Co-operation
FTA	free-trade area
G-7	Group of Seven
G-8	Group of Eight
GAFTA	Greater Arab Free Trade Areas
GDP	gross domestic product
GMEI	Greater Middle East Initiative
GNP	gross national product
HIPC	heavily indebted poor countries

IAEA	International Atomic Energy Agency
ICG	International Crisis Group
IDPs	internally displaced persons
IEPAs	Interim Economic Partnership Agreements
IGAD	Intergovernmental Authority on Development
IMF	International Monetary Fund
INOGATE	Interstate Oil and Gas Transport to Europe
IPU	Integrated Police Unit
JCIE	Japan Center for International Exchange
JHA	Justice and Home Affairs
KEDO	Korean Energy Development Organisation
LDCs	least developed countries
MAFTA	Mediterranean Arab Free Trade Area
MDGs	Millennium Development Goals
MDRP	Multi-country Demobilisation and Reintegration Programme
MEDA	Mediterranean Co-operation Programme
MEP	Member of the European Parliament
MLC	Mouvement pour la Libération du Congo
MONUC	Mission de l'Organisation des Nations Unies en République Démocratique du Congo
NAO	national authorising officer
NATO	North Atlantic Treaty Organisation
NCRI	National Council of Resistance of Iran
NEPAD	New Partnership for Africa's Development
NGO	non-governmental organisation
NPT	Nuclear Non-proliferation Treaty
NPTR	Nadym-Pur-Taz region
OAU	Organisation of African Unity
OPEC	Organisation of the Petroleum Exporting Countries
OSCE	Organisation for Security and Co-operation in Europe
PA	Palestinian Authority
PAO	principal authorising officer
PIF	Pacific Islands Forum
PLA	People's Liberation Army
PM	Prime Minister
PNC	National Congolese Police
PSC	Political and Security Committee of the EU
PSoC	Political and Social Committee
RCD	Rassemblement Congolais pour la Démocratie
REC	Regional Economic Community
SAARC	South Asian Association for Regional Co-operation
SACU	Southern Africa Custom Union
SADC	Southern African Development Community
SALW	small arms and light weapons

SARS	severe acute respiratory syndrome
SCGP	South Caucasus gas pipeline
SCO	Shanghai Co-operation Organisation
SIS	Schengen Information System
SPLA/M	Sudan People's Liberation Army/Movement
SSA	Sub-Saharan Africa
SSR	security sector reform
TAC	Treaty of Amity and Co-operation
TCA	Trade and Co-operation Agreement
TPLF	Tigrayan People's Liberation Front
TWN	Third World Network
UMA	Arab Maghreb Union
UN	United Nations
UNDP	United Nations Development Programme
UNHCR	United Nations High Commissioner for Refugees
UNSC	United Nations Security Council
UNSCR	United Nations Security Council Resolution
US	United States (of America)
USSR	Union of Soviet Socialist Republics
WAEMU	West African Economic and Monetary Union
WMD	weapons of mass destruction
WTO	World Trade Organisation

Introduction

Global actors competing or co-operating?

Valeria Bello and Belachew Gebrewold

Background

The urgency attached to the agenda of international terrorism and human and drugs trafficking has forced the European Union (EU) into new co-operation with various regional actors. In this context Africa and Asia have become increasingly significant. Such inter-regional relations have taken on new dimensions in the context of contemporary international politics framed by new security challenges and new competitive forces particularly from Asia. Africa is a significant actor mainly as a supplier of natural resources and as the origin of an increasing number of illegal migrants to Europe. The EU presents itself as an international 'civilian power' (Duchêne 1972; Telò 2006; Whitman 1998, 2002), which attempts to use soft power to influence international affairs and to strengthen its relationships with Asia and Africa, and a 'normative power' (Archibugi 1995; Manners 2002), which tries to commit other areas of the world to regulated global governance, insisting that international anarchy will not benefit anyone in the long term. Described as a unique political community with its particular form of regional integration and non comparable governance model, the EU is moving beyond its territory, and attempting to promote regional integration in Asia and Africa. The EU's policies towards Africa and Asia are intended to shape its role as a global player, and to enhance the prospects for peace, security and development in Europe, Asia and Africa.

On 10 November 2008 the Council of the EU issued its conclusions on trilateral talks and co-operation between the EU, China and Africa. The primary objectives of these trilateral talks and co-operation are to promote peace and security, and to achieve the Millennium Development Goals (MDGs) in Africa. Africa is already a strategic partner of the EU, within the framework of the Action Plan adopted at the 2007 Lisbon Africa–EU Summit. China is not only an important economic partner of the EU, but it has also become a very significant player in Africa, challenging the EU's role there. China's commitments have been boosted by the establishment of the Forum on China–Africa Co-operation (FOCAC). Following these developments the EU, which is very sensitive about AU–China relations, in accordance with its postulated normative approach to international relations, instead of competing directly with China, has pushed to co-ordinate efforts around priorities which reflect the common needs of all (Council of the EU 2008). The 2006 EU–China Summit showed the increasing importance of EU–Chinese co-operation and interdependence. This relationship is a logical consequence of the process to strengthen the EU's bilateral partnerships with both China and Africa and to identify common interests and areas for co-operation. The European Council has already proposed trilateral co-operation regarding peace and security in Africa, support for African infrastructure, sustainable management of the environment and natural resources, and agriculture and food security. Such trilateral co-operation aims to contribute to the stability of African countries and to strengthen African crisis management capabilities (Council of the EU 2008).

It is widely acknowledged that both the attainment of security and responses to security threats are a multifaceted process. Through a 'comprehensive security' strategy the EU underlines the interdependence of the political, socio-economic, cultural, ecological and military dimensions of security (Council of the EU 2003).

Comprehensive security implies the need to formulate integrated policies on all of them. This comprehensive approach is translated into the overall objective of 'effective multilateralism', i.e. a stronger international society, well functioning international institutions and a rule-based international order. At the global level, the EU seeks to pursue this objective mainly through the United Nations (UN), which the EU Strategy 2003 sees as the core of the international system, and through other global and regional partnerships and organisations (Biscop 2005: 23–4). Its co-operation with Asia and Africa is part of this strategy. However, the question is whether this effective multilateralism is realistic or whether states are destined to betray such glorious ambitions while pursuing national or regional interests.

In practice, the EU has developed various strategies towards Africa and the Asian regions. The Commission issued to the Council on 4 September 2001 a communication called 'Europe and Asia: A Strategic Framework for Enhanced Partnerships'. In this communication the EU set out a comprehensive strategic framework for relations to strengthen its political and economic presence in Asia and its regions. The strategy focuses on the following key points: engagement in the political and security fields, mutual trade and investment flows, partnership in reducing poverty, human rights, democracy, good governance and the rule of law, global alliances to address global challenges within international organisations, and mutual awareness respect and understanding between the EU and Asia (Council of the EU 2001).

Faced with China's increasing activity on the international scene, its desire for respect and recognition from the international community, and its re-emergence as a major global power, the EU's engagement with China has increased accordingly. The EU and China are co-operating to promote sustainable development and improve trade and economic relations. They have strengthened bilateral co-operation in various fields including science and technology, migration and non-proliferation of weapons of mass destruction. This shows that there is a strong desire on both sides to deepen and expand their relations (CEC 2006). However, the EU's demands that China should strengthen the rule of law, implement reforms to protect human rights and minorities, and increase transparency on military expenditure and objectives, still remain a point of friction between the EU and China.

Besides China there is another emerging global player: India. Through the Communication from the Commission to the Council, the European Parliament and the European Economic and Social Committee of 16 June 2004 an 'EU–India Strategic Partnership' was proposed. The objectives include strengthening co-operation through multilateralism, promoting peace, combating terrorism, non-proliferation of weapons of mass destruction, enhancing commercial and economic interaction, co-operation on sustainable development, protecting the environment, mitigating climate change and combating poverty and the improvement of human rights and strengthening of civil society (CEC 2008).

In the EU–Africa strategic partnership agreed in December 2007 the African Union and the EU expressed their intention to pursue four political objectives: to work in a partnership of equals, to promote peace and security, good governance, human rights, trade and the regional and continental integration of Africa and to offer joint responses to global challenges, including migration, mobility and employment. Migration policy has become a key area for co-operation between Europe and Africa due to the increasing number of illegal migrations from Africa to Europe, which are seen as a threat to European economic and political security. In June 2006 in Rabat (Morocco) and in November 2006 in Tripoli (Libya) both sides endorsed these objectives and areas of co-operation in order to address the migration–security nexus.

Because of its economic power the EU has been able to enjoy its role and a great power as a dominating and inscrutable actor, not only while pursuing its economic interests but also as a value-based actor, promoting human rights (Bretherton and Vogler 2006: 88). Addressing transnational crime is one of the key components of the European Security Strategy of 2003. However, the fight against transnational crime focuses not only on individuals within EU territory; the objective is to secure the Union as a political system in the global context. This demands a structuring of external relations. Using its political and economic resources the EU has been playing a leading role in the definition of models used for international co-operation in the fight against transnational crime (Longo 2003: 168–70). Co-operation with Asia and Africa has become indispensable for this. But both Asia and Africa are sceptical about the EU's intentions when they feel that the EU attempts to export its values in the form of human rights, the rule of law and democracy. Through this 'soft diplomacy' of political conditionality the EU has politicised its co-operation by proposing values (Petiteville 2003:

134). Furthermore, the EU sees itself as a 'normative power' which represents certain normative positions; specific models of development associated with core values such as good governance and democracy. Such norms and values have pervaded the EU's negotiations with foreign partners (Smith 2007: 534–5). Indeed, what we sustain in this book is that, rather than proposing its values to others, the EU is trying to defend them from the dislocating effect of globalisation on production and the consequent loss of employment in societies and countries with a responsible approach to environmental and social rights. If the EU does not try to defend its social model from the effects of unregulated globalisation, it is likely that we will assist to the dismantling in Europe of social, political and environmental rights.

However, conditionality and in particular the social and environmental clauses imposed by the EU have been the focus of most of the criticisms from those (scientists, economists, non-governmental and governmental organisations) who consider economic development to be the only feasible solution to the problems of developing countries, even if it results in an unfair distribution of benefits across their societies. In addition, the EU's political conditionality has led to the strengthening of relations between Africa and Asia (mainly China), in an attempt to sideline the EU, as illustrated in this book.

China and India have taught the EU, and its member states, the economic significance of Africa. Previously, Africa has been generally regarded by the EU as the origin of problems such as illegal migration and disease, or as a security threat, and as an immature player. But the EU's perception has started to change, thanks to China and India, and to the consequent ability of the African Union (AU) to make the EU take Africa seriously. For the EU, Asian involvement in Africa has been a late wake-up call.

Outline of the book

This book analyses the interactions between EU, Africa and Asia; it explores the main EU strategies towards these regions, in the context of the Common Foreign and Security Policy (CFSP) and the Security Strategy Paper of 2003: fighting terrorism and conflicts, and promoting economic co-operation and poverty alleviation. It examines the effects of the EU–Africa strategy, and the prospects for the EU's political conditionality towards Africa and Asia, taking into account the growing involvement of the competing economic giants, India and China.

The key question addressed in this book is the extent to which the core of EU foreign policy (the promotion of human rights and democracy) will be modified in competition with these emerging players in the global market. To what extent will the suggested trilateral talks be effective? Obviously, China and Africa appreciate the EU's consensus seeking approach in its international diplomacy. But at the same time they do not like its political conditionality.

Mary Farrell's chapter assesses the degree to which social learning and norm transfer is taking place and the 'appropriateness' and 'relevance' of particular models of regional integration for regional groupings. The chapter contrasts the role of ideas and epistemic communities as agents of the policy process, and examines the ideas, actors and institutions that shaped the particular conception of regional integration in contemporary policy discourse. The objective of the chapter is to assess whether difficulties in exporting the 'EU model' in fact reflect a failure to develop a truly normative agenda in the community's international relations policy more generally and to compare the vision of regional integration held by other countries and regional groupings with the European model. The EU's self-perception as a model for other integrations is based on perceptions of threats from within as well as from outside.

An analysis of the view of members of the European Parliament, ambassadors to the EU in the Political and Security Committee (PSC), and officials of the European Commission and the General Secretariat of the Council of Ministers is indispensable to understand the security threat perceptions and institutional responses of the EU to Africa and Asia. The chapter by Emil Kirchner and Maximilian B. Rasch examines the threat perceptions of European political elites, emphasising the geographical and issue-specific nature of the threats, and the temporal and global nature of particular challenges to security and stability. It assesses the extent to which the EU relies on non-military (economic, financial and political means) rather then military policy instruments, the effectiveness of European security policy and the quality and quantity of the European expenditure in this area.

The EU is increasingly seen as a civilian or normative actor, using soft power to spread its values and norms and its model of regional integration to other areas of the world. Since 2004 the EU has established a new strategic partnership with Africa to support its efforts to reach the UN Millennium Development Goals. This partnership means the beginning of constant interaction with African partners in the area, primarily with the AU, but also with individual countries. At the same time the EU has been strengthening its relationship with Asia and the Association of South East Asian Nations (ASEAN). Valeria Bello argues that the formation of the EU's international identity and the effectiveness of its policies depend both on the identification of these parties involved – Africa and Asia – with the norms, goals and values embedded in the European model of governance and also on the interaction actually taking place in the official meetings between the different regional organisations. Her chapter assesses the impact of the EU on the regional integration processes of Africa and Asia and its possible future impact on the addressing of global challenges.

The second part of the book concerns Africa. The African regional integration process has accelerated significantly in the last decade and the EU has played a significant role in this development. With the creation of New Partnership for Africa's Development (NEPAD) and the AU many African political elites and intellectuals welcomed these new developments as an

'African Renaissance'. These initiatives are considered vital to the linking of economic development, social stability and political security with the need to redefine Africa's own responsibility for – and to encourage a stronger popular ownership of – the future of the continent. But since the emergence of these initiatives many critical voices have been heard. It has been said that the priority of African states should be to address urgent needs such as hunger, disease, malnutrition, lack of democracy, etc., at the state level, rather than creating such big continental institutions. In his chapter Ludger Kühnhardt analyses the added value of regional integration in Africa and the EU's impact on, and interests in, the process. Kühnhardt argues that there is no law of nature that requires that every integration process begins with the same tools and follows the same or similar paths. Africa and Europe have taken quite different historical paths. Kühnhardt compares both Unions and shows that the rationale of European integration was the idea of reconciliation based on a gradually emerging common rule of law; whereas the rationale for African integration could be the formative idea of continental stability through socio-economic progress based on a gradually emerging regionalised common rule of law.

Kühnhardt says that the EU can set criteria defined by normative principles for the management of bi-regional relationships, but only a political approach culminating in coherent, comprehensive and multidimensional bi-regional association agreements with the existing regional groupings in Africa can serve as the basis of a new, mature and equal relationship between the EU and Africa within which they can together manage global challenges through global governance.

Migration is one of these increasingly globalised challenges. Immigration and asylum are tightly intertwined with other issues; such as housing, welfare, security, labour markets, health and education. This means that migration policy must find complex solutions to complex problems. Since 1990 domestic policy on immigration and asylum in the EU have increasingly been shaped by EU institutions. EU authorities are facing various challenges. Governments of the member states are unwilling to lead an open debate on the question of migration for fear of provoking public hostility. Heinrich Neisser argues that this is due to lack of information of the real situation. Because of the increasing influence of populist and far-right parties in many EU countries, migration and asylum policies are becoming very strict. Demands for tightly controlled migration and asylum policies are also increasing at the EU level. According to Neisser, within the EU measures taken in different policy fields must be coherent; coherence is a prerequisite for effectiveness. Neisser's chapter discusses the historical development of European migration policy. He stresses that even if the general migration policy of the EU is on the right track, there is still a danger for the European humanitarian tradition and values of human rights coming from the individual states' migration policy.

The EU's Hague Programme stresses the importance of the organisation's active role outside its territory in keeping Europe secure. As Belachew Gebrewold underlines, the 'external dimension' of the Hague Programme envisages realising this strategy. The EU's joint military action plan in the Democratic Republic of Congo (DRC) in 2003 (Operation Artemis), approved by the European Council (Council Joint Action 2003/423/CFSP) under the mandate set out in United Nations Security Council Resolution 1484 (2003) is a good example of this. The EU contributed a significant amount of money to the Demobilisation and Reintegration Programme for the Great Lakes Region, it financed a disarmament programme in Congo Brazzaville, allocated a considerable amount of money to support the establishment of an Integrated Police Unit (IPU) in the DRC; and implemented many other co-operative actions. So the EU is still a major player in the DRC. Nevertheless, Belachew Gebrewold argues, the success of the EU in the DRC will depend not on how well equipped its troops are, nor on the amount of money it allocates, but on how coherent the policies of the EU, of its member states and other global actors are there.

The EU is the leading economic actor in Africa. One of the aims of the 'external dimensions' of the Hague Programme's EU security policy is to empower Africa economically in order to ensure security in both African and Europe. It is becoming increasingly apparent that promising growth rates, increased aid and the competition of major global players for African resources are boosting the development and bargaining power of Sub-Saharan Africa (SSA) in relation to the EU. However, Dirk Kohnert argues that, as a legacy of its colonial past, Africa remains vulnerable to external shocks. Self-interested EU trade policy contributes to poverty and unsatisfactory development in SSA. Progress towards the Millennium Development Goals is being made, but far too slowly. According to Dirk Kohnert, the political and economic dominance of African states by the EU and its former colonial powers tends to perpetuate asymmetrical power relations in the new Partnership Agreements. Kohnert analyses the economic relationship between the EU and Sub-Saharan Africa, including the EU's trade policies vis-à-vis Sub-Saharan Africa, current Economic Partnership Agreements (EPAs) negotiations, its impact on pro-poor growth, regional integration and the development of African states. He examines African migration to the EU and its impact in home and receiving countries. This chapter also considers how these objectives are suffering due to the new competition between Asia and Europe, exploring the implications of this competition for EU–Africa economic relations. Kohnert describes how China contributes much to general economic development without the use of clause or conditionality, and, in contrast, the EU has a more 'pro-society' approach: thus the two might be seen as allies of different societal levels of the African states.

The EU and Africa have had an official strategic partnership since 2007, which purportedly offers a comprehensive, common frame for all EU actors in the spheres of foreign and development policy. It is hoped that future measures can be taken to support African states. For the first time ever, a strategy that takes the entire African continent into account is meant to allow more coherent foreign and trade policies to be pursued by both the EU as a whole and the Union's individual member states. Peace and security, good governance, and the acceleration of economic growth are all intended to aid African states in realising ambitious millennium goals. Partnership is a further important element. The adoption of what Louis Michel, EU Commissioner for Development and Humanitarian Aid, has referred to as a 'comprehensive, integrated and long-term' strategy marks the result of an intensive consultation process, during which the African Union and the Regional Economic Communities associated with it were called upon to comment on the EU's policy goals and visions for its relations with Africa. Taking Ethiopia as a case study, Stefan Brüne shows the dilemma of the EU in dealing with African allies when the latter do not implement democracy and good governance.

As Part III illustrates, the EU has increasingly become a model of regional integration in East Asia. Philomena Murray argues that the response of third countries to the process of Europeanisation, and to EU external relations policies, is relatively under-researched. While there has been some scholarly analysis of the EU as a putative paradigm, Murray contends that third countries, in their relationship with the EU, are increasingly obliged to shift their focus from exclusively state-to-state relations to regional bilateralism and multilateralism. According to Murray, considerable attention has been accorded in the literature to both the advantages of membership of regional integration blocs (such as the EU) and possible lessons for other parts of the world. The conditions, advantages and disadvantages of regional integration have been the subject of considerable debate. The EU is commonly regarded as having fulfilled these conditions. Murray's chapter examines the institutional architecture of regional integration and compares the various European and Asia Pacific perspectives. Further she argues that the experiences differ according to historical context, actors, leadership and external hegemonies, and urges a comparative interdisciplinary approach that seeks to broaden debates beyond ideal-type paradigms. The issue of the EU projecting itself as a civilian power and exporter of norms is examined, in the context of the EU's promotion of its experience of regional integration in East Asia.

Europe's dependence on the supply of energy from the Caspian Basin and Central Asia has security implication for the continent. Russia knows this too well. In the confrontation between the United States (US) and Russia on the US missile defence shield planned in Eastern Europe, the major EU states decided to take a soft position instead of obviously supporting the US because energy security has become a central part of all external EU relations. Geopolitical security and economic stability are essentially interconnected. Martin Malek argues that although Russia depends on the EU as its largest oil and gas customer, currently Moscow and not Brussels sets the rules of the game. Gazprom aspires to control natural gas supply and distribution networks in Europe. By gaining control of the infrastructure in transit countries, Russia limits other potential suppliers' access to markets.

The EU's foreign policy strategies are determined by its search for both political security and energy security. They determine its behaviour of external relations. Paolo Foradori assesses the role of the EU in the fight against nuclear proliferation in the Middle East, exploring the strengths and weaknesses of the specific European approach to non-proliferation. The Middle East is arguably the most politically and militarily volatile region in the world. Countries such as Egypt, Jordan, Saudi Arabia, Syria and the Gulf States wish to become nuclear powers. The quest for nuclear weapons is not only confined to state actors in the Middle East, and even some terrorist groups – of which Al Qaeda is one among many – are thought to be seeking them. The EU has unequivocally identified the spread of Weapons of Mass Destruction (WMD), and nuclear weapons in particular, as 'the single most important threat to peace and security' (Council of the EU 2003: 5) and in recent years it has emerged as one of the key players in non-proliferation and disarmament. Over the last decade, the EU has proved itself able to develop a specific approach to non-proliferation, the main strength of which lies in the appropriate use of the instruments of soft power. Its defining characteristic is its comprehensive nature, which aims to create a stable security environment for the whole region. Foradori first analyses the EU's development of its non-proliferation policy and its strategic documents; discussing its successes and failures, and the impediments to a more successful policy, and assessing future prospects. Then, he examines the EU's specific involvement in the Middle East, focusing on the successful American–European co-operation in the case of Libya and then on European efforts to contribute to the dialogue with Iran towards a resolution of the nuclear issue. Lastly, he considers the interconnectedness of security-related issues in Europe, the Middle East and north-eastern Africa.

India is increasingly becoming a partner as well as a rival of the EU. Anton Pelinka compares the similarities and differences between India and the EU at the institutional level. One of the significant similarities between India and the EU is the federal system, though India's federation is a top-down federative structure, whereas that of the EU is a bottom-up federation-in-the-making. From the point of view of Comparative Politics the Indian system is a combination of 'Westminster' plus Federalism, whereas the EU is still a system *sui generis*. From the point of view of Party Theory, the Indian style party system is dominated by 'people, not parties', whereas the EU-style party system is volatile, because it is dominated by national parties, since no European parties yet exist. In India, which is officially secular, religion is one of the driving forces of politics, thus leading to both Hindu and Muslim fundamentalism. The EU includes officially secular states, officially non-secular but in reality secular states and states dominated semi-officially by one church. Pelinka argues that in the international *arena*, India is potentially a global power that speaks with one voice, whereas the EU, while is also potentially a global power, seems unable to speak with one voice. There are converging interests and common values shared by India and the EU: democracy (though the caste system is still existent in India), human rights, religious tolerance. Both entities favour a multi-polar and balanced structure in world politics. However, according to Pelinka, they do not see eye to eye on globalisation, and have diverging interests at the international level: India seems to profit from globalisation more than does Europe. Regarding nuclear weapons, the EU is a strong advocate of non-proliferation; India the most prominent violator of non-proliferation. Pelinka considers whether diversity is an obstacle or a precondition for the establishment of a democratic federation, and how such differences can shape approaches to foreign policy and the emergence of consensus on international relations. These ideas are explored further in the discussion of how India, as a global military and economic power with growing interests in Africa, is likely to affect EU–Africa relations. Pelinka concludes that India can learn from the EU how to balance a market economy and social welfare: the 'European social model'; whereas the EU can learn from India how to shape one democratic actor from an extremely diverse giant.

Like India–EU relations, China–EU relations are characterised by competition and co-operation. Liselotte Odgaard argues that the consequence of the strategic partnership between the EU and China is that political dialogue between them has increased in recent years, but co-operation remains limited, because for China, security co-operation is still an experimental concept. Therefore, the EU cannot be sure that the compromises inherent in multilateralism will continue to form a central part of Chinese foreign policy strategies. The uncertainty about China's future intentions constitutes a barrier towards extensive security co-operation between the EU and China.

According to Liselotte Odgaard, Chinese foreign policy focuses on limiting the possibilities of violent conflict in its neighbourhood, without compromising the right to use force against entities defined by China as separatists or aggressors threatening Chinese sovereignty. This policy is intended to allow Beijing to concentrate resources on internal economic development and is pursued by co-operating with states that are at least partially supportive of Chinese foreign policy goals.

The traditional role of the EU as a normative player in human rights and democracy issues has gradually been challenged by others, not least India and China. Taking such challenges as his starting points, Michael Schulz's chapter gives an overview of the EU's political visions, ambitions and strategies in relations to the Israeli–Palestinian conflict. The chapter also attempts to describe the complex relations the EU has with regional players in the Middle East (North Africa, the Arab League and Asian countries). It investigates how the EU has approached Israeli and Palestinian societies and examines these interactions at the three levels: the grass roots, civil society, and at the level of political leaders. Schulz asks in what ways different sectors of the EU have contributed to strengthen/worsen the peace building capacities at these three levels of Israeli and Palestinian societies? Also, what role can the EU play in combination with the US, the UN and Russia, with whom the so-called road map was formulated?

This book addresses a broad range of issues: European security, EU migration policy, the African Union and its peace and security policy, terrorism and international security, the impact of Asian (in general) and Chinese (in particular) economic growth on global economic and security structures. It compares the EU, Asia and Africa in a single volume in order to show how these three regions interact politically and economically to address global challenges, and provides an assessment of the multilateralism which the EU clearly stated in its Security Strategy paper of 2003.

References

Archibugi, D. (1995) *Cosmopolitan Democracy: An Agenda for a New World Order*, Cambridge: Polity Press.

Biscop, S. (2005) *The European Security Strategy*, Aldershot: Ashgate.

Bretherton, C. and Vogler, J. (2006) *The European Union as a Global Actor*, London: Routledge.

CEC (2006) 'EU–China: closer partners, growing responsibilities', Com (2006) 632. Online. Available: http://eur-lex.europa.eu/smartapi/cgi/sga_doc?smartapi!celexpl us!prod!DocNumber&lg=en&type_doc=COMfinal&an_doc=2006&nu_doc=631 (accessed 10 October 2008).

—— (2008) 'EU–India strategic partnership', Com (2004) 430. Online. Available: http://eur-lex.europa.eu/LexUriServ/LexUriServ.do?uri=COM:2004: 0430:FIN:EN:PDF (accessed 19 October 2008).

Council of the EU (2001) 'Europe and Asia: a strategic framework for enhanced partnerships', Com (2001) 469. Online. Available: http://eur-lex.europa.eu/LexU-riServ/LexUriServ.do?uri=COM:2001:0469:FIN:EN:PDF (accessed 29 November 2008).

—— (2003) 'A secure Europe in a better world: European Security Strategy', Brussels, 12 December 2003. Online. Available: consilium.europa.eu/uedocs/cmsU-pload/78367.pdf (accessed 12 July 2008).

—— (2008) 'Council conclusions on trilateral dialogue and co-operation between the European Union, China and Africa', Brussels, 10 November 2008. Online. Available: www.consilium.europa.eu/uedocs/cmsUpload/Eu-Africa103901.pdf (accessed 29 November 2008).

Duchêne, F. (1972) 'Europe's role in world peace', in R. Mayne (ed.) *Europe Tomorrow. Sixteen Europeans Look Ahead*, London: Fontana.

Longo, F. (2003) 'The export of fight against organized crime policy model and the EU's international actorness', in M. Knodt and S. Princen (eds) *Understanding the European Union's External Relations*, London: Routledge.

Manners, J. (2002) 'Normative power Europe: a contradictions in terms?' *Journal of Common Market Studies* 40 (2): 235–58.

Petiteville, F. (2003) 'Exporting values? EU external co-operation as a soft diplomacy', in M. Knodt and S. Princen (eds) *Understanding the European Union's External Relations*, London: Routledge.

Smith, M. (2007) 'The European Union and International Political Economy: Trade, Aid and Monetary Policy', in K. E. Jørgensen *et al.* (eds) *Handbook of European Union politics*, London: Sage Publications.

Telò, M. (2006) *Europe: a Civilian Power? European Union, Global Governance, World Order*, Basingstoke: Macmillan.

Whitman, R. (1998) *From Civilian Power to Superpower? The International Identity of the European Union*, Basingstoke: Macmillan.

—— (2002) 'The fall, and rise, of civilian power Europe', National Europe Centre Paper 16. Online. Available: https://dspace.anu.edu.au:8443/handle/1885/41589 (accessed 18 November 2008).

Part I

General framework

1 The EU's promotion of regional integration

Norms, actorness and geopolitical realities

Mary Farrell

Having attained a degree of internal integration, consolidated in large part by internal market liberalisation, the introduction of a single currency, and a raft of economic and social policies, the European Union (EU) has over the past decade sought to extend its presence on the international stage. Until now, this aspiration has been hindered by the lack of a common European voice in foreign policy, unlike the cohesiveness of international trade policy where the legitimacy of the European Commission to speak and negotiate for the member states is uncontested both inside and outside the community. In one area of external relations, however, the EU appears to be sidestepping the weaknesses of the foreign policy framework, building co-operative relations and political dialogue with other regional communities in Africa, Asia, and the Americas. The EU has gone so far as to declare its support for regional integration in other parts of the world, entering into a growing number of inter-regional co-operation agreements, and creating a variety of instruments intended to support the region-building process elsewhere.

To what extent does inter-regional co-operation serve to enhance the role of the EU as an international actor, and to enhance its power and influence in other regions? Is the EU promoting a form of regional integration modelled on its own structures and institutions? Does the EU adopt a single approach to this policy, or take account of the diversity of conditions in each region? On preliminary examination, this region-to-region dialogue is distinctive in comparison with the bilateral dialogue that characterises much of foreign policy and the international relations of states. Though the EU member states still conduct bilateral foreign policy, the promotion of multilateralism ranks high with the promotion of democracy, rule of law, and the respect for human rights – to the extent of having such provisions included in all its international agreements as a legal requirement (European Commission 2003; European Council 2003).

The EU's promotion of regional integration elsewhere can be understood in the context of the broader support, and indeed preference for, multilateralism as a 'normal' way of conducting international relations, of resolving disputes and conflicts, and in the collective effort to provide such public goods as a liberal trade regime, development and poverty reduction, and environmental protection. Hence, is region-to-region co-operation a form of multilateralism on a scale below the global level that allows the EU to act as a political actor with a legitimacy that it does not have at the global level? In the powerful institutions of global governance, notably the United Nations (UN), the International Monetary Fund (IMF), and the World Bank, where sovereign states are the principal and legitimate actors, the EU has mainly observer status with the more limited capacity that this entails to shape global governance. However, in its growing inter-regionalism, the EU has the chance to explore and indeed exploit the possibilities for expanding regional governance beyond its own boundaries to other regions in the world, and thus to shape the external milieu according to certain interests and priorities.

This chapter explores the nature of the EU's regional integration promotion in different areas of the world, and seeks to identify the general approach taken by EU actors, the objectives and the policy instruments adopted in this latest phase of European external relations. The chapter is structured as follows: the first section details the broad context and rationale for the EU's 'regional integration as external policy', and this is followed in the second by an examination of the policy used to promote regional integration. The third looks at how the EU institutional framework has been adapted to the case of EU–Africa co-operation. The fourth section explores the possibility of expanding regional governance through inter-regionalism, while the fifth considers the normative potential in the EU's promotion of regional integration elsewhere. The sixth section takes a critical look at the prospects for exporting European governance.

Rationale and context

In practice, regional integration can vary from loose co-ordination among participating countries of selected policies and practices in some areas such as trade (regional co-operation), to deeper integration at the political level, a pooling of sovereignty and the creation of supranational institutions (regional integration). Over time, as integration processes continue, the recognition of common interests and values can promote a sense of identity, and a regional political community acts as a subject with its own identity, an actor with capability, and the structures to facilitate region-wide decision-making. The EU's policy on regional integration elsewhere appears as a mix of policy instruments, and strategic objectives ranging from security to trade, inter-regional co-operation in technical and financial assistance, and development policy. This diversity is exemplified in the frameworks of EU–Africa and EU–Asia relations.

In *The EU and Africa: Towards a Strategic Partnership*, adopted by the European Council in December 2005, the primary goals of the EU's Africa strategy were identified as the achievement of the Millennium Development Goals (MDGs), and the promotion of sustainable development, security and good governance in Africa. Regional integration was linked to the Economic Partnership Agreements (EPAs) and to a whole array of objectives around Africa's integration into the global economy, as well as improved governance and the compliance with EU standards and rules, aid for trade, and environment and climate policies.

The EU–Africa summit meeting in Lisbon (December 2007) agreed a long-term strategic partnership, reiterating the commitment to the MDGs, and identifying four main objectives around which specific strategies would be developed (1) peace and security; (2) governance and human rights; (3) trade and regional integration; (4) key development issues. This Joint Africa–EU Strategy builds upon the historical co-operation between the two regions, but goes further to offer a comprehensive and multi-dimensional focus on development, security, investment, trade, migration, social development, agriculture and food security, infrastructure, water and sanitation (Kühnhardt 2005; chapter 4 in this volume). The inter-regional co-operation framework is also multi-level, recognising the 'need for a more defined division of roles and responsibilities between the pan-African, sub-regional, national and local levels and between the different actors on the EU side, as well as for coherence and complementarity with other international actors' (Kühnhardt 2005: 30).

The new strategic partnership between the EU and Africa will rest upon a dense institutional architecture that is very much resonant with the multi-level governance model that applies to the internal EU regional polity – thus three-yearly Africa–EU summit meetings of the heads of state and government, supported by a troika of senior officials from each side,[1] regular co-operation between the EU and African Commissions, and a strengthened formal structure for dialogue between the European Parliament, the Pan-African Parliament and the AU's Economic, Social and Cultural Council.

In the case of EU relations with the Middle East, inter-regional co-operation and regional integration promotion initiatives are very much determined by the former's capacity as an actor reliant upon civilian power, and driven by the geo-strategic objectives of improved political stability in the region, and a desire to reduce the inflow of economic migrants from the region into Europe. EU efforts have revolved around the discourse of trade integration among the participating states, fostering intra-regional trade and policy co-ordination between the Middle East states under the framework of the Barcelona process. In recent years, the promotion of regional trade agreements has been the EU's preferred policy instrument, simultaneously signing bilateral trade agreements with individual countries while pushing for trade liberalisation at the intra-regional level. Given the constraints of the EU as a coherent foreign policy actor, policy towards the Middle East has tended at times to be *ad hoc* or reactive, with very limited positive outcomes even in the economic arena.

Despite the EU's continued support for and encouragement of regional integration and co-operation, there has been little intro-regional co-operation or economic integration, with relations among the Middle East states more often characterised by tension and conflict. In an effort to revitalise efforts to promote co-operation in the region and to 'transform the Mediterranean into an area of peace, democracy, co-operation and prosperity', the Euro-Mediterranean Heads of State and Government meeting in Paris in July 2008 issued a joint declaration stating their intention to enhance intra-regional co-operation and to strengthen multilateralism. The Paris declaration on the *Barcelona Process: Union for the Mediterranean* is effectively an effort to address common goals, in security, peace and stability within the region, building on what was initiated with the 1995 Barcelona Process and proposing an extended set of institutional structures to support an upgrading of the EU's political relations with the Mediterranean partners.[2] This means that heads of state and government have agreed to hold biennial summits and to decide jointly on concrete regional projects.

According to the Paris declaration, EU bilateral relations with these countries will continue under existing policy frameworks, such as the Association Agreements, and the European Neighbourhood Policy. It is envisaged that the Barcelona Process will be coherent and complementary with the Joint Africa–EU Strategy, but will remain independent from the EU enlargement process, the accession negotiations and the pre-accession process. Unlike the case of EU–Africa relations, however, the institutional framework for inter-regional co-operation is much less dense, partly due to the absence in the Mediterranean region of the kind of regional integration arrangements to be found on the African continent. However, there is a Euro-Mediterranean Parliamentary Assembly, and the heads of state and government have agreed to establish a Joint Secretariat tasked with the responsibility to identify and promote regional projects.

The security imperative is less influential in shaping the EU's relations with Asia generally (Hemner and Katzenstein 2002). Instead, an economic rationale underpins the programmes and policies that emerged with the European Commission's 1994 publication 'Towards a New Asia Strategy'. Trade flows and inter-regional economic co-operation have increased significantly on a regional and bilateral basis, with a few individual countries (China, Singapore, Japan, India) taking the lion's share of economic flows.

Market access and strengthening the EU's political and economic presence across the region as a global economic actor are the key objectives in the EU's Asia strategy. Unlike other regions, the EU has tended to downplay the policy of promoting regional integration in Asia, and mainly confines this discourse on regional integration promotion to the case of south Asia, and the South Asian Association for Regional Co-operation (SAARC) regional grouping. Instead, inter-regional co-operation is conducted in a series of *fora* and institutional frameworks: the pure inter-regional, or bloc-to-bloc co-operation taking place in EU–ASEAN (Association of South East Asian Nations), EU–SAARC, and the Asia–Europe Meeting (ASEM); and the hybrid inter-regional, bilateral co-operation characterised in EU–China dialogue, EU–India, and EU–Japan (Balme and Bridges 2008). The ASEM continues as a forum for informal dialogue and co-operation between the EU, the European Commission, and the Asian states (Brunei, China, Indonesia, Japan, South Korea, Malaysia, the Philippines, Singapore, Thailand, and Vietnam), and, while the wide-ranging agenda of topics reflects a broad-based set of interests, action is largely confined to the economic, technical and trade-related concerns of all actors (Farrell 2009).

The mix of bilateral/multilateral co-operative agreements continues to characterise the EU's relations with most other regional communities, and the extent to which emphasis is placed upon the promotion of regional integration per se varies quite considerably from region to region. There is clearly some gap between the rhetorical statements of the European authorities and the actual policy practice.

Promoting regional integration: the practis

While other areas of foreign policy have yet to be elaborated coherently, the EU policy on regional integration attracted little opposition at national or European level, raising no threat to national sovereignty, or to the common interests shared by the community of states.

Driven by the European Commission, a number of directorates quickly adopted the regional integration policy and the changing approaches to development policy ('trade, not aid') brought the Development Directorate into closer contact with external relations and trade directorates. Even if this emerging consensus across different areas of the European Commission did not dispel the normal rivalries and competition between them, there was enough common interest among the supranational bureaucracy to drive this policy forward. In practice, the EU policy (implemented largely through the European Commission) has operated not through the kind of common approach to be found in other policy areas (such as trade, competition, agriculture) but instead by a diversified strategy based on a range of policy instruments and a mix of conditionalities and incentives, tailored to the economic, security and geopolitical interests of the EU.

Three broad approaches to the promotion of regional integration can be distinguished, exemplified by the differences in instruments and a qualitative distinction in strategic intent (Farrell 2007). First, the promotion of regional integration through enlargement has provided a very direct and comprehensive way of implementing this policy, at the same time spreading the regulatory system and the legal order to new member states. Driven by the need to construct a security community on the eastern borders, the multi-faceted and highly politicised policy was implemented by the European Commission and relied heavily on a series of conditionality instruments and a mix of carrot-and-stick mechanisms to engender domestic political change in the applicant countries. The intended outcome of the process was of course eventual membership of the EU. But the use of conditionality in the enlargement process served also to enforce the EU rules and to shape the institutions in the applicant states. Conditionality was coercive, securing compliance with the policy outcome and with the Commission's highly politicised demands that the individual applicant states adopt the full array of rules, regulations, standards and policies in the *acquis communautaire.*

Second, the EU can and has been able to influence regional integration in a broad and general way through normative suasion, where other regional communities adopt certain practices, institutional arrangements, or other forms of governance modelled on the European regional governance system (Acharya and Johnston 2007). The role of norms in shaping outcomes has long been recognised in the literature, and even in the absence of a specific policy, agreement, or other form of intervention targeted at a region it can be possible for the EU to exert influence. In practice, the same policy approach is not adopted for all regional groupings and for individual countries, so that the EU's effectiveness as a norm exporter is determined by the nature of each arrangement and how the target region responds to the EU. Agreements that are politically rather than legally binding tend to commit the contracting parties only if there is a strong interest at stake. Where non-compliance with EU norms and values is not sanctioned, the adherence to agreements is purely voluntary. Since 1992 all EU agreements with third countries contain a clause defining respect for human rights and democracy as 'essential elements' in the EU's relationship, so that the EU can suspend the agreement (under international law) where there is a breach of the agreement as evidenced by human rights infringements. So far, the EU has not taken this opt-out option, and it is clear that the application of such political conditionality is extremely inconsistent across countries and regions generally.

Third, the promotion of regional integration has developed through the inter-regional agreements between the EU and other regional groupings, such as the Asia–Europe meeting (ASEM) or the Cotonou Agreement with the African, Caribbean and Pacific group. The inter-regional agreements also take different forms, distinguishing between pure interregional co-operation (involving formal regional blocs, such as EU–Mercosur) and hybrid inter-regionalism (co-operation between a formal regional community and a group of countries that do not constitute a formal regional entity). Inter-regional co-operation takes a variety of forms and policy instruments, ranging across aid programmes, regional trade agreements, support for regional integration and more comprehensive regional strategies – sometimes embracing all of these components. Generally, the inter-regional agreements cover a whole range of issues (trade, environment, technical assistance, development, infrastructure, political reform), though the individual agreements tend also to include specified objectives, such as the Cotonou Agreement with its emphasis on the integration of the African countries into the global economy. However, there is no standard approach adopted by the EU in concluding inter-regional co-operation agreements, and the outcomes reflect the bargaining strength and negotiation between both parties.

Complexity and diversity of content, policy instruments, and outcomes characterise all inter-regional co-operation agreements. European Commission official publications do, however, broadly agree on the impetus for this departure in the EU's external relations. The genesis of these agreements is a shift in the EU's strategic priorities, with geographical proximity prioritising the regions of greatest importance. Newly independent states emerging after the collapse of the Soviet Union generated uncertainty over security and a threat of instability on the EU's eastern borders, thus posing the question of how to manage relations with those states. Ultimately the concerns were addressed through the offer of membership. Furthermore, new geo-strategic priorities were emerging, to underline the need for new actions and programmes located in the strategic priorities of the EU rather than those of the individual states. In essence, the policy towards the promotion of regional integration can be seen as part of a dual strategy, the preservation of regional order and the enhancement of the EU's global presence.

Not all three approaches identified in this section are mutually exclusive: enlargement was about spreading regional integration, and also disseminating European norms to the prospective members; and, inter-regional co-operation also facilitates norm transfer, though without the prospect of accession. Conditionality is used pervasively in all the European Commission's negotiations, though its impact is highly variable across countries and regions. Similarly, the link between regional integration and development emerges in both EU–Africa and EU–Asia relations, though clearly there are significant variations not only in the underlying structural conditions but also in the receptivity to European norms and ideas.

The African approach to regional integration reflects much from the European experience, most noticeably in the preference for supranational institution-building (Babarinde 2007). Like its European counterpart, the African Union embodies a pan-African Parliament, a Commission, an Executive Council of Ministers, Permanent Representatives' Committee, a Court of Justice, a Peace and Security Council, and financial institutions (African Central Bank, African Monetary Fund, and African Investment Bank). The proposal for West African monetary integration included many of the elements of the European model, including convergence criteria for public borrowing, inflation, and interest rates, and planned for a phased introduction of a new currency (the eco), though the deadline has now been pushed back by several years. ECOWAS, though intended as an economic community, has evolved into a regional security organisation (Nivet 2006).

In Asia, the European policy is implemented against a different set of political and economic conditions, as well as fewer power asymmetries and a strong commitment generally to the principle of domestic non-intervention (Camilleri 2003). Though the EU continues to push the human rights agenda in bilateral and multilateral negotiations with Asian countries, the latter have not been so receptive to the explicitly normative European agenda nor to any extension of policy discussion beyond the trade and economic arena, with the result that the EU has not been able to press conditionality with the same fervour as elsewhere.

However, the ASEAN grouping has begun in recent years to address regional integration, emphasising trade, strengthening security and addressing the 'war on terror' in the region, as part of a reappraisal of the regional group's role and relevance in the contemporary Asian and global order (Conde 2007).

In recent years, much of the EU's inter-regional co-operation has been dominated by trade agreements, a trend to European external policy that contrasts sharply with the failure to secure agreement in the WTO trade liberalisation negotiations under the Doha Development Round. Negotiations for a free trade area (FTA) started with the ASEAN group, with the Andean Community, and Central America. These essentially economic inter-regional agreements are supported by a range of bilateral agreements between the EU and individual countries that represent diverse strategic interests – China, India, South Africa, and Brazil rating particularly strong as important partners for the EU. This 'search for partnership' characterises much of the EU's external trade relations over the past five years, with the European Commission as principal actor and lead negotiator representing the member states. Mostly, the issues and agenda cover trade and economic matters, where the European Commission has negotiating authority and the mandate to represent the member states.

Institutions for integration: the case of EU–Africa co-operation

Inter-regional co-operation between the EU and Africa has a long history, based upon an institutionalised framework that pre-dated any other inter-regional co-operation policies currently implemented by the EU. The Cotonou Agreement of 2000 marked a departure from its predecessor in several respects.[3] Growing criticism of the Lomé agreements for their failure to deliver real results in terms of increasing the market access for ACP producers, or even to secure the development and modernisation of primary production among the countries of the region, combined with a more critical concern within Europe towards the need to secure 'value for money' in the financial resources allocated under the category of development policy led to a reappraisal of the agreements. The review of the Lomé agreements took place amidst growing donor fatigue and increased public concern about the effectiveness of European aid expenditure and the appropriate use of public finance in the recipient countries. A further decisive factor in changing the nature of the EU–Africa co-operation policy was the shift in EU development policy towards an emphasis on 'trade, not aid' as a key route to development, taking the European policy into line with the broad approach adopted by the international institutions, notably the World Bank and the International Monetary Fund. By the mid-1990s, there was a strong international consensus favouring a neo-liberal approach to development and support for market-based activities.

The Cotonou agreement reflected these various concerns, emphasising trade liberalisation (dropping the non-reciprocity of the predecessor Lomé accords), with the specific proposal for regional economic integration agreements between the EU and groups of countries within the ACP bloc and, in parallel, the establishment of regional integration among the countries of the African, Caribbean and Pacific region. These Economic Partnership Agreements (EPAs), constituted a departure from previous policy by emphasising broad-based economic liberalisation – across countries, products, sectors and markets – and broadening the policy agenda, at the instigation of the European Commission, to include competition, trade and environmental considerations, trade and labour standards, consumer policy and consumer health, the protection of intellectual property rights, and standardisation and certification.

In parallel with the EPA negotiations, the European Commission was actively developing an Africa strategy, with the publication of the EU Strategy for Africa in 2005, followed soon after by the Joint Africa–EU Strategy adopted at the Lisbon summit meeting in December 2007 (European Council 2007).[4] The joint declaration issued in Lisbon referred to the intention 'to build a new strategic political partnership for the future, overcoming the traditional donor–recipient relationship and building on common values and goals in our pursuit of peace and stability, democracy and rule of law, progress and development' (EU–AU 2007: para. 4). This joint strategy goes far beyond the parameters of previous EU inter-regional co-operation to propose an expanded institutional framework, with the African Union as the voice of continental issues and the most important institutional partner for the EU. Emanating from this strategy and the new institutional framework is an interconnected set of policies and action plans with specified time frames and indicated outcomes, exemplified in the First Action Plan (2008–10), which sets out eight lines of action covering areas such as peace and security, trade and regional integration, democratic governance and human rights, the millennium development goals, and migration/mobility/employment.[5]

Governance issues and challenges

The EU approach to promoting regional integration is based on a hierarchical set of priorities linked to strategic goals, with the most stringent requirements and conditions imposed on the countries seeking membership of the EU, while other countries face lower conditionality levels, and region-to-region co-operation is based upon loose institutional arrangements to facilitate dialogue and co-operation over mainly economic and sometimes security issues. As we saw earlier, the EU is adopting a diverse approach in promoting regional integration outside the European arena, where a clear geopolitical and geo-economic strategy is shaping inter-regional relations.

While Asia is not regarded as a single entity, the EU does have particular bilateral strategic partnerships in the region, most notably with China, Japan, South Korea, India and Taiwan. However, when we look closer at these relations with Asia and the individual countries in the region, the set of complex intra-regional relations and dynamics make any attempt to assess the influence of the EU at a multilateral level rather difficult. The main forum for inter-regional dialogue and co-operation remains the ASEM framework, and though this continues to link the leaders and policy-makers of Europe and a large part of the Asian region in regular political discussions and mutual economic/technical co-operation, it has tended to operate as a low-key institution with high politics issues largely sidelined.

Though regional co-operation has been strengthened in Asia over the past three decades, it remains very much a product of intergovernmental political relations conducted amidst the ongoing mix of big power politics by a few states and balance-of-power strategies by the rest (Kühnhardt 2005). This shared geopolitical motivation stems from the diverse yet strong concerns with national sovereignty in the individual Asian countries, and the belief that regional co-operation should not be allowed to undermine sovereignty or national political autonomy. The idea of developing regional co-operation (intergovernmental co-ordination) or going the route of regional integration (supranational institutions and a legal order) fashioned on the European model could never find strong support among the Asia states, where modernisation and nationalism have co-existed with diverse cultural and political traditions. Even the calls for a form of regional monetary integration, in the wake of the Asian financial crisis of 1997, have not materialised into anything stronger than a rescue fund for the region.

After the Asian financial crisis the ten ASEAN members together with China, Japan and South Korea opted to create a network of bilateral currency swaps rather than to take the more weighty political decision on deeper monetary co-operation with institutions to formulate common policies. The Chiang Mai Initiative therefore reflected the political preferences of countries unwilling to see control of monetary policy ceded to a supranational institution. While there are options short of a full monetary union that countries could take, in the Asian case the possibility of linking the currencies to a strong currency within the region (as the European countries did with the Exchange Rate Mechanism, pegging to the German Mark (DM) and hence to German monetary policy) was not considered possible in the absence of a strong co-ordinating institution along the lines of Germany's Bundesbank. Perhaps also, the rivalry, suspicion and lack of trust among the countries and the surprisingly small economic integration and trade flows between the particular countries proved obstacles to even such limited monetary integration.

By contrast, in West Africa, where monetary integration modelled on the European experience has been considered, the countries have gone some way to create the supranational monetary institutions that will replace the national central banks, introducing convergence criteria and co-ordination of macroeconomic policies as part of the phased introduction of a single currency. However, the West African countries still do not have the level of real economic integration, measured in the density of trade patterns and capital flows, to allow the economies to support a single monetary policy and to withstand the pressures of an asymmetrical currency union arrangement (Kenen and Meade 2007). For now, the New Partnership for Africa's Development (NEPAD) adopted by the African Union at the 2001 Lusaka summit stands as the continent's main economic blueprint for co-ordinated policy action, and the peer review mechanism which encourages member states to submit their macroeconomic policy programmes to an independent review has some resonance with the EU's open method of co-ordination (Babarinde 2007).[6]

The EU has not actively promoted regional monetary integration as part of its external relations or inter-regional co-operation. Neither in the case of Africa nor Asia has the EU sought to endorse a model of monetary integration closely or even loosely modelled on the euro-zone arrangements. This does not preclude the model, or parts of it, being considered by African or Asian states as a form of regional co-operation or even integration. At the start of 2009, with the world undergoing a new global financial and economic crisis, no advance towards a level of regional monetary integration similar to the European experience had been contemplated. For its part, the EU has concentrated on economic and trade liberalisation in its dealings with the African countries through the Economic Partnership Agreements (EPAs) negotiations, and a growing series of bilateral trade agreements across Asia.

Is there any evidence to support the export of a European model of governance? To the extent that this is happening, it takes place largely through the trade liberalisation arrangements of the EU's bilateral and multilateral trade agreements. It is not surprising that the aspects of the EU governance model most likely to be promoted externally or adopted as part of inter-regional relations concern trade liberalisation – as a global economic powerhouse, with the largest share of world trade and a major share of global foreign direct investment, the search for new markets and the spread of competition norms help to secure fundamental European strategic economic and political goals. In the global economy, norms on competition and trade liberalisation become more widely adopted internationally, and as other countries seek to strengthen economic and trade ties with the EU there is scope for the European Commission as the collective representative of the individual member states in external trade negotiations to act as the catalyst in the international transfer of European-derived trade and competition norms.

The extent to which the spread of EU trade and competition norms can be considered to promote regional integration does, however, depend on the conditions in the recipient host region. The degree of intra-regional trade within ASEAN is still significantly lower than that of the EU, while other parts of Asia also show weak though improving levels of trade integration among neighbouring countries. In North East Asia there are numerous free-trade agreements and proposed agreements, and a number of preferential trade agreements, most of which stem from a preference for bilateral rather than a multilateral engagement on the part of the participants.[7] These trade agreements are in line with the World Trade Organisation regulatory framework, but as Kühnhardt observes, 'free trade agreements *per se* are expressions of regional co-operation, not of regional integration' (Kühnhardt 2005: 30).

Conditions in the host region affect the receptivity to regional integration norms, and to the arrangements, procedures, policies and institutions that foster co-operation on common policies; similarly, the political context of inter-state relations impacts upon the capacity to accept and recognise the political legitimacy of supranational institutions, including legal and political norms. As the preceding section suggests, a tendency towards free-trade agreements provides a limited basis for region-building, for the creation of a regional political community based on some degree of common governance. The increasing tendency of the EU itself to engage in bilateral trade agreements can also undermine regional integration or at least slow down the process, and even call into question the EU's own commitment to multilateralism, as evidenced in the latter's inability or unwillingness to seek progress in the latest negotiations under the WTO's Doha Development Agenda.

More generally, the absence of any apparent prioritisation with regard to regional versus bilateral agreements with third countries and regions (beyond those in close proximity to EU borders) suggests that the EU adopts a rational view towards the calculation of the costs and benefits, and will be guided by a realist assessment of the European self-interest. The plethora of bilateral agreements amidst a host of inter-regional agreements (and region and country strategy papers) attest to the EU's mix-and-match approach.

As one example in the EU relations with Southern Africa, recent EPA negotiations involved the SADC countries in two sets of negotiations with the countries eventually split, some negotiating under the SADC framework and the rest with COMESA, while South Africa as the most powerful member of SADC was already subject to a bilateral trade agreement negotiated separately with the EU. In Asia, the EU is seeking to strengthen co-operation with SAARC, while also contemplating a free-trade agreement with its most powerful member state, India. And the ASEM inter-regional forum stands alongside a range of bilateral agreements and strategic partnerships, with countries such as Japan, China, South Korea and individual ASEAN member states.

Normative aspects

The normative identity of the EU has been argued and fought over by proponents and sceptics alike. The Lisbon Treaty asserts the normative principles upon which the union is based – principles of democracy, respect for the rule of law and for human rights, principles of equality and solidarity, and respect for international law (including the principles of the United Nations Charter); it also contains an ambitious vision for the EU's external action, including such goals as peace, security, sustainable development, free and fair trade, eradication of poverty, and solidarity and mutual respect among peoples. How does the promotion of regional integration fit in with these principles?

The legal requirement that all agreements between the EU and third countries (or regions) must include clauses on democracy and human rights is an established part of practice since the early 1990s. Far from being a straightforward non-negotiable clause, however, the EU negotiators have to convince the other parties of the seriousness of these principles in the European legal order, and must respond to the contestation of normative principles in what are frequently trade-related agreements (seen by the other party in essentially economic rather than normative terms). Where other regional communities do not share the EU's normative vision, inter-regional co-operation is less likely to ensure a transfer of normative values. Norm transfer has been most successful in the case of enlargement, where the EU was able to impose stronger requirements on accession countries, and better placed to enforce normative conditions in return for the guarantee of membership.

Democracy promotion by the EU has been most successful in the post-Soviet states that were accepted as members of the EU. In fact, enlargement has been regarded as a very successful democracy promotion programme, where the prospect of membership 'created powerful incentives for successful governments to improve democratic standards and also pursue economic reforms' (Vachudova 2007: 105). With the European Neighbourhood Policy, the Commission is taking its role and authority as democracy promoter into the community of states that constitute the EU's neighbours. The latest phase of the Barcelona Process brings together thirty-nine governments and over 700 million people, making it one of the largest of the EU's inter-regional co-operation programmes.[8] Covering political, economic and cultural dialogue, the programme also includes priorities on terrorism, the non-proliferation of nuclear, chemical and biological weapons, support for the Israeli-Palestine peace process, and economic development. In this case, the same tools and policies are being applied, though the promise of membership is mostly absent from the negotiations. The exclusion of the incentive of membership for the neighbourhood countries in a programme with extremely broad scope and ambition, and 'a commitment to peace, democracy, regional stability and security through regional co-operation and integration' across countries with different values and diverse political and economic development, suggests that the prospect of successful democracy promotion is significantly diminished.

Elsewhere, democracy promotion is, at least notionally, on the agenda of EU external relations. But there is less likelihood of imitating the results of the enlargement process for a variety of reasons. Democracy promotion and human rights have been central to EU relations with Africa for almost two decades, included in development and foreign policy arenas generally, as well as forming part of the provisions within the Cotonou Agreement and now also in the Joint Africa–EU Strategy. However, the broad statements of European support for democracy promotion to be found in these declarations often do not translate into practical programmes of assistance for democratic institutions in individual states targeted for development assistance.

As one of the largest donors with respect to development assistance to Africa, European efforts have largely concentrated upon projects related to rural development, technical assistance, transport, capacity building programmes, good governance, and HIV/AIDS (Crawford 2004). The European Commission, as the co-ordinator of EU development policy, has tended to shy away from more political type initiatives in the implementation of programmes of action within the individual African countries. In a continent where poverty and underdevelopment, child malnutrition, ill health and inadequate physical and social infrastructure remain such evident and immediate challenges to societal welfare and development prospects, development agencies have followed the Millennium Development Goals to focus on the objectives of poverty reduction. The result has been less emphasis upon democracy promotion.

But it has to be considered that a major constraint in implementing more imaginative policies on democracy promotion was the lack of a European common foreign policy, and the institutional arrangements in the EU which allowed the European Commission to be a central player in external relations – but only in the trade arena. In development policy, while there is shared competence between national and European development policies, it has not been possible for the European Commission to step into the more political policy initiatives (with the important exception of its role as policy entrepreneur in the enlargement negotiations).

In the Asian context, the regional co-operation is much more geared to the pursuit of globalisation-related goals, so economic co-operation is considered to be more in tune with national interest objectives and the shared common interests of the region. Democracy promotion in ASEAN, where its membership is characterised by a diversity of regimes, governance and political cultures, is not an immediate goal likely to be adopted by the group or the individual member states. China, a major strategic partner of the EU, is not going to adopt this programme with its potential to undermine the fabric of the state and national political culture anytime soon. This is not to suggest that the EU has no significant normative role to play in the different Asian sub-regions. On the contrary, the growth of economic ties has brought benefits to both sides, and raised the European profile in political as well as public circles.

The EU is recognised as an international actor with some degree of influence (though not necessarily a powerful actor), and is identified as different in its approach compared with the US which many Asian countries regard as a dominant and aggressive power with a penchant for unilateralist actions. The willingness and capacity of the EU to respond to this goodwill in a politically constructive way is in large part determined by how far the union can advance with the Common Foreign and Security Policy, and the potential of the new foreign policy and security architecture in the Lisbon Treaty.

In the area of human rights, the EU identifies itself as the promoter and defender of human rights established under the United Nations Charter, and the European Convention on Human Rights. The EU's almost self-referential normative position is well known and acknowledged throughout the world, and the reputation as the 'better peoples of the United Nations', though somewhat sanctimonious, is largely borne out in practice (Fassbinder 2004). This is due to a combination of the shared traditions of the European member states in the area of human rights and the fact that human rights are one of the defining principles upon which the Union operates, with all new member states being required to adopt the principle as a condition of membership. Since the Treaty on European Union (the Maastricht Treaty) the member states have agreed to co-ordinate their positions on foreign policy at the international level, resulting in an increase in the common positions adopted at the United Nations (Laatikainen and Smith 2006).

While this improved co-ordination of actions by the member states helps to shape and consolidate the human rights dimension of external policy, including the promotion of regional integration, the strong intergovernmental bias in external actions generally means that the European Commission's capacity to enforce these provisions is much weaker than the authority and influence it can wield in the area of external economic relations and international trade agreements. Inter-regional agreements that include provisions on non-trade issues, including provisions on such normative areas as human rights, are therefore likely to be characterised by implementation gaps and the outcomes anticipated by the signatories of such agreements. Even when the EU uses its influence as a (largely undisputed) trade power, and links such provisions to the trade clauses of a proposed regional trade agreement, the degree to which the EU can exert influence is mixed due to the tensions between the principles and objectives of the EU.

These tensions imply that the EU struggles even in external trade policy as it tries to balance regionalism and multilateralism, non-discrimination and bilateral preferences, and to find its identity somewhere between Western hegemony and a mediating power, leading to what Meunier and Nicolaïdis have described as a 'conflicted trade power' (Meunier and Nicolaïdis 2006). Whatever the difficulties facing the attempts of the EU to promote regional integration with normative dimensions, and these will undoubtedly continue in the future, there is no real alternative focus that could be taken without undermining the identity and even credibility of the EU as an international actor. To quote Bardo Fassbinder, 'the European Union would get into serious trouble if as an international actor it stopped being faithful to the values which are its own spiritual foundation. This is the true reason why the EU, as long as it retains its identity, cannot engage in selfish power politics, a diplomacy of coercion, or military interventions contrary to international law' (Fassbinder 2004: 884).

Exporting governance?

The EU remains committed to the promotion of regional integration elsewhere as inter-regionalism and regional integration continue to shape relations between states at the international level. This external policy of promoting regional integration is highly diversified in both the substance and objectives, and varied according to geo-economic, political, and strategic considerations. Trade remains always a fundamental component of the policy, though other more political elements that make up the internal EU structure can be found in the external agreements. Though motivated by market access considerations, trade clauses are now accompanied by provisions on competition rules, product standards, environmental protection rules, and intellectual property rights, leading some analysts to see in these developments the export of the European model of governance (Lavenex 2008).

The enlargement of the EU does indeed constitute a case of exporting European governance, and the conditionality clauses attached to accession negotiations (including the requirement on meeting the *acquis communautaire*) imposed an absolute requirement on the new member states to adopt the European regulatory and legal order. Different structural and political conditions operate in the countries that are subject to the European Neighbourhood Policy where, in the absence of the promise of membership, the approach has been based on a less hierarchical attempt at inducing other countries to adapt to predetermined EU norms and regulations by fostering horizontal networks of actors and organisations, based more on voluntary participation and co-operation rather than vertical authority by government and bureaucracy. As Lavenex (2008) describes it, 'integration occurs no longer through law but through co-ordination'.

While network governance has taken hold within the EU, there is mixed evidence of its potential beyond the European political and geographical boundaries. For one thing, effective policy networks depend upon the creation of joint regulatory structures to bind the EU and its partner region and, second, the existence of networks to spread knowledge and diffuse best practice, implement and enforce rules and laws, as well as regulatory networks to formulate new common rules and standards. In the ENP, targeted towards a region of growing strategic importance and geographically close to the EU, the outcome or 'export of governance' has been very much determined by the governance capacity of the third countries ability to participate as equal partners, and positively influenced by the existence of ongoing co-operation within existing institutional frameworks. In areas of high politics, network governance faces greater difficulty as the EU generally prefer to interact in the more traditional hierarchical (often intergovernmental) manner with third countries.

Though region-to-region co-operation has been conducted on traditional hierarchical lines, it has had the effect of promoting a regional political community, pushing states to work collectively towards common positions in order to negotiate with the EU. In Asia, this has happened via the ASEAN community, though less so with ASEM. The fact that functional co-operation has expanded within the ASEAN grouping, and is now emerging within the ASEM structures, suggests there is scope for the growth of this type of network governance as different actors negotiate their way through policy networks and the integrative potential is explored further.

With regard to EU–Africa relations, African countries have so far gone along with the European top-down approach to regional integration and inter-regional co-operation. The EPA negotiations have largely followed the traditional, hierarchical method, driven by the heavy hand of the European Commission to secure reciprocal market access, while enforcing product standards and competition rules. The highly institutionalised European model of regional integration has been emulated in the continental-level African Union, and to some extent in the sub-regional economic communities. Yet at the sub-regional level, regional economic communities have developed in an *ad hoc* manner, with ill matched institutional structures and political strategies – a case in point being the Economic Community of West African States (ECOWAS), where the fifteen member states decided on market liberalisation but then failed to realise substantive policies for the agreed-upon free movement of people.

Political decisions to cover the adjustment costs associated with greater competition under regional economic integration have not been made, either in Africa or Asia, though in Europe the compensatory redistributive mechanisms of the Structural Funds have proved instrumental in retaining the broad-based political support and legitimacy of the integration project. When the African, Caribbean and Pacific countries raised the issue of a fund to compensate the ACP countries adversely affected by liberalisation once the EPAs came into effect, they were told by the European Commission that this was an arrangement for the countries themselves to establish.

The European regulatory model, with the competition laws at the core, remains very much a unique legal framework and it has not been replicated in any of the existing regional governance systems around the world. Even when the requisite degree of political support and consensus among the participating states (in Africa, Asia or Latin America) can be established, there would still be the issue of creating a supranational legal framework to enforce the competition laws, and the governance capacity to implement them. But the European model is more than competition law – it embodies a supranational legal order and a set of supranational institutions, with a whole host of policies in trade, economic and monetary relations, social, environmental and other issue areas implemented in a multi-level governance system – a state-like polity comprising sovereign states. However, as Andrew Hurrell has noted 'there is no evidence that Europe is indicative of a post-Westphalian order or that it is likely to serve as a model for other regions' (Hurrell 2007: 143). It is, nonetheless, a regional polity that can exercise external influence in international trade, and it is through trade that the EU has shaped the regional integration processes in other parts of the world.

Conclusion

This chapter has examined the way in which the EU has sought to influence regional integration in other parts of the world, distinguishing between different approaches according to the political and strategic imperatives facing the member states. Enlargement has provided the best instance of successful regional integration, expanding the regulatory, legal and political order in return for membership. Much less successful have been the attempts to 'export' a significant part of the European governance to the neighbouring countries in the context of the European neighbourhood policy, though the EU member states signified renewed efforts in 2008 to deepen co-operation with the Mediterranean countries, and to promote regional co-operation and integration among the countries of the region.

Beyond the neighbourhood, the promotion of regional integration through inter-regional co-operation and, normatively, with the EU as an exemplar has yielded mixed results. In any event, the EU acts as a regional actor in negotiations and dialogue with other regions, processes of interaction and communication that pressure the other 'partner' to think and act regionally. Inter-regional co-operation also provides a basis for agreeing common norms, and ultimately paves the way towards common standards and shared governance. Whether this will ultimately result in the widespread 'Europeanisation' of governance at the international level only time will tell.

Certainly there is scope through the promotion of regional integration, where the EU uses its trade policy as an instrument of leverage in the hands of the European Commission to influence other countries. But there remain some constraints on this capability in the lack of consistency to the approaches used by the EU, and sometimes the credibility of the European actor in the face of internal contradictions and tensions that inevitably weaken external policy action. In the absence of a coherent and co-ordinated external policy and the architecture to support foreign policy proposed in the Lisbon Treaty, these constraints will compromise any efforts to promote and support regional integration.

Finally, there are two promising lines of further research that are taking the study of 'Europe in the world' in new and interesting directions, and that may help to deepen the analysis of how and to what extent the EU can promote regional integration, or indeed whether it should. One is the study of 'Europeanisation' beyond Europe, which offers a fruitful research agenda, and the opportunity to undertake an analysis of the politics of inter-regional co-operation, and of regional polity-building, by going beyond the discussions of EU as civilian or normative power to analyse external policies with the explicit focus on 'Europeanisation' but looking at processes from the target countries (Schimmelfennig 2007). The second, and related line of enquiry focuses on the EU's position in relation to global governance, and to the interaction between regional and global governance systems generally. Much criticism has been directed at the contemporary global governance system, mostly a product of the immediate post-war period and perceived as unevenly representing the contemporary global system of states – the effectiveness, democracy and legitimacy of the system has long been questioned by academic and political analysts in non-core and core states alike. As Hurrell concludes, 'the organisation of regions, the capacity of regions to generate and promote ideas of global order, and the claim of different regions to be represented more fully and more equally are likely to play a central role in the coming struggle for global political legitimacy' (Hurrell 2007: 146).

Notes

1 On the EU side, the troika consists of the current and incoming EU presidency (until the Lisbon Treaty comes into effect), the European Commission and the EU Council Secretariat; on the African side, representation comprises the current and outgoing presidencies of the African Union, and the AU Commission.

2 The Mediterranean countries are Albania, Algeria, Bosnia-Herzegovina, Croatia, Egypt, Israel, Jordan, Lebanon, Libya, Mauritania, Monaco, Montenegro, Morocco, the Palestinian Authority, Syria, Tunisia and Turkey.

3 The Cotonou Agreement covers relations between the EU and Sub-Saharan Africa. Relations with the countries of north Africa are based on the Euro-Mediterranean Partnership and Association Agreements, and the European Neighbourhood Policy and ENP Action Plans.

4 The Africa–EU Strategic partnership applies to the whole of the African continent.

5 The eight partnership and priority actions are: Africa–EU partnership on peace and security; democratic governance and human rights; trade, regional integration and infrastructure; Millennium Development Goals; energy; climate change; migration, mobility and employment; science, information society and space.

6 Under the open method of co-ordination the European Commission prepares a set of broad guidelines to which the member states adhere while maintaining their own individual national policies and strategic objectives – member states report annually to the Commission but retain the freedom to set policies appropriate to the national contexts and political priorities. The loose co-ordination approach contrasts with other methods of European governance, in particular with the policy harmonisation in the policy areas such as trade, competition, agriculture and the single currency.

7 North East Asia includes some of the largest countries in the region, as well as small trade-oriented economies – Japan, South Korea, China, as well as Hong Kong and Taiwan.

8 See the Joint Declaration of the Paris Summit for the Mediterranean, 13 July 2008, Paris, announced during the French presidency.

References

Acharya, A. and Johnston, A. I. (2007) *Crafting Co-operation: Regional International Institutions in Comparative Perspective*, Cambridge: Cambridge University Press.

Aggarwal, V. A. and Fogarty, E. (2004) *EU Trade Strategies between Regionalism and Globalism*, Basingstoke: Palgrave.

Babarinde, O. (2007) 'The EU as a Model for the African Union: the Limits of Imitation', University of Miami Jean Monnet/Robert Schuman Paper 7 (2). Online. Available: www.miami.edu/eucenter (accessed 18 December 2008).

Balme, R. and Bridges, B. (2008) *Europe–Asia Relations: Building Multilateralisms*, Basingstoke: Palgrave.

Camilleri, J. (2003) *Regionalism in the New Asia-Pacific Order*, Cheltenham: Edward Elgar.

Conde, C. (2007) 'Reality intrudes on dreams of EU-like pact for Asean', *International Herald Tribune*, 28 January. Online. Available: http://carlosconde.com/2007/01/ (accessed 24 October 2008).

Crawford, G. (2004) 'The European Union and democracy promotion in Africa: the case of Ghana', *European Journal of Development Research* 17 (4): 571–600.

EU–Africa Summit (2007) 'The Africa–EU Strategic Partnership: a Joint Africa–EU Strategy'. Online. Available http: www.eu2007.pt/NR/rdonlyres/D449546C-BF42–4CB3-B566–407591845C43/0/071206jsapenlogos_formatado.pdf (accessed 16 October 2008).

EU–AU (2007) 'Lisbon Declaration : EU Africa Summit', 8–9 December 2007, Lisbon. Online. Available: http://euroafrica-ict.org/downloads/Lisbon_declaration.pdf (accessed 12 December 2008).

European Commission (2003) 'The European Union and the United Nations: the choice of multilateralism', Communication Com (2003) 526, 10 September 2003. Online. Available: http://europa.eu/scadplus/leg/en/lvb/r00009.htm (accessed 24 October 2008).

European Council (2003) 'A Secure Europe in a Better World: a European Security Strategy', European Security Strategy adopted on 12 December 2003. Online. Available: http://consilium.europa.eu/uedocs/cmsUpload/78367.pdf (accessed 22 October 2008).

—— (2007) 'European Council Meeting. Presidency Conclusions', Brussels, 14 February. Online. Available: www.consilium.europa.eu/ueDocs/cms_Data/docs/pressData/en/ec/97669.pdf (accessed 24 October 2008).

Farrell, M. (2006) 'EU Representation and Co-ordination within the United Nations', in K. V. Laatikainen and K. E. Smith (eds) *The European Union at the United Nations: Intersecting Multilateralisms*, London: Palgrave.

—— (2007) 'From EU model to external policy? Promoting regional integration in the rest of the world', in S. Meunier and K. R. McNamara (eds) *Making History: European Integration and Institutional Change at Fifty*, Oxford: Oxford University Press.

—— (2009) 'EU–Asia co-operation: from interregionalism to bilateralism?' in F. Söderbaum and P. Stälgren (eds) *The European Union and the Global South*, Boulder, CO: Lynne Rienner.

Fassbinder, B. (2004) 'The Better People's of the United Nations? Europe's practice and the United Nations', *European Journal of International Law* 15 (5): 857–84.

Hemner, C. and Katzenstein, P. (2002) 'Why is there no NATO in Asia? Collective identity, regionalism and the origins of multilateralism', *International Organisation* 56 (3): 575–607.

Hoffmeister, F. (2007) 'Outsider or front runner? Recent developments under international and European law on the status of the European Union in international organisations and treaty bodies', *Common Market Law Review* 44: 41–68.

Hurrell, A. (2007) 'One world? Many worlds? The place of regions in the study of international society', *International Affairs* 83 (1): 127–46.

Kenen, P. B. and Meade, E. E. (2008) *Regional Monetary Integration*, Cambridge: Cambridge University Press.

Kühnhardt, L. (2005) 'Northeast Asia: obstacles to regional integration. The interests of the European Union', ZEI Discussion Paper C152. Online. Available: www.zei.de (accessed 28 December 2008).

Laatikainen, K. V. and Smith, K. E. (2006) *The European Union at the United Nations: Intersecting Multilateralisms*, London: Palgrave.

Lavenex, S. (2008) 'A governance perspective on the European neighbourhood policy: integration beyond conditionality?' *Journal of European Public Policy* 15 (6): 938–55.

Meunier, S. and Nicolaïdis, K. (2006) 'The European Union as a conflicted trade power', *Journal of European Public Policy* 13 (6): 200–32.

Nivet, B. (2006) 'Security by proxy? The EU and (sub)regional organisations: the case of ECOWAS', Institute for Security Studies Occasional Paper 63, Paris: ISS. Online. Available: www.iss-eu.org (accessed 14 December 2008).

Savino, M. (2006) 'The role of transnational committees in the European and global orders', *Global Jurist Advances* 6 (3). Online. Available: www.bepress.com/gj/advances/vol. 6/iss3/art5 (accessed 17 October 2008).

Schimmelfennig, F. (2007) 'Europeanization beyond Europe', *Living Rev. Euro. Gov.* 2 (1) 2007. Online. Available: www.livingreviews.org/lreg-2007–1 (accessed 29 December 2008).

Toniatti, R. (2007) 'The European Security and Defence Administration within the Context of the Global Legal Space', NYU School of Law Jean Monnet Working Paper 7/2007. Online. Available: www.jeanmonnetprogram.org/papers/07/070701.pdf (accessed 29 December 2008).

Vachudova, M. A. (2007) 'Historical institutionalism and the EU's eastward enlargement', in S. Meunier and K. R. McNamara (eds) *Making History European Integration and Institutional Change at Fifty*, Oxford: Oxford University Press.

Wouters, J. (2007) 'The United Nations and the European Union: Partners in Multilateralism', EU Diplomacy Papers 4 (2007). Online. Available: www.coleurope.eu/file/content/studyprogrammes/ird/research/pdf/EDP%204–2007%20Wouters.pdf (accessed 29 December 2008).

2 EU threat perceptions and governance

Emil J. Kirchner and Maximilian B. Rasch

There is increasing acceptance that the European Union (EU) is becoming an important actor in foreign and security matters (Hill and Smith 2005; Keukeleire and MacNaughtan 2007; Meyer 2005; Smith 2004). A significant factor in the rising importance of EU security activities derived from the 1999 decision by EU leaders to add European Security and Defence Policy (ESDP) to the scope of its security activities. As a consequence, the EU has not only improved its institutional and decision-making capacity, but has also augmented its policy activities in this field, especially through a number of civil–military missions in various parts of the globe. Apart from contributing to peace and stability in the European context through, for example, enlargement rounds and the European Neighbourhood Policy and Stability and Association Process for the Western Balkans, the EU has also extended its security activities to places as far afield as Africa (ESDP missions to the Democratic Republic of Congo) and Asia (ESDP mission to Aceh). Yet, while this phenomenon is unfolding, and while the so-called European Security Strategy of 2003 has identified perceived security threats to the EU and outlined a general response approach to these threats, few specific data exist on how EU decision-makers rank these threats or which instruments they deem appropriate for dealing with the ranked threats (Kirchner and Sperling 2002). It is the aim of this chapter to examine threat perceptions by EU elites across both military and non-military type of threats, and to explore which type of instruments EU policy-makers prefer in response to given threats. A further objective is to assess what importance policy-makers assign to the EU as a security actor, and whether a strengthened EU security dimension is viewed as detrimental to the role of North Atlantic Treaty Organisation (NATO) and US commitments to European security.

The chapter will first focus EU policy-makers' threat perceptions and then proceed with an analysis of the institutions and instruments policy-makers prefer in response to threats. This will be followed a review of EU policy-makers' perceptions of interstate interactions and security conceptions. The empirical findings presented herein are based on a survey, which was conducted between June 2006 and February 2007. It consisted of 43 respondents: 12 Members of the European Parliament (MEPs), 14 civil servants, including 6 Ambassadors of the EU member states in the Political and Social Committee (PSoC), and 17 academic security experts. Further details of this survey can be found in Kirchner and Rasch (2007).

Threat perceptions

While traditional security studies were primarily concerned with threats emanating between states and in which territorial defence or survival were seen as core aspects, studies in the 1990s, and particularly in the last five years, have expanded the rubric of security threats through the inclusion of a number of so-called non-military threats. The pros and cons of this expansion have been subject to a debate among scholars (see, for example, Baldwin 1997; Krause 1998). No effort will be made here to rehearse this debate but rather concentrate on the actual perceptions EU policy-makers have about security threats and the instruments or measures they deem necessary in response to those threats. The following will assess the major findings and implications of the above-mentioned survey on security threats.

In the survey, EU policy-makers were asked to choose, from a list of thirteen given threats, the five gravest threats the EU is facing today. Within those five threats identified respondents had to rank-order between 1 (gravest threat) and 5 (least grave threat). This classification was done for both 2006 and 2010. Only very few respondents cited threats other than those provided in the list.

The top three gravest security threats of the three target groups are quite similar for both 2006 and 2010 (see Tables 2.1–2.2). For 2006, MEPs and academic experts identified 'terrorist attacks against state or society' as the gravest threat (with a mean of 1.60 and 2.13 respectively). For the civil servants, this category ranked only fourth. They regarded 'macroeconomic instability' as the gravest threat to the EU (mean of 1.86). Only minor differences occur between the three groups of respondents when looking at the second and third gravest threats, as in all three cases 'migratory pressures' and 'terrorism against critical infrastructure' come up, even though not in the same order. Civil servants and academic experts assign the second highest rankings for 2006 to 'terrorism against critical infrastructure' (with a mean of 2.00 and 2.27 respectively); MEPs rank this threat as third highest (mean of 2.86). For MEPs the second highest average ranking is attributed to 'migratory pressures' (mean of 2.67), a threat seen by civil servants and academic experts as third-ranked (with a mean of 2.29 and 2.70 respectively).

The three target groups agree that terrorism is expected to remain a key threat in 2010 (see Tables 2.1 and 2.3): concerning 'terrorist attacks against state or society', MEPs assign the top rank to this category (mean of 1.78), while civil servants and academic experts both put it in third position (mean of 2.50 and 2.93 respectively). 'Terrorism against critical infrastructure' ranks first in 2010 for academic experts and is placed second by MEPs (mean of 2.27 and 2.57 respectively). An issue not among the top three in 2006

Table 2.1 Mean perceptions of security threats, 2006 and 2010

Threat	Year	Civil servants (n = 14)	MEPs (n = 12)	Academic experts (n = 17)	Overall (n = 43)
Biological/chemical	2006	3.33 (6)	0.00 (0)	3.00 (7)	3.15 (13)
	2010	3.50 (6)	3.00 (1)	3.29 (7)	3.36 (14)
Conventional war	2006	3.00 (2)	3.00 (1)	3.00 (1)	3.00 (4)
	2010	3.00 (2)	1.00 (1)	3.00 (1)	2.50 (4)
Criminalisation of	2006	3.57 (7)	3.00 (5)	2.33 (3)	3.13 (15)
economy	2010	3.43 (7)	4.00 (5)	2.00 (3)	3.33 (15)
Cyber-attack	2006	3.25 (4)	3.50 (2)	4.00 (2)	3.50 (8)
	2010	3.67 (6)	4.50 (4)	3.33 (3)	3.85 (13)
Ethnic conflict	2006	4.00 (3)	3.67 (6)	2.86 (7)	3.38 (16)
	2010	3.33 (6)	3.25 (4)	2.80 (5)	3.13 (15)
Macroeconomic	2006	1.86 (7)	3.33 (3)	2.33 (6)	2.31 (16)
instability	2010	2.20 (5)	4.00 (2)	3.14 (7)	2.93 (14)
Man-made	2006	2.36 (11)	3.57 (7)	2.83 (12)	2.83 (30)
environmental	2010	2.00 (12)	3.13 (8)	2.58 (12)	2.50 (32)
Migratory pressures	2006	2.29 (7)	2.67 (6)	2.70 (10)	2.57 (23)
	2010	2.91 (11)	2.71 (7)	3.46 (13)	3.10 (31)
Narcotics trafficking	2006	3.00 (8)	2.50 (2)	4.00 (5)	3.27 (15)
	2010	3.00 (5)	3.00 (1)	4.20 (5)	3.55 (11)
Natural disasters/	2006	2.56 (9)	3.67 (3)	3.63 (8)	3.15 (20)
pandemics	2010	2.00 (9)	4.00 (1)	3.00 (7)	2.53 (17)
Nuclear/radiological	2006	3.00 (4)	0.00 (0)	3.33 (3)	3.14 (7)
	2010	3.20 (5)	0.00 (0)	2.00 (4)	2.67 (9)
Terrorism: critical	2006	2.00 (9)	2.86 (7)	2.27 (11)	2.33 (27)
infrastructure	2010	2.63 (8)	2.57 (7)	2.27 (11)	2.46 (26)
Terrorism: state or	2006	2.70 (10)	1.60 (10)	2.13 (15)	2.14 (35)
society	2010	2.50 (8)	1.78 (9)	2.93 (14)	2.48 (31)

Note
Numbers in brackets indicate how many respondents have chosen each threat. Only when this number represents at least 50 per cent of the respondents in each target group were the results used later on in the evaluation.

gains considerable prominence in 2010: 'man-made environmental threats'. Civil servants assumed that this thematic complex would pose the gravest threat to the EU in 2010 (mean of 2.00) and academic experts rank it second highest (mean of 2.58). Besides both categories of terrorism and 'man-made environmental threats' two other categories were ranked within the top three security threats: Civil servants put 'natural disasters and pandemics' at

Table 2.2 Top three security threats, 2006

Rank	Civil servants (n = 14)	MEPs (n = 12)	Academic experts (n = 17)	Overall (n = 43)
1	Macroeconomic instability	Terrorism: state or society	Terrorism: state or society	Terrorism: state or society
2	Terrorism: infrastructure	Migratory pressures	Terrorism: infrastructure	Terrorism: infrastructure
3	Migratory pressures	Terrorism: infrastructure	Migratory pressures	Migratory pressures

second position (mean of 2.00[1]), whereas MEPs ranked 'migratory pressures' third (mean of 2.71).

Only measured differences are ascertainable between PSoC ambassadors and the other civil servants interviewed (see Tables 2.4–6). However, there was a slight tendency on the part of PSoC ambassadors to give more importance to soft threats. Accordingly, 'man-made environmental threats', 'macroeconomic instability' and 'natural disasters and pandemics' ranked highest for 2006. For 2010, the threat perceptions of PSoC ambassadors and the other civil servants are even more congruent.

When looking at the overall mean perceptions of security threats it is notable that the two categories on terrorism are the ones most salient in 2006 and 2010, while 'migratory pressures' (2006) and 'man-made environmental threats' (2010) rank third. This reflects that European elites remain very much influenced by the direct impact that terrorism has on strategy, decision-making and action-taking since 11 September 2001.

Having examined types of security threat, attention will now turn to the origin of security threats. This will provide a more rounded picture when considering the response to security threats.

Table 2.3 Top three security threats, 2010

Rank	Civil servants (n = 14)	MEPs (n = 12)	Academic experts (n = 17)	Overall (n = 43)
1	Environmental threats	Terrorism: state or society	Terrorism: infrastructure	Terrorism: infrastructure
2	Disasters and pandemics	Terrorism: infrastructure	Environmental threats	Terrorism: state or society
3	Terrorism: state or society	Migratory pressures	Terrorism: state or society	Environmental threats

Table 2.4 Civil servants: mean perceptions of security threats, 2006 and 2010

Threat	Year	PSC ambassadors	Other civil servants	Overall civil servants
Biological/chemical	2006	3.50 (2)	3.25 (4)	3.33 (6)
	2010	4.00 (2)	3.25 (4)	3.50 (6)
Conventional war	2006	1.00 (1)	5.00 (1)	3.00 (2)
	2010	1.00 (1)	5.00 (1)	3.00 (2)
Criminalisation of economy	2006	3.50 (2)	3.60 (5)	3.57 (7)
	2010	3.00 (2)	3.60 (5)	3.43 (7)
Cyber-attack	2006	3.50 (2)	3.00 (2)	3.25 (4)
	2010	3.33 (3)	4.00 (3)	3.67 (6)
Ethnic conflict	2006	3.50 (2)	5.00 (1)	4.00 (3)
	2010	3.50 (2)	3.25 (4)	3.33 (6)
Macroeconomic instability	2006	1.75 (4)	2.00 (3)	1.86 (7)
	2010	3.00 (2)	1.67 (3)	2.20 (5)
Man-made environmental	2006	1.50 (4)	2.86 (7)	2.36 (11)
	2010	1.60 (5)	2.29 (7)	2.00 (12)
Migratory pressures	2006	2.50 (2)	2.20 (5)	2.29 (7)
	2010	3.20 (5)	2.67 (6)	2.91 (11)
Narcotics trafficking	2006	2.67 (3)	3.20 (5)	3.00 (8)
	2010	3.50 (2)	2.67 (3)	3.00 (5)
Natural disasters/pandemics	2006	2.60 (5)	2.50 (4)	2.56 (9)
	2010	1.80 (5)	2.25 (4)	2.00 (9)
Nuclear/radiological	2006	2.50 (2)	3.50 (2)	3.00 (4)
	2010	2.00 (2)	4.00 (3)	3.20 (5)
Terrorism: critical infrastructure	2006	2.50 (2)	1.86 (7)	2.00 (9)
	2010	3.00 (2)	2.50 (6)	2.63 (8)
Terrorism: state or society	2006	2.67 (3)	2.71 (7)	2.70 (10)
	2010	3.34 (3)	2.00 (5)	2.50 (8)

Note
Numbers in brackets indicate how many respondents have chosen each threat. Only when this number represents at least 50 per cent of the respondents in each target group were the results used later on in the evaluation.

Origins of threats

Respondents were asked to state the origins of the five gravest threats they had selected previously from the list of thirteen threats. They could do so by naming specific cases in two categories: 'states and regions' and 'non-state actors'.

Table 2.5 Civil servants: top three security threats, 2006

Rank	PSC ambassadors	Other civil servants	Overall civil servants
1	Man-made environmental	Terrorism: critical infrastructure	Macroeconomic instability
2	Macroeconomic instability	Migratory pressures	Terrorism: infrastructure
3	Natural disasters/ pandemics	Natural disasters/ pandemics	Migratory pressures

The overall impression is that no clear preference prevails for one of the two categories (see Tables 2.7a–b). Even though 'non-state actors' have been chosen 124 times and 'states or regions' only 108 times, the difference between these results does not seem large enough to be significant.

Man-made environmental threats, migratory pressures and terrorism against state or society are ranked as the top three threats having their *origins in states and regions* (see Table 2.7a). Industrialised regions and countries, especially the US, China and India are listed as responsible for man-made environmental threats. Particularly Africa, but also Asia and in general failed states, are seen as the origins of migratory pressures. Terrorism against state or society rooting in specific states or regions is regarded as originating in the Middle East, Iran, Pakistan and also Afghanistan.

Non-state actors of origins of threats were most often mentioned in connection with the two categories of terrorism (see Table 2.7b); third came man-made environmental threats. Not surprisingly, terrorists and fundamentalists, most often with Islamist or other religious motivations, are regarded as the main actors involved in terrorism directed against state, society or critical infrastructure. Man-made environmental threats are seen by the survey participants to be caused above all by industry and corporations, but also militant activists and globalisation are mentioned.

Table 2.6 Civil servants: top three security threats in 2010

Rank	PSC ambassadors	Other civil servants	Overall civil servants
1	Man-made environmental	Terrorism: state or society	Environmental threats
2	Natural disasters/ pandemics	Natural disasters/ pandemics	Disasters and pandemics
3	Migratory pressures	Man-made environmental	Terrorism: state or society

Threat response

Given the diverse picture presented on types and origin of security threat, which policy instruments are most suitable to address current security threats? This question has been answered by the survey participants for the five gravest threats they had chosen out of the list of thirteen threats in the previous question. They were able to choose among five policy instruments, namely 'diplomacy', 'economic and financial assistance', 'police co-operation

Table 2.7a Percentage naming states and regions as origins of security threats

Threat	Civil servants (n = 12)	MEPs (n = 12)	Security experts (n = 14)	Overall (n = 38)
Biological/chemical attack			21.4 (3)	7.9 (3)
Conventional war	8.3 (1)	8.3 (1)		5.3 (2)
Criminalisation of economy	33.3 (4)	16.7 (2)		15.8 (6)
Cyber-attack	8.3 (1)	8.3 (1)		5.3 (2)
Ethnic conflict	8.3 (1)	33.3 (4)	28.6 (4)	23.7 (9)
Macroeconomic instability	33.3 (4)	25.0 (3)	21.4 (3)	26.3 (10)
Man-made environmental	58.3 (7)	41.7 (5)	50.0 (7)	50.0 (19)
Migratory pressures	33.3 (4)	41.7 (5)	50.0 (7)	42.1 (16)
Narcotics trafficking	33.3 (4)	16.7 (2)	14.3 (2)	21.1 (8)
Natural disaster/pandemics	33.3 (4)	16.7 (2)	35.7 (5)	29.0 (11)
Nuclear/radiological attacks	16.7 (2)		7.1 (1)	7.9 (3)
Terrorism: critical infrastructure	8.3 (1)	33.3 (4)	14.3 (2)	18.4 (7)
Terrorism: state or society	16.7 (2)	50.0 (6)	28.6 (4)	31.6 (12)

Table 2.7b Percentage naming non-state actors as origins of security threats

Threat	Civil servants (n = 12)	MEPs (n = 12)	Academic experts (n = 14)	Overall (n = 38)
Biological/chemical attack	33.3 (4)		28.6 (4)	21.1 (8)
Conventional war		8.3 (1)		2.6 (1)
Criminalisation of economy	41.7 (5)	41.7 (5)	14.3 (2)	31.6 (12)
Cyber-attack	16.7 (2)	16.7 (2)		10.5 (4)
Ethnic conflict	16.7 (2)	41.7 (5)	21.4 (3)	26.3 (10)
Macroeconomic instability	25.0 (3)	8.3 (1)	14.3 (2)	15.8 (6)
Man-made environmental	50.0 (6)	41.7 (5)	28.6 (4)	39.5 (15)
Migratory pressures	8.3 (1)	25.0 (3)	21.4 (3)	18.4 (7)
Narcotics trafficking	41.7 (5)	8.3 (1)	14.3 (2)	21.1 (8)
Natural disaster/pandemics	33.3 (4)	8.3 (1)	14.3 (2)	18.4 (7)
Nuclear/radiological attacks	16.7 (2)			5.3 (2)
Terrorism: critical infrastructure	58.3 (7)	33.3 (4)	57.1 (8)	50.0 (19)
Terrorism: state or society	66.7 (8)	58.3 (7)	71.4 (10)	65.8 (25)

and intelligence sharing', 'traditional military' and 'special operations'. In addition, respondents could name other policy instruments they deemed important, and select as many instruments as they wished.

A full overview of the results of this part of the survey is given in Table 2.8. The values in brackets behind the percentages show how many individuals have chosen a specific policy instrument for each of the thirteen threats. Boxes remain empty if none of the participants selected the policy instrument.

When looking at the overall frequency with which the individual policy instruments have been selected, it becomes clear that there is a preference for 'police co-operation and intelligence sharing' (see Table 2.9). 26.5 per cent of all entries fell into this category. 'Economic and financial assistance' and 'diplomatic' policy instruments obtained about a fifth each of all selections.

The hard security instruments 'traditional military' and 'special operations' only rank at fourth and fifth position. In particular, the low output for military instruments implicates a shift in thinking towards a wider definition of security, reflecting the multi-faceted dimension of current threats, and the fact that threats come from distant parts of the world, for which reason defence in traditional terms is ineffective.

For seven of the thirteen security threats 'police co-operation and intelligence sharing' are given as the best policy instrument when looking at the overall results. The threats are biological and chemical attacks, criminalisation of the economy, cyber-attacks, narcotics trafficking, nuclear and radiological attacks, as well as the two categories of terrorist attacks. 'Economic and financial assistance' was seen as the best instrument to address four security threats, namely macroeconomic instability, man-made environmental threats, migratory pressures and natural disasters and pandemics. And finally, conventional war and ethnic conflict was regarded to be tackled most suitably via 'diplomatic' means.

The analysis of group internal preferences for policy instruments displays interesting differences between civil servants, MEPs and academic experts (see Table 2.10). Civil servants have the lowest preference for soft security instruments, i.e. 'diplomacy' and 'economic and financial assistance'. On the other hand they most often selected the hard security instruments available, namely 'military', 'police co-operation' and 'special operations'. This is even more surprising as the majority of these civil servants work at the 'soft end' of EU power. In contrast, security experts, many of whom are academics, tended most often to choose soft security instruments. The MEPs participating in the survey took a middle course between civil servants and academic experts in all categories and most often suggested alternative policy instruments being important, such as control of demographic developments, intercultural dialogue and the proactive fight against AIDS.

Differences also occurred within the target group of civil servants (see Table 2.10). While PSoC ambassadors and the other civil servants shared the view that 'police co-operation' is the most important policy instrument,

Table 2.8 Best policy instruments to address security threats (%)

Threat	Civil servants, (n = 14)	MEPs (n = 12)	Academic experts (n = 17)	Overall (n = 43)
Biological/chemical attacks				
Diplomatic			11.8 (2)	4.7 (2)
Economic/financial assistance			11.8 (2)	4.7 (2)
Police co-operation/ intelligence sharing	28.6 (4)		35.3 (6)	23.3(10)
Traditional military	14.3 (2)		5.9 (1)	7.0 (3)
Special operations	21.4 (3)		29.4 (5)	18.6 (8)
Other				
Conventional war				
Diplomatic	14.3 (2)	8.3 (1)	5.9 (1)	9.3 (4)
Economic/financial assistance			5.9 (1)	2.3 (1)
Police co-operation/ intelligence sharing			5.9 (1)	2.3 (1)
Traditional military	7.1 (1)			2.3 (1)
Special operations	7.1 (1)			2.3 (1)
Other				
Criminalisation of economy				
Diplomatic	7.1 (1)	8.3 (1)	11.8 (2)	9.3 (4)
Economic/financial assistance	35.7 (5)	8.3 (1)	17.7 (3)	20.9 (9)
Police co-operation/ intelligence sharing	35.7 (5)	41.7 (5)	11.8 (2)	27.9(12)
Traditional military				
Special operations	7.1 (1)	8.3 (1)	5.9 (1)	7.0 (3)
Other		8.3 (1)		2.3 (1)
Cyber-attack				
Diplomatic			5.9 (1)	2.3 (1)
Economic/financial assistance	7.1 (1)		5.9 (1)	4.7 (2)
Police co-operation/ intelligence sharing	28.6 (4)	16.7 (2)	11.8 (2)	18.6 (8)
Traditional military				
Special operations		8.3 (1)		2.3 (1)
Other	7.1 (1)			2.3 (1)
Ethnic conflict				
Diplomatic	14.3 (2)	25.0 (3)	23.5 (4)	20.9 (9)
Economic/financial assistance	14.3 (2)	8.3 (1)	29.4 (5)	18.6 (8)
Police co-operation/ intelligence sharing	7.1 (1)	16.7 (2)	17.7 (3)	14.0 (6)
Traditional military	14.3 (2)	8.3 (1)	5.9 (1)	9.3 (4)
Special operations	14.3 (2)	8.3 (1)		7.0 (3)
Other		16.7 (2)	11.8 (2)	9.3 (4)

Table 2.8 continued

Threat	Civil servants (n = 14)	MEPs (n = 12)	Academic experts (n = 17)	Overall (n = 43)
Macroeconomic instability				
Diplomatic	14.3 (2)	16.7 (2)	11.8 (2)	14.0 (6)
Economic/financial assistance	35.7 (5)	25.0 (3)	29.4 (5)	30.2 (13)
Police co-operation/ intelligence sharing			5.9 (1)	2.3 (1)
Traditional military				
Special operations				
Other	7.1 (1)	8.3 (1)	11.8 (2)	9.3 (4)
Man-made environmental threats				
Diplomatic	57.1 (8)	33.3 (4)	41.2 (7)	44.2 (19)
Economic/financial assistance	42.9 (6)	41.7 (5)	52.9 (9)	46.5 (20)
Police co-operation/ intelligence sharing	21.4 (3)	8.3 (1)	5.9 (1)	11.6 (5)
Traditional military	7.1 (1)			2.3 (1)
Special operations		16.7 (2)		4.7 (2)
Other	28.6 (4)	16.7 (2)	41.2 (7)	30.2 (13)
Migratory pressures				
Diplomatic	35.7 (5)	33.3 (4)	47.1 (8)	39.5 (17)
Economic/financial assistance	42.9 (6)	25.0 (3)	58.8 (10)	44.2 (19)
Police co-operation/ intelligence sharing	28.6 (4)	25.0 (3)	23.5 (4)	25.6 (11)
Traditional military				
Special operations	7.1 (1)			2.3 (1)
Other		16.7 (2)	5.9 (1)	7.0 (3)
Narcotics trafficking				
Diplomatic		8.3 (1)	23.5 (4)	11.6 (5)
Economic/financial assistance	14.3 (2)	8.3 (1)	17.7 (3)	14.0 (6)
Police co-operation/ intelligence sharing	57.1 (8)	16.7 (2)	23.5 (4)	32.6 (14)
Traditional military				
Special operations	42.9 (6)	16.7 (2)	11.8 (2)	23.3 (10)
Other	7.1 (1)	8.3 (1)		4.7 (2)
Natural disasters/pandemics				
Diplomatic	14.3 (2)		11.8 (2)	9.3 (4)
Economic/financial assistance	28.6 (4)	16.7 (2)	29.4 (5)	25.6 (11)
Police co-operation/ intelligence sharing	71.1 (1)		11.8 (2)	7.3 (2)
Traditional military	14.3 (2)			4.7 (2)
Special operations	7.1 (1)	8.3 (1)	17.7 (3)	11.6 (8)
Other	42.9 (6)	8.3 (1)	5.9 (1)	18.6 (8)

continued

Table 2.8 continued

Threat	Civil servants (n = 14)	MEPs (n = 12)	Academic experts (n = 17)	Overall (n = 43)
Nuclear/radiological attacks				
Diplomatic	7.1 (8)		11.8 (2)	7.0 (3)
Economic/financial assistance			5.9 (1)	2.3 (1)
Police co-operation/ intelligence sharing	21.4 (3)		17.7 (3)	14.0 (6)
Traditional military	21.4 (3)			7.0 (3)
Special operations	21.4 (3)		11.8 (2)	11.6 (5)
Other				
Terorist attacks: critical infrastructure				
Diplomatic	21.4 (3)	25.0 (3)	17.1 (3)	20.9 (9)
Economic/financial assistance	7.1 (1)	16.7 (2)	17.7 (3)	14.0 (6)
Police co-operation/ intelligence sharing	57.1 (8)	50.0 (6)	52.9 (9)	53.5 (23)
Traditional military	42.9 (6)	16.7 (2)		18.6 (8)
Special operations	50.0 (7)	33.3 (4)	47.1 (8)	44.2 (19)
Other		8.3 (1)	11.8 (2)	7.0 (3)
Terrorist attacks: state or society				
Diplomatic	28.6 (4)	50.0 (6)	47.1 (8)	41.9 (18)
Economic/financial assistance	7.1 (1)	33.3 (4)	29.4 (5)	23.3 (10)
Police co-operation/ intelligence sharing	64.3 (9)	75.0 (9)	76.5 (13)	72.1 (31)
Traditional military	35.7 (5)	16.7 (2)	11.8 (2)	20.9 (9)
Special operations	42.9 (6)	33.3 (4)	64.7 (11)	48.8 (21)
Other		25.0 (3)	11.8 (2)	11.6 (5)

PSoC ambassadors thought that 'economic and financial assistance' and 'traditional military' rank second (both with the same percentages). The other civil servants, however, believed that 'diplomacy' would be the second most important policy instrument, followed by 'special operations'.

What becomes apparent from the survey is that EU policy-makers have a preference for the non-military instruments in response to the most pressing security threats. This raises questions about the role of the EU as a security provider and its relationship with NATO and the US. These issues will be dealt with next.

Importance of the EU

How important is the EU at present to address the security threats facing Europe today? To deal with this question, respondents were asked to give their impression for each of the thirteen threats listed in Table 2.11. This time higher mean values imply higher importance, as the participants in the

Table 2. 9 Analysis: preferences for policy instruments

Policy instrument	Civil servants		MEPs		Academic experts		Overall	
	No.	%	No.	%	No.	%	No.	%
Diplomatic	30	16.8	25	22.3	46	22.7	101	20.4
Economic/financial assistance	33	18.4	22	19.6	53	26.1	108	21.9
Police co-operation/ intelligence sharing	50	27.9	30	26.8	51	25.1	131	26.5
Traditional military	22	12.3	5	4.5	4	2.0	31	6.3
Special operations	31	17.3	16	14.3	32	15.8	79	16.0
Other	13	7.3	14	12.5	17	8.4	44	8.9
Total	179	100.0	112	100.0	203	100.0	494	100.0

Note

This table shows how often the individual policy instruments have been selected within each target group. For instance, all civil servants taken together have selected 'diplomacy' thirty times as one of the most appropriate policy instruments to address the gravest security threats.

survey could choose between 0 ('not important at all') and 5 ('absolutely essential'). When looking at the overall results, the EU is seen as having the most important role to play in tackling macroeconomic instability, migratory pressures and man-made environmental threats. That very much reflects the notion of the EU as a 'soft power'. This impression is underpinned by the choices of the three threats the EU is regarded as being least important to address: cyber-attack, conventional war and biological or chemical attacks. In terms of hard security the Union is apparently seen as a comparably weak actor.

Table 2.10 Analysis: civil servants' preferences for policy instruments

Policy instrument	PSC ambassadors		Other civil servants		Overall civil servants	
	No.	%	No.	%	No.	%
Diplomatic	7	10.6	23	20.4	30	16.8
Economic/financial assistance	13	19.7	20	17.7	33	18.4
Police co-operation/intelligence sharing	16	24.2	34	30.1	50	27.9
Traditional military	13	19.7	9	8.0	22	12.3
Special operations	10	15.2	21	18.6	31	17.3
Other	7	10.6	6	5.3	13	7.3
Total	66	100.0	113	100.0	179	100.0

Table 2.11 Mean importance of the European Union

Threat	Civil servants (n = 8–12)	MEPs (n = 11–12)	Academic experts (n = 13–14)	Overall (n = 33–38)
Biological/chemical attack	2.92	2.50	2.79	2.74
Conventional war	2.33	2.67	3.00	2.68
Criminalisation of economy	3.08	4.00	3.36	3.47
Cyber-attack	2.17	2.73	2.64	2.51
Ethnic conflict	3.08	3.27	3.71	3.38
Macroeconomic instability	3.83	4.25	4.57	4.24
Man-made environmental	3.50	3.75	4.36	3.90
Migratory pressures	3.88	3.83	4.08	3.94
Narcotics trafficking	3.25	3.00	3.64	3.32
Natural disaster/pandemics	3.08	3.42	3.43	3.32
Nuclear/radiological attacks	2.67	2.50	3.07	2.76
Terrorism: critical infrastructure	2.67	3.08	3.00	2.92
Terrorism: state or society	2.92	3.25	3.14	3.11

Note

n may vary by question.

It is interesting that the average importance of the EU for all threats combined is rated the lowest by civil servants, and the highest by security experts. Apparently the people most closely involved in EU policy-making judge the impact of the organisation in terms of concrete threat response less positively than the observers in academic circles or 'think tanks' (see also Table 2.12).

Table 2.12 Civil servants: mean importance of the European Union

Threat	PSC	Civil servants	Overall civil servants
Biological/chemical attack	3.17	2.67	2.92
Conventional war	2.50	2.17	2.33
Criminalisation of economy	3.00	3.17	3.08
Cyber-attack	2.33	2.00	2.17
Ethnic conflict	3.50	2.67	3.08
Macroeconomic instability	3.67	4.00	3.83
Man-made environmental	3.33	3.67	3.50
Migratory pressures	3.00	4.17	3.88
Narcotics trafficking	3.33	3.17	3.25
Natural disaster/pandemics	3.17	3.00	3.08
Nuclear/radiological attacks	3.33	2.00	2.67
Terrorism: critical infrastructure	2.50	2.83	2.67
Terrorism: state or society	3.00	2.83	2.92
Base *n* (may vary by question)	2–6	6	8–12

It is worth while to compare elite and public views on the putative importance of the EU in addressing key threats. According to the latest Eurobarometer survey, the most positive role of the EU is seen by the public in fighting terrorism, as well as in defence and foreign affairs (European Commission 2007: 117). Only concerning the third rank within the Eurobarometer survey is the public in agreement with elite security experts about the Union's role by naming the protection of the environment. Nevertheless, these and other Eurobarometer figures suggest that the public in the twenty-seven EU member states perceives the EU much more as a hard security actor than do the experts.

Spending on threat response

Appropriate and effective threat response to a large extent depends on adequate investment in capacities, instruments and resources. It is therefore important to analyse whether the overall funding used for hard security, and the way the money is spent, stand in apt relation to the security situation.

The majority of experts in all three target groups share the view that budgetary resources and manpower are misaligned with the threats Europe faces today (see Table 2.13). It is noteworthy, however, that three-quarters of civil servants and security experts see a misalignment, while only half the MEPs share this sentiment.

However, it is not simply the size of national defence budgets which causes the misalignment. When looking at the overall results of the survey, more than half the respondents believe that the budgets are just the right size (see Table 2.14). Only the majority of academic experts regard the budgets as too small.

The key to why there is a perceived misalignment of resources while the resources are largely considered of appropriate size can be found in resource distribution and military modernisation. On average, 78.4 per cent of all respondents believe that the distribution of defence budgets does not meet the needs resulting from the current security environment (see Table 2.15). The highest proportion of people within the three target groups which regard the distribution as appropriate are security academic experts (35.7 per cent). On the other hand, 91.7 per cent of MEPs think that that the distribution is unsuitable to address the security threats.

Table 2.13 Alignment of budgetary and manpower resources with threats (%)

Alignment	Civil servants (n = 12)	MEPs (n = 11)	Academic experts (n = 14)	Overall, in % (n = 37)
Aligned	25.0 (3)	45.5 (5)	28.6 (4)	32.4 (12)
Misaligned	75.0 (9)	54.6 (6)	71.4 (10)	67.6 (25)

Note
Numbers in brackets indicate how many respondents chose each alternative. *n* = number of respondents.

Table 2.14 Evaluations of EU member states' national defence budgets and military modernisation (%)

Size of budget	Civil servants (n = 12)	MEPs (n = 11)	Academic experts (n = 14)	Overall (n = 37)
Too large	0.0 (0)	0.0 (0)	0.0 (0)	0.0 (0)
Just about right	50.0 (6)	63.6 (7)	42.9 (6)	51.4 (19)
Too little	50.0 (6)	36.4 (4)	57.1 (8)	48.7 (18)

Note
Numbers in brackets indicate how many respondents chose each alternative. *n* = number of respondents.

Table 2.15 allows conclusions to be drawn as to where the problems within budget distribution are located. The overall results show that too much or enough money is being spent on personnel, but too little on procurement and research and development. In particular research and development is seen by all three target groups as a sector in which funding is inappropriate. Of all respondents 96.6 per cent share this view.

An effective and operational military also needs to experience constant modernisation. But are European armies seen as receiving enough funding for modernisation efforts? The majority of civil servants, MEPs and security experts (70.3 per cent) think that too little money is made available to that

Table 2.15 Satisfaction with distribution of defence budget spending

Level of satisfaction	Civil servants (n = 9–11)	MEPs (n = 10–12)	Academic Experts (n = 9–14)	Overall (n = 28–37)
Distribution of defence budget meets needs?				
Yes	18.2 (2)	8.3 (1)	35.7 (5)	21.6 (8)
No	81.8 (9)	91.7 (11)	64.3 (9)	78.4 (29)
Personnel				
Too much	44.5 (4)	45.5 (5)	44.5 (4)	44.8 (13)
Just about right	11.1 (1)	27.3 (3)	33.3 (3)	24.1 (7)
Too little	44.5 (4)	27.3 (3)	22.2 (2)	31.0 (9)
Procurement				
Too much	11.1 (1)	10.0 (1)	0.0 (0)	7.1 (2)
Just about right	0.0 (0)	10.0 (1)	11.1 (1)	7.1 (2)
Too little	88.9 (8)	80.0 (8)	88.9 (8)	85.7 (24)
Research and Development				
Too much	0.0 (0)	0.0 (0)	0.0 (0)	0.0 (0)
Just about right	11.1 (1)	0.0 (0)	0.0 (0)	3.5 (1)
Too little	88.9 (8)	100.0 (11)	100.0(9)	96.6 (28)

Note
Numbers in brackets indicate how many respondents chose each alternative. *n* = number of respondents.
n may vary by question.

end (see Table 2.16). Only a third (27 per cent) of all survey participants believe that just enough funds are being devoted to military modernisation. It is noteworthy that the civil servants have the most positive impression in this question, while security experts see the situation most negatively.

Notably, on all budgetary questions PSoC ambassadors assess the situation slightly more negatively than the other civil servants. In all following examinations the views of both subgroups are almost identical.

ESDP, US commitment and NATO

Security policies of the EU and the US, on the one hand, and the EU and NATO, on the other, are linked and often *de facto* complementary. However, with the emergence of an ever more institutionalised, effective and resourceful European Security and Defence Policy (ESDP), tensions over power and influence have emerged between the US-dominated NATO and the European security framework ESDP, also with repercussions on transatlantic relations.

But, according to the results of the survey, a prospering ESDP does not significantly impair NATO's status. Almost 70 per cent of all respondents believed that a more autonomous ESDP would not, or would only to a limited extent, weaken NATO further (see Table 2.17). Only around 15 per cent of all participants attributed some or very much weakening impact to the ESDP. Interestingly, civil servants saw the least likelihood of such a negative impact.

The three target groups are divided on the question whether a weaker NATO would lead to a retrenchment of US commitment to European security (see Table 2.17). The majority of civil servants surveyed (41.7 per cent) believe that such a scenario is not likely. Most MEPs (45.5 per cent), however, think exactly the opposite and see the possibility of a retrenchment of US commitment to European security as a consequence of a weaker NATO. Half the security experts then opt for a 'maybe', followed by 35.7 per cent of those who disregard such an outcome. The discord between the groups is reflected in the overall results on this question, showing no clear preference.

Table 2.16 Funding for military modernisation

Level of satisfaction	Civil servants (n = 11)	MEPs (n = 12)	Academic experts (n = 14)	Overall (n = 37)
Sufficient funds to military modernisation?				
Too much	9.1 (1)	0.0 (0)	0.0 (0)	2.7 (1)
Just about right	36.4 (4)	33.3 (4)	14.3 (2)	27.0 (10)
Too little	54.6 (6)	66.7 (8)	85.7 (12)	70.3 (26)

Note
Numbers in brackets indicate how many respondents chose each alternative. *n* = number of respondents.

Nevertheless, the majority of respondents believe that the US commitment to European security is important (see Table 2.17): 36.8 per cent regard the US commitment as essential. A staggering 94.7 per cent of all the participants' views can be found in the top three categories 'essential', 'very important' and 'important'. Only two security experts saw the US commitment as being 'not very important' and not a single respondent as 'inessential'.

Interstate interactions and security conceptions

The aspect of US and NATO relations raises wider questions about EU policy-makers' perceptions on multilateralism and their definition of security in a broad or narrow sense. Respondents were asked to choose a position on a scale from 1 (solely unilateral) through 5 (strictly bilateral) to 9 (always multilateral), with intermediate stages between the three categories. As Table 2.18 illustrates, the means of the three target groups are remarkably similar, with around 7 suggesting an inter-state interaction pattern just between bilateral and multilateral. The lowest values obtained in the individual groups were 4, i.e. between unilateral and bilateral interaction. Interestingly MEPs had only 6 as the lowest value. With 8 and 9 as the extremes

Table 2.17 Perceptions of ESDP and US commitment to European security (%)

Perception	Civil servants (n = 12)	MEPs (n = 11–12)	Academic experts (n = 14)	Overall (n = 37–38)
More autonomous ESDP weaken NATO?				
Not at all	33.3 (4)	41.7 (5)	28.6 (4)	34.2 (13)
Little	41.7 (5)	25.0 (3)	35.7 (5)	34.2 (13)
Some	16.7 (2)	8.3 (1)	21.4 (3)	15.8 (6)
Very much	8.3 (1)	16.7 (2)	14.3 (2)	13.2 (5)
Don't know	0.0 (0)	8.3 (1)	0.0 (0)	2.6 (1)
Weaker NATO leads to retrenchment of US commitment to European security?				
Yes	25.0 (3)	45.5 (5)	7.1 (1)	24.3 (9)
Maybe	33.3 (4)	27.3 (3)	50.0 (7)	37.8 (14)
No	41.7 (5)	18.2 (2)	35.7 (5)	32.4 (12)
Don't know	0.0 (0)	9.1 (1)	7.1 (1)	5.4 (2)
American commitment to European security…?				
Essential	58.3 (7)	41.7 (5)	14.3 (2)	36.8 (14)
Very important	16.7 (2)	33.3 (4)	28.6 (4)	26.3 (10)
Important	25.0 (3)	25.0 (3)	42.9 (6)	31.6 (12)
Not very important	0.0 (0)	0.0 (0)	14.3 (2)	5.3 (2)
Inessential	0.0 (0)	0.0 (0)	0.0 (0)	0.0 (0)

Note
Numbers in brackets indicate how many respondents chose each alternative. *n* = number of respondents.

on the other end of the spectrum, the multilateral behaviour of their governments was communicated by a number of respondents.

When respondents were asked to assess the EU security conception, the
range of responses was broader (see Table 2.18). The idea was to find out if
the EU was seen as conceiving of security narrowly (i.e. focusing on issues
where hard power is required) or broadly (i.e. concentrating on issues where
soft power is necessary). The position had to be marked on a continuum
ranging from 'narrow' (1) through 'medium' (5) to 'very broad' (9). The
means of the three target groups were again located around 7, i.e. 'broad'.
The fact that the answers ranged from 1, 2 or 3 at one end of the scale to 9
at the other shows how different the perceptions of the EU are.

It should be noted that EU policy-makers often hover between a so-called
national and an EU outlook. Further research is required to differentiate
more clearly between the two viewpoints. This is particularly crucial with
regard to an understanding of the views of security experts on a specifically
European security culture.

Conclusion

What conclusion, then, can be drawn from EU policy-makers' perception of
security threats, institutional response and the role of the EU as a security
actor? A number of key characteristics prevail. Foremost among them is the
importance attributed by these actors to 'new' security threats. But not all
three groups agree on the ranking of these 'new threats'. Both MEPs and
security experts identified 'terrorist attacks against state and society' as the
gravest threat. However, civil servants ranked them fourth. Migratory pressures and 'terrorism against critical infrastructure' come second and third for
all three categories of respondent. While the picture for 2010 again has terrorism as the main threat for MEPs and security experts, civil servants rate
environmental threats and pandemics first and second.

Table 2.18 Mean evaluations of inter-state interactions and security conceptions

Evaluation	Civil servants (n = 12)	MEPs (n = 12)	Academic experts (n = 14)	Overall (n = 38)
Interstate interaction				
(1 solely unilateral; 5 strictly bilateral; 9 always multilateral; with intermediary stages)				
Mean	7.42	7.58	7.14	7.37
Minimum/maximum	4/9	6/9	4/8	4/9
Security conceptions				
(1 narrow; 5 medium; 9 very broad', with intermediary stages)				
Mean	7.08	6.42	6.93	6.82
Minimum/maximum	2/9	1/9	3/9	1/9

A similar picture emerges with regard to EU policy-makers' perceptions of appropriate response to threats, with civilian or 'soft power' aspects being singled out as the preferred instruments in dealing with security threats. Specifically, there is a preference for police co-operation and intelligence sharing, economic and financial assistance and diplomatic instruments. 'Hard' security instruments 'traditional military' and 'special operation' rank only in fourth and fifth position. The particularly low ranking for military instruments is in line with the adoption by MEPs, civil servants and security experts of a broad definition of security, and may also reflect that MEPs and civil servants work at the 'soft end' of EU power. In similar vein, MEPs, civil servants and security experts see EU actions as most relevant in response to threats constituting the 'new' security agenda, i.e. in tackling macroeconomic instability, migratory pressures and man-made environmental threats.

EU policy-makers felt that the national defence budgets were 'just about right'. They indicated, however, that the distribution of defence budgets does not meet the security requirements of the external environment, with too little being spent on procurement, research and development, and modernisation efforts.

Judging from the survey, the EU-level actors perceive a more autonomous ESDP as not significantly impairing NATO. A more differentiated picture emerges on the question of whether a weaker NATO would lead to a retrenchment of US commitment to European security. Whereas civil servants see such a development as unlikely, MEPs see it as likely, and security experts are split on this issue. Nevertheless, all three categories place a very high premium on US commitment to European security. In a broader sense, this also connects with the high value the EU-level actors have placed on multilateralism as the preferred means of interstate interaction.

Note

1 The mean has the same value as the one for 'man-made environmental threats', but only nine chose the 'natural disasters and pandemics' category (three fewer than for 'man-made environmental threats'). Thus it seems to be appropriate to rank 'natural disasters and pandemics' second.

References

Baldwin, D. (1997) 'The concept of security', *Review of International Studies* 32 (1): 47–79.

European Commission (2007) 'Eurobarometer 65: public opinion in the European Union', July 2006, Brussels. Online. Available: http://ec.europa.eu/public_opinion/archives/eb/eb65/eb65_first_en.pdf (accessed 17 July 2008).

Hill, C. and Smith, M. (eds) (2005) *International Relations and the European Union*, Oxford: Oxford University Press.

Keukeleire, S. and MacNaughtan, J. (2007) *The Foreign Policy of the European Union*, Basingstoke: Palgrave Macmillan.

Kirchner, E. J. and Rasch, M. (2007) 'Supranational Threat Perceptions: Survey Results from the EU', Garnet Working Paper 18. Online. Available: www.garnet-eu.org/fileadmin/documents/working_papers/1807/5.3.2%20contents.pdf (accessed April 2008).

Kirchner, E. J. and Sperling, J. (2002) 'The new security threats in Europe: theory and evidence', *European Foreign Affairs Review* 7 (4): 423–52.

Krause, K. (1998) 'Theorising security, state formation and the "third world" in the post-Cold War world', *Review of International Studies* 24 (1): 125–36.

Meyer, C. (2005) 'Convergence towards a European Strategic Culture? A constructivist framework for explaining changing European norms', *European Journal of International Relations* 11: 523–49. Online. Available: http://ejt.sagepub.com/cgi/reprint/11/4/523 (accessed 13 June 2008).

Smith, M. (2004) *Europe's Foreign and Security Policy: the Institutionalization of Co-operation*, Cambridge: Cambridge University Press.

3 The European international identity considered from outside

European, African and Asian interaction

Valeria Bello

The concept of identity is currently one of the most discussed in the social sciences. Its use within debates concerning regional contexts – for instance, the European Union (EU) – has resulted in several interesting works, which demonstrate its relevance in the field of international relations.[1] On the ground, questions of identity have arisen again since the end of the Cold War, when so-called 'ethnic conflicts' and wars *justified* in terms of identity broke out again, no longer frozen by the two superpowers (Kaldor 1999). In addition, postmodern theories of international relations differ from other approaches in their assertion of identity as a strong affecting factor in the definition of actors' international strategies (Checkel 1998: 325–7; Wendt 1999).

In an interesting chapter on identity in regional integration processes, Slocum and Van Langenhove (2005), after considering the difference between the static concept of identity used by Cerutti and Enno (2001: 4) and the dynamic one used by Von Busekist (2004: 81–2), argue that 'Being a concept, "identity" – like other concepts – is used by actors towards various ends (Austin 1961). Its meaning is dependent upon the way it is used in a particular context and is thus situation-specific' (Slocum and Van Langenhove 2005: 139).

I would add that the identity is not just a concept but, considering its dynamic and situational aspects, actually a scheme of reference for action and of meaning for communication (Bello 2007: 10–11, 15, 24; Holzner 1978; Schutz 1970). Thus it can explain to those members who share it what the boundaries of their actions are and how to communicate this to others. On the basis of my previous study (Bello 2007, 2008), I would also say that identity depends not only on a situation, but also on the particular interactions which take place between actors in a specific context (Bello 2007: 10–11). In other words, amongst the various elements which compose the scheme of reference and the meanings through which an actor expresses itself, those used in a specific context depend on the interactions which actually takes place there. According to this view, the EU identity, like any identity, interacts with that of others and adapts itself by reacting to what they say and do, and according to the idea that the EU itself has of the others.

This means that the identity of the EU perceived in a context by a particular player (let's say the African Union) is necessarily different from the EU identity perceived in the same context by another actor who is also participating (for instance, the Association of South East Asian Nations, ASEAN), because, in fact, the EU acts differently towards the two. This definition of identity helps us to understand why there are a number of different perceptions of EU identity, as shown for example in the remarkable 'Beyond self-perception: the others' view of the European Union' edited by Sonia Lucarelli (2007). Moreover, this concept of identity has already proved to be useful for the comprehension of inter-regional relations, as illustrated by Julie Gilson.

> One way to comprehend the distinctiveness of a region-to-region framework is to focus on the way it posits a given 'self' interacting with a specific 'other'. [...] the self may be understood as being formed from the start by the very act of being in a relationship with an other. In this way, the identity of the self is intrinsically linked with the process of 'engaging' with that other. Put simply, interregionalism may not only represent the conjoining of two independent regions, but may be regarded as a process whereby, through their mutual interaction, the regions of East Asia and Europe come to recognize themselves as such.
>
> (Gilson 2005: 309–10)

In the case of the inter-regionalism, the variety of interaction is increased by the fact that regional players are composed of different member states, each with their own culture, history and political views. In addition, even when considered as a single unit, the EU's collective identity (like that of similar regional actors) should always be understood as a construction of the individuals who compose it (officials, Ministers, experts, chairman).[2]

Does this mean that it is not possible to predict the nature of interactions between actors, in particular collective ones? Indeed, we can understand the limits of possible interactions because they are established by the frames given by the schemes of reference and meanings described above. This is exactly what this chapter intends to do. I have analysed fifty documents by different international actors – governmental and non-governmental – related to EU activities and links with Africa and Asia and in particular with the two important regional organisations, ASEAN and the African Union (AU), and within the Asia–Europe Meeting (ASEM) process. Using this analysis I can explain the interactions between the actors involved and what can be expected in future situations.

As will be illustrated, Duchêne's concept of a 'civilian power Europe' (Duchêne 1972; Telò 2006) and the concept of a normative Europe (Archibugi 1995; Delanty and He 2008; Smith 2003) are empirically grounded, but cannot alone explain the complexity of the EU position and vision. Since the EU created its European Security and Defence Policy (ESDP) authors have been suggesting the possibility that the normative power of Europe could suffer. The empirical findings show that this has not happened, as argued by Whitman (2002). In this chapter I suggest that the EU, far from denying its normative approach, uses it rationally to achieve its goals and to spread what is a different model of global governance compared with that which follows from the advanced capitalistic model of unregulated liberalism and globalisation. In other words, the EU is proposing its own interpretation of the liberal agenda. However, the EU has a problem caused by its inability to be frank about the fact that the search for what it considers a better, regulated globalisation, to be achieved by a normative approach to global governance, cannot have negative reverberations on its societies. Otherwise it will seem an oral opportunistic talk which is then belied by what is actually done. The EU, as a political international player, is entitled to propose its own model for managing global dynamics, which the EU considers good for societies, both within and without the EU, as being fair to people, the environment and workers, and providing the same (or even higher) levels of well-being as those attainable through unregulated trade. In this chapter I will illustrate, by investigating identity perceptions and interactions, if in Africa and Asia there is agreement with this model and room for its implementation.

Perceptions of the EU by governmental and non-governmental organisations

This study of external perceptions of EU identity was done through an interpretative analysis of fifty documents (official reports, press releases, non-official and official positions[3]), produced by non-governmental organisations (NGOs, e.g. Amnesty International, Third World Network) and institutional players such as the AU, ASEM and ASEAN. The interpretative analysis differs from a discourse analysis because it does not only refers to claims but mainly to relations between different lines of reasoning (here called *codes*). Arguments are codified and then related to other assertions and those taken into consideration in the analysis are those more interrelated to the most frequent codes (sensitising concepts), which direct the theoretical explanations of events (Blumer 1954; Bowen 2006; Lincoln and Guba 1985). The scientific software used was ATLAS.ti, initially invented to serve grounded theory and then also applied as a useful scientific tool for both quantitative and qualitative analysis.

The most obvious finding I obtained from documents related to Africa and the EU's dealings with it was that the latter is considered a self-interested actor in its trade and market strategies, not an enthusiastic view of a normative actor in the international arena. Indeed, trade is the area in which the EU has brought most criticism upon itself in recent years. For instance, the Third World Network (TWN), 'an independent non-profit international network of organisations and individuals involved in issues relating to development, Third World and North–South affairs' (TWN Web site: introduction, accessed 12 September 2008), tends to be very hostile to the EU. In the ten press release documents of the TWN analysed, the main condemnations regard the fact that the EU is supposed to use aggressive trade strategies (TWN, 15 October 2005, 23 January 2007) and that it uses the Green box[4] in order to increase the international competitiveness of its food sector (TWN, 31 October 2005, 24 August 2007). There are no positive accounts of the EU to be found in the TWN documents. This is because the network concentrates on the World Trade Organisation (WTO) rounds, and meetings, reports, news and positions produced in that context. Therefore its perspective on the EU is influenced by the disputes that the EU has had *in loco* in recent years and, particularly by the interruption of the Doha round. This is also the main source of criticism of the EU made by the African Union, as will be outlined in the next section.

Another aspect of the EU criticised by the TWN is its use of environmental and social clauses and the conditionality included in its agreements. These allow the EU to suspend agreements if a state does not respect the principles established in particular clauses, an element of the EU approach that the TWN does not appreciate at all. Unfortunately, this is a difficult point to resolve, because the EU cannot avoid such conditionality without betraying its principles, values and interests. The EU – as a regional institutional player – is committed to protecting the environment and social rights both within its territory and globally. This fact – a consequence of the European social model and identified by Derrida and Habermas, and by Antony Giddens (Habermas and Derrida 2003; Giddens 2007) as the main feature of the EU – is an important characteristic of its activity, policy and identity (Bello 2007). A different approach from the EU to these questions is hard to imagine. 'It is increasingly held that competitive pressure should not be allowed to endanger our social model if the exporters derive their competitive advantage from a blatant disregard for minimal labour standards' (Foqué and Steenbergen 2005: 57). As the two authors point out, the EU tries to respond to the dislocating effect of globalisation on production and the consequent loss of employment in societies and countries with a responsible approach to environmental and social rights (Foqué and Steenbergen 2005: 55–7, 59).

So, paradoxically, the EU's international image is most tarnished in the eyes of both developing countries, particularly in Africa, and those organisations which understand development in purely economic term, by the EU's very nature. This means that if the EU wishes to maintain its own identity, it cannot satisfy the present demands of developing countries, the WTO liberalisation system and all those NGOs, organisations and networks which share the idea of an economics-driven development. Is this problem irresolvable? It seems just a question of the EU needing to manifest itself and its values with sufficient certainty? The EU seems to speak with ambiguity, because it does not make clear that its international strategies simply do not coincide with the process of unregulated globalisation, nor with the WTO regulated globalisation process.

The criticism would carry no weight if the EU affirmed its own identity coherently, firmly and without double standards.

European regional integration started in the economic sector. However, the EU has always asked its members to meet certain social and environmental standards, and so has not had a purely economic perspective; in other words, it has not believed that the dismantling of tariff and non-tariff barriers is necessarily entirely beneficial. It has imposed a distributive system based on solidarity amongst members, through its social dimension, and in particular the European Social Fund and the structural funds. As Mary Farrell points out:

> For economists, the point of departure is the set of economic linkages formed through trade in an integrated area, where the removal of tariffs and non-tariffs barrier is expected to produce significant increases in overall economic welfare for the countries involved, even if the gains are unevenly spread across economic sectors and societal groups.
>
> (Farrell *et al.* 2005: 5)

However, the EU has acted internally in order to avoid the unfair distribution of gains across societies, and it also tries to apply these standards with its partners in the international arena.

Unfortunately, this EU attitude is discredited by double standards and lack of clarity. The above mentioned criticisms hold until the EU clearly expresses its position and stops trying to please everybody, ending up pleasing nobody.

The double talk is also considered in other chapters in this volume:[5] it is the main argument against the EU from the perspective of developing countries and discredits the EU as an actor operating normatively in the field of international relations. This will not help the EU to improve its relations with developing countries.

A similar problem concerns the human rights issue. Considering documents and press releases produced in 2006–08 by Amnesty International (AI) – one of the most well known and respected NGOs in this field – about EU activities (in particular in Africa and Asia but also on European soil), the EU is seen to have two sides. On the one hand, it is constantly asked by Amnesty International to defend human rights in various part of the world, frequently in Africa and Asia. Thus the NGOs try to ally with the EU on the issue of human rights, as argued even by Andretta and Doerr (2007). However, the other main factor that emerges from the analysis is the demand that the EU should solve the human rights issues it has on its own territory, mainly with minority communities (for instance, the Roma in Italy; violations of the human rights of immigrants in several European countries; and gender issues – the lack of freedom for, and crimes against, gay, lesbian, bisexual and transgender people – in Poland and Latvia (AI, 15 November 2006, 12, 20 June 2007).

The EU lacks credibility as long as it is unable to face and solve human rights issues in its region. With the exception of this criticism, the EU is shown to be a staunch ally of NGOs such as Amnesty International, thanks to its activities in support of human rights around the world (activities often possible because of the conditionality criticised by the WTO delegations and the TWN). The European Parliament, as Amnesty International points out (AI, 30 April 2007), has spoken several times in support of concrete action to protect human and minority rights even within the EU itself. The main problems here are thus the contradictions within some EU member states, depending on whether they are acting at the Brussels or the national level.

> In Poland, the person who replaced the director for the national teaching agency – dismissed for accepting a standard Council of Europe manual on anti-discrimination – has recently declared that homosexuality is contrary to human nature. These examples contradict the assurances presented by the Polish President during his visit to Brussels in August.
>
> (AI, 15 November 2006: para. 4)

In this case, the EU member states' inconsistency falls on the shoulders of the EU as a whole, and undermines the EU's credibility with its international partners, limiting its power to influence countries towards development strategies respectful of human, social and environmental rights. In particular, the violation of the fundamental freedoms and human rights of immigrants in several EU member states reduces the credibility of the EU's normative power with respect to African countries, from where most of immigrants who reach the EU by sea have come and whose citizens are therefore the majority of the victims of human rights abuse.

> *Three major human rights tests for EU Justice and Home Affairs Council (Brussels, 12–13 June).* Amnesty International hopes that tomorrow's JHA Council will not shy away from confronting a number of urgent issues that put EU human rights commitments to the test: 1. ensuring safety for irregular immigrants from Africa who try to reach Europe by sea; 2. responding adequately to the Iraqi refugee crisis; 3. adopting fair trial safeguards.
>
> Failure to address these pressing questions adequately will strain the EU's credibility as a responsible international actor and its ambition to create an area of freedom, security and justice in Europe.
>
> (AI, 12 June 2007: para. 1)

Instead, in Asia, the EU activities are considered very positively by Amnesty International, because the EU has been able to persuade some countries in the region to abolish the death penalty; therefore, it is asked to carry on contributing to the improvement of the human rights situation in Asia.

In a letter to the German EU Presidency (available at www.amnesty-eu. org), Amnesty International noted the progress that has already been achieved, with the creation of the 'Anti Death Penalty Asia Network' and the fact that last year, with EU support, the Philippines abolished the death penalty for all crimes. South Korea also considered a parliamentary bill to ban capital punishment. 'The EU should challenge Asia's execution rates but also build on the positive signs within the continent and suggest ways in which Europe and Asian can work together towards abolition.'

(AI, 28 May 2007)

Therefore, based on the analysis of this important international NGO, Asia, and in particular South East Asia, seems to be the area of the world where the EU is most successful at influencing attitudes with its normative model. The following analysis of those official documents produced by regional organisations in Africa and in Asian areas explains the differences in the EU's attitudes and approaches to the two continents, the different perceptions these regional players have of the EU and the effects of their reciprocal relations.

The perceptions of regional organisations

In order to investigate the interactions between Europe, Africa and Asia at a regional level, I have analysed twenty-two official reports and documents produced by the communication offices of the AU, ASEAN and ASEM.[6] I have thus been able to determine what the main elements associated with the EU as a global player are. The documents analysed were produced from 2003 to 2007 and concern the meetings occurred between these regional players. They are based on official meetings and were drawn up to record and communicate strategies agreed upon and positions undertaken, sometimes jointly, sometimes by the AU's and ASEAN's communication offices alone. In the analysis I have taken the different sources into account. The study of the second type of documents (those produced by the AU's or ASEAN's communications offices alone) is important because through them one can recognise the positions and points of view of the EU's counterparts. Through the investigation of joint documents, one obtains a suggestion of the interaction between the EU and other regional players (EU and AU or EU and ASEAN, or within ASEM meetings). Jointly produced documents give us more than the points of view of these external actors on the EU's strategies and more than pictures of the situations. The interaction shows us the frames inside which actions take place, and which structure players' behaviours. These frames are then useful tools for the interpretation of future circumstances, because they consist of the elements which configure relations between players, and around which relations (and behaviours) are organised. Therefore, through this analysis, one can understand both the different positions which the EU has had in relation to the two regional actors in recent years, and the different views that these actors actually have of the EU, together with the substance of their interaction.

From the observation of the EU's interaction with the two regional actors, one can see that it has similar strategies towards the two, with a number of common elements: the main goals of the EU at the moment. These are: first the increase of regional integration in the two areas concerned and research on security and peace. Then, secondly, development and the definition of common interests in the context of international relations. The methods used by the EU to achieve these goals are the creation of institutional commitments with the two partners; exchanges of experience, financial support and economic co-operation.

So the first frame of the EU's international action is the commitment to a regulated economy and its consequent advocacy of the EU regional integration model as an alternative to the liberal agenda. However, the EU also shows fundamentally different attitudes towards its partners in Africa and in Asia. The AU is treated as a 'junior partner', in need of help and support, while ASEAN is considered a more mature player and within the ASEM meetings the EU acts as an equal. Indeed, from 2005 to the beginning of 2007 the institutional tool used with the AU was the EU 'Strategy for Africa', whose title doubtless expressed the unidirectional way in which reciprocal relations are conceived of in parts of the EU. Therefore these are the two frames that the EU has of these two areas.

The EU interacts with ASEAN and within the ASEM meetings as an equal, speaking of common interests, of economic co-operation, of the standardisation of rules, of trade and investment. In contrast, the AU was not considered by the EU ready to act as a mature regional player, even though the Organisation of African Unity (the predecessor of the AU) was created in 1963 – four years before ASEAN was formed by Indonesia, Malaysia, the Philippines, Singapore and Thailand – and despite the fact that since 1999 it has constituted a union, formed by political bodies charged with taking care of the political as well as of the socio-economic integration of the continent.

Taking this fact into consideration, the realisation of a memorandum of understanding on exchange of staff between the two institutions (AU–EU, 26 September 2006) looks like an attempt by the EU to help the African Union to reach maturity and gain experience, a measure in line with the EU objective of contributing to the development of regional integration processes around the world. The EU's attitude revealed a low opinion of the AU's role and capacity, which was probably offensive to the AU. However, the EU's attitude also seems to feed off the way the AU views its relations with the EU. Consequently, a frame which guides the action of this area in relation to the EU can be traced, as can be done with the Asian regions.

In fact, the EU's contrasting attitude to the two regional institutions coincides with the divergent views that they, in turn, have of the EU. Both the AU and ASEAN consider the EU to be a positive and successful model, whose experience should be shared and imitated. However, the AU is more critical of the EU in several respects, and seems to use it principally as a source of funding and economic development assistance. In the documents analysed, the AU has expressed its appreciation for those EU's concrete initiatives which involved providing financial support (AUC–EC, 26 September 2006; AUC–EC, 29 September 2006; AU–EU, 29 September 2006; cf. AU, 20 January 2007; AUC–EU, 9 March 2007). Despite this, the AU has continued to be very critical of the EU, particularly of its economic and trade strategies, criticised openly by AU Trade and Industry Commissioner Tankeu in a press release of January 2006 (AU, 16 January 2007). Soon after, the AU requested greater coherence from the EU ('between facts and norms' one might say) mainly with the relaunch of the Doha round and the reduction of its internal subsidies for some products (AU, 20 January 2007).

It is impossible to establish where this particular dynamic begins; if it is because the EU degrades the AU by considering it as a junior actor to be helped and supported and the AU therefore acts on this base and uses the EU just as a source of funding; or vice versa: if it is because the fact that the AU just asks for financial support that the EU belittles its role. In any interaction, the participants' thoughts and actions are so interconnected that they have to be considered simultaneous and therefore the relations of cause–effect cannot be further investigated. It is worth noting that, since the AU strongly criticised the EU at the end of 2006 and in January 2007, things have changed. It was no coincidence that great emphasis was given in a joint press release of 2 February 2007 to the launch of the first joint strategy, the 'EU Africa Strategy', then adopted at the Lisbon Summit in the second half of 2007 (AU–EU, 2 February 2007). The AU criticism was thus essential to the future development of relations between the EU and the AU. The AU's criticisms were accompanied by open appreciation of China (AU, 16 January 2007). This was of course a signal to the EU, and it clearly indicates that Africa–China relations are a sensitive point for the EU, and the AU knows this and turns it to advantage.

On the other hand, in Asia, we have to distinguish the different role that the European regional integration process has had for the distinct Asian regions. Countries such as China, India and Japan have clearly fewer reasons to act within inter-regional dialogue, and this could be the reason of the negative European evaluation of the first ASEM decade contained into the European Background Study, prepared by the University of Helsinki.

> To sum up, stocktaking of the accomplishments of the Asia–Europe Meeting (ASEM) in its first decade inevitably leads to the conclusion that the dialogue forum has not entirely lived up to the initial expectations and has not been exploited to the full. The paucity of tangible outcomes has led to a perceived emergence of 'disaffection', or 'forum fatigue' among partners. Also in the interregional context ASEM had

limited influence as a balancing, institution-building, rationalizing, agenda-setting, and identity-building framework.

(University of Helsinki NES 2006: 198)

Nevertheless, the report prepared jointly by the Japan Center for International Exchange (JCIE) and the University of Helsinki contains more positive concluding remarks than those expressed in the European Background Study, as it also includes the Asian perspective. In the eyes of Asian countries, what has been done within ASEM is good, taking into account the expected lack of interest on the part of huge countries such as China and India in multilateral action.

> At the same time, the research teams understand and recognize the fundamental reality and the constraints of having to accommodate different perspectives, interests and expectations among its thirty-nine members. The modest recommendations above propose piecemeal changes to answer some of the main criticisms and challenges identified during the research. [...] The Chairman's Statement of the seventh Foreign Ministers Meeting in Kyoto noted that co-operation among the ASEM partners, which now represent about 40% of the earth's population, 50% of global GDP and 60% of world trade, is becoming increasingly important in addressing key global issues the international community is facing. With such figures, Asia–Europe co-operation is no longer a luxury but a necessity. Asia and Europe therefore need to use whatever frameworks available to deepen their co-operation and share the burdens of global responsibility. The ASEM process is one such framework, and several issues such as those highlighted in the recommendation need to be addressed with urgency and tenacity.
>
> In the long run, as Asia and Europe become more integrated, ASEM could become an important and highly effective region-to-region dialogue and co-operation framework to build sustainable peace, prosperity and stability.
>
> (JCIE and the University of Helsinki 2006: 16–17)

This final consideration, and in particular its difference compared with the European Background Study, shows the will of Asian countries to co-operate at regional level, even if they admit the diversity of interests and ideas amongst them. For example, South East Asian countries reunited in ASEAN have an enthusiastic approach towards the EU. With the exception of a regret concerning the cancellation of a meeting, the ASEAN has voiced its appreciation of EU initiatives and actions in several occasions, in particular its efforts in sustaining the ASEAN integration process with different tools: financially and through exchanges of experience (ASEAN, 28 January 2003, 10 March 2005, ASEAN, 5 June 2007). Even if the EU is actually mainly an economic partner, and trade and investment are the basis of their co-operation, the ASEAN–EU partnership involves several areas and is considered by both players an excellent partnership, simply because it works.

> The Ministers acknowledged the full implementation of all previously agreed co-operation in particular in the field of regional integration, renewable energy, higher education, biodiversity conservation, standards and intellectual property rights.
>
> (ASEAN–EU, 10 March 2005)

One essential aspect of the EU–ASEAN dialogue is the identification of common interests in international relations, based on mutual understanding of cultures and mutual respect. The definition of this common strategy is connected with the aim of combating terrorism, a factor which came up only once in the AU-related documents (AU–EU, 28 February 2007). In the ASEAN–EU dialogue, it is said that the only successful way to combat terrorism is through reciprocal respect for and understanding of culture and the possibility of building upon common interests in the global arena. In a press release from the ASEAN Secretariat on 27 January 2003, 'The ministers [ASEAN and EU Foreign Ministers] said there is an urgent need for a comprehensive approach to the threat of terrorism which must be addressed through political, economic, diplomatic, military and legal means. They also acknowledged the need to strengthen dialogue and promote mutual understanding between cultures' (ASEAN, 27 January 2003). In a joint statement of March 2005:

> The Ministers reaffirmed their commitment to combat terrorism in accordance with international obligations, the UN Charter and general norms of international law, including respect for human rights and humanitarian law. In this connection, the Ministers emphasized the importance of addressing the root causes of terrorism and avoiding the identification of terrorism with any particular religion or ethnic group or nationality.
>
> (ASEAN–EU, 10 March 2005)

To sum up, in Asia the sole region that seems to be willing to follow the EU's model is South East Asia, while the other Asian countries have not yet shown relevant interest in developing inter-regional relations and actions. Therefore, drawing parallels between the two most advanced regional integration processes in Asia and in Africa – the AU and ASEAN – the findings show that the EU was able to convince its partners to base their international strategies on the construction of regional integration processes and the search for peace and stability; pursuing economic and social wealth through these means. Consequently, the EU is successful in presenting its regional integration process as a model to be imitated in such areas.

However, the AU considers the EU to be an inconsistent partner whenever its economic interests are at stake, and to be vying fiercely with China over Africa. These factors, though not new, are worth underlining, because they demonstrate some of the EU's weakness as a global player. ASEAN seems to be an excellent partner from the European point of view, as it is willing to follow the EU model unsceptically. Despite the greater physical distance, mutual understanding with South East Asian countries appears to be easier than with Africa. The EU possibility to convince also other Asian countries to undertake important regional initiatives depends on its ability to be fully successful in other areas, and mainly in Africa. If in the past the US and the Soviet Union competed to impose their models on the 'Third World', nowadays the liberal agenda is generally accepted by Asian and African countries. Nevertheless, there is still a challenge between different visions: the unregulated globalisation and the European social model. Will the European member states allow the EU's model to be successful?

Conclusion

Until the beginning of this century – or at least until the end of the Cold War – the European social model could be considered an alternative to US capitalism. As Habermas and Derrida noted, the welfare state and the self-limitations of sovereignty are two recent examples of the EU's main characteristics and achievements (Habermas and Derrida 2003: 9), and indeed this peculiarity was the inspiration for the 'third way' theory (Giddens 1999). However, as Antony Giddens outlined in his work 'Europe in the Global Age' (Giddens 2007), the welfare state, which is the foundation of the European social model, is now challenged by globalisation, and a number of different social reforms are being implemented in the European countries. However, the European method of protecting its internal welfare state model is by spreading its norms and values to other areas of the globe, frequently through co-operation agreements. That is why it has been described as a 'normative actor'. Therefore the EU environmental and social clauses are first of all tools to protect European interests, identity and beliefs. They are also principles that protect societies and the environment.

Thus, while being an integral part of the European normative approach towards international relations and the international economy, the clauses system also contributes to an approach to welfare which considers not only economics but also social aspects of life and the environment. In doing so, it is clear that the EU is also protecting its own territory and its societies. But the EU is also convinced that this behaviour does not really harm the poorest countries. The EU considers that African and Asian states will not damage their citizens by respecting social and environmental clauses, as well as political conditionality. The EU proposes its own vision of the liberal agenda, arguing that unregulated liberalism and purely 'economic' welfare cannot balance the uneven gains within a society. The real problems are communicating this logic clearly and firmly and avoiding double standards. It is true that most of the problems related to human rights in

Europe are caused by some European member states and not by the EU itself, but how can one insist on these clauses internationally if the EU is not able to enforce them within its own territory? Issues concerning immigrants, minorities, gender and sexual orientation still have to be resolved within European countries and by some European governments in particular. This problem, and the EU's unwillingness to advocate forcefully enough its model as an alternative to the phenomenon of unregulated globalisation and to that of advanced economic liberalism, seem to be the critical points of the EU's external relations, which must be resolved before further advances of its normative – in the sense of non-anarchic – global governance can be made.

Notes

1 This is not an exhaustive list, but on the question of European identity in particular it is worth consulting: Burgess (2002), Cerutti and Lucarelli (2008), Delanty (1995, 2002), Delanty and Jones (2002), Eder (2005), Eliasson (2004), Farrell *et al.* (2005), Fossum (2001, 2005), Freres (2000), Kantner (2006), Lucarelli (2008), Olsen (2005, 2005); Risse and Maier (2003), M. Sassatelli (2002, 2006) and Slocum and Van Langenhove (in Farrell *et al.* 2005).

2 If we neglect this, we can be accused of hypostatisation, as highlighted in the past by Berger and Luckmann with respect to the concept of collective identity (1966: 235). In its defence, see Holzner (1983).

3 Due to length constraints, the full list of documents is not included in this chapter. However, the author will be happy to produce it at any time under request by e-mail (valeria.bello@soc.unitn.it). The documents here listed are only those directly quoted into the text.

4 The Green box is a category of domestic support permitted under the WTO agreement which should be minimally trade-distorting and that is excluded from reduction commitments under the Uruguay Round Agreement on Agriculture (URAA) because it is unrelated to production or prices but is justified by environmental protection and regional development.

5 See particularly Chapters 5 (Belachew Gebrewold), 7 (Dirk Kohnert) and 8 (Stefan Brüne).

6 I have taken into account documents produced by the two most advanced and oldest (hence comparable) regional integration process in Africa and Asia (the AU and ASEAN), and documents produced within the ASEM context (even if it is rather a new entity), because the latter is an interregional forum where Europe and Asia discuss global issues. Consequently, it is apt to show what happens at regional level between the two continents.

References

AI (15 November 2006) 'EU: ensure Poland and Latvia respect rights of minorities', Amnesty International press release EUR 01/020/2006 (Public). Online. Available: www.amnesty.org/en/library/asset/EUR01/020/2006/en/dom-EUR010202006en.html (accessed 10 October 2008).

—— (30 April 2007) 'EU–US Summit: no more business as usual, please', Amnesty International press release IOR 61/012/2007 (Public). Online. Available: http://asiapacific.amnesty.org/library/Index/ENGIOR610122007?open&of=ENG-2M4 (accessed 10 October 2008).

—— (28 May 2007) 'EU–ASEM: involve Asian nations in efforts to abolish the death penalty', Amnesty International press release IOR 30/011/2007 (Public). Online. Available: http://asiapacific.amnesty.org/library/Index/ENGIOR300112007?open&of=ENG-2AS (accessed 10 October 2008).

—— (12 June 2007) 'Three major human rights tests for EU Justice and Home Affairs Council', Amnesty International press release IOR 61/017/2007 (Public). Online. Available: http://asiapacific.amnesty.org/library/Index/ENGIOR610172007?open&of=ENG-369 (accessed 10 October 2008).

—— (20 June 2007) 'EU summit: acknowledge, repair and prevent CIA renditions', Amnesty International press release IOR 61/016/2007 (Public). Online. Available: www.amnesty.org/en/library/asset/IOR61/016/2007/en/dom-IOR610162007en.html (accessed 10 October 2008).

Andretta, M. and Doerr, N. (2007) 'Imagining Europe: internal and external non-state actors at the European crossroads', *European Foreign Affairs Review* 12 (3): 385–400.

Archibugi, D. (1995) *Cosmopolitan Democracy: an Agenda for a New World Order*, Cambridge: Polity Press.

ASEAN (27 January 2003) 'News release. ASEAN and EU Foreign Ministers team up to combat terrorism', ASEAN release. Online. Available: www.aseansec.org/14032.htm (accessed 23 November 2008).

—— (28 January 2003) 'Joint Co-chairmen's Statement, fourteenth EU–ASEAN Ministerial Meeting', Brussels, 27–28 January 2003. ASEAN Documents. Online. Available: www.aseansec.org/14034.htm (accessed 21 November 2008).

—— (5 June 2007) 'Press release. European Commission provides €7.2 million to support ASEAN integration process', Jakarta, 5 June 2007. ASEAN Documents. Online. Available: www.aseansec.org/20649.htm (accessed 23 November 2008).

ASEAN–EU (10 March 2005) 'Joint Co-chairmen's Statement of the fifteenth ASEAN–EU Ministerial Meeting', ASEAN Documents. Online. Available: www.aseansec.org/17354.htm (accessed 23 November 2008).

AU (16 January 2007) 'Press release. African Union Ministers of Trade meet to evaluate the state of negotiation with the WTO and the EPA', AU press release. Online. Available: www.africa-union.org/root/au/Conferences/Past/2007/January/TI/16jan/TRADE_en.doc (accessed on 21 November 2008).

—— (20 January 2007) 'Communiqué de presse no. 04/2007', AU press release. Online. Available at: www.africa-union.org/root/AU/Conferences/Past/2007/January/summit/press/PRESSE%20RELEASE%20ANNONCE%20FRENCH1%2004.doc (accessed 21 November 2008).

AU–EU (15 May 2007) 'Final communiqué. Eighth EU–Africa Ministerial Troika Meeting', AU documents. Online. Available: www.africa-union.org/root/AU/News/Communique/2007/may/final_Communique.doc (accessed 21 November 2008).

—— (28 February 2007) 'Communiqué de presse conjoint. Stratégie conjointe UE–Afrique', AU press release. Online. Available: www.africa-union.org/root/ua/Actualites/2007/fevrier/JOINT%20PRESS%20RELEASE%20EU-AU%20FRANCAIS%2028fev07.doc (accessed 21 November 2008).

—— (2 February 2007) 'Communiqué de presse conjoint', AU press release. Online. Available: www.africa-union.org/root/UA/index/COMMUNIQUE_DE_PRESSE_CINJOINT_AU_EU%5B1%5D.doc (last accessed 21 November 2008).

—— (29 September 2006) 'Joint communiqué. Third Meeting of the African Peace Facility Joint Co-ordination Committee', AU press release. Online. Available: www.africa-union.org/root/AU/News/Press/2006/September/Joint_co-ordination_meeting_AU_EU.pdf (accessed 21 November 2008).

AUC–EC (9 March 2007) 'Joint press release. AUC and EC joint task force meets to review progress on co-operation', AU press release. Online. Available at: www.africa-union.org/root/UA/Actualites/2007/mars/AU%20EC%20JOINT%20PRESS%20RELEASE%2009_03_07.doc (accessed 21 November 2008).

—— (26 September 2006) 'Press release 47/2006', AU press release. Online. Available at: www.africa-union.org/root/UA/Actualites/2006/sept/AU-EU%20commission%20to%20commission%20meeting%2026sept06.pdf (accessed 21 November 2008).

—— (29 September 2006) 'Press release. Meeting between the European Commission and the Commission of the African Union', AU press release. Online. Available: www.africa-union.org/root/AU/News/Press/2006/September/PR_EU_AU_29_september.pdf (accessed 22 November 2008).

Austin, J. L. (1961) *How to do Things with Words*, Oxford: Clarendon Press.

Bello, V. (2007) 'Questioni di identità nel sistema globale: la rappresentazione politica dell'UE e il processo di europeizzazione', unpublished thesis, University of Florence.

—— (2008) 'Europeanisation and Social Identity: an Interpretative Analysis carried out on Italian Civil Society Representatives', paper presented at the IIS XXXVIII World Congress, Budapest, Jean Monnet Working Papers, Trento Jean Monnet European Studies Centre. Online. Available: www4.soc.unitn.it:8080/poloeuropeo/content/e2611/e6560/IISBudapestPaperBello_eng.pdf (accessed 18 November 2008).

Berger, P. and Luckmann, T. (1966) *The Social Construction Of Reality*, New York: Doubleday; trans. *La realtà come costruzione sociale* (1969), Bologna: Mulino.

Blumer, H. (1954) 'What is wrong with social theory?' *American Sociological Review* 18: 3–10.

Bowen, G. A. (2006) 'Grounded theory and sensitizing concepts', *International Journal of Qualitative Methods* 5 (3). Online. Available: www.ualberta.ca/~iiqm/backissues/5_3/HTML/bowen.html (accessed 18 November 2008).

Burgess, P. (2002) 'What's so European about the European Union? Legitimacy between institution and identity', *European Journal of Social Theory* 5 (4), London: Sage Publications.

Cerutti, F. and Enno, R. (2001) *A Soul for Europe: on the Political and Cultural Identity of the Europeans*, Sterling, VA: Peeters Leuven.

Cerutti, F. and Lucarelli, S. (eds) (2008) *The Search for a European Identity: Values, Policies and Legitimacy of the European Union*, London: Routledge.

Checkel, J. (1998) 'The constructivist turn in international relations theory', *World Politics* 50 (2): 324–48.

Delanty, G. (1995) *Inventing Europe: Idea, Identity, Reality*, London: Macmillan.

—— (2002) 'Models of European identity: reconciling universalism and particularism', *Perspectives on European Politics and Society* 3 (3): 345–59.

Delanty, G. and He, B. (2008) 'Cosmopolitan perspectives on European and Asian transnationalism', *International Sociology* 23 (3): 323–44.

Delanty, G. and Jones, P. R. (2002) 'European identity and architecture', *European Journal of Social Theory* 5 (4): 453–66, London: Sage Publications.

Duchêne, F. (1972) 'Europe's role in world peace', in R. Mayne (ed.) *Europe Tomorrow: Sixteen Europeans Look Ahead*, London: Fontana.

Eder, K. and Sphon, W. (2005) *Collective Memory and European Identity: the Effects of Integration and Enlargement*, Aldershot: Ashgate.

Eliasson, J. (2004) 'Traditions, Identity and Security: the Legacy of Neutrality in Finnish and Swedish Security Policies in Light of European Integration', European Integration Online Papers 8 (6), ECSA-A. Online. Available: http://eiop.or.at/eiop/texte/2004–006a.htm (accessed 18 November 2008).

Farrell, M., Hettn, B. and Van Langenhove, L. (2005) *Global Politics of Regionalism: Theory and Practice*, London: Pluto Press.

Foqué, R. and Steenbergen, J. (2005) 'Regionalism: a constitutional framework for global challenges?' in M. Farrell (ed.) *Global Politics of Regionalism*, London: Pluto Press.

Fossum, J. E. (2001) 'Identity politics in the EU', Arena Working Papers WP 01/17, Oslo: Centre for European Studies. Online. Available: www.arena.uio.no/publications/wp01_17.htm (accessed 18 November 2008).

—— (2005) 'Conceptualizing the EU's social constituency?' *European Journal of Social Theory* 8 (2): 123–47, London: Sage Publications.

Freres, C. (2000) 'The European Union as a global 'civilian power': development cooperation in EU–Latin American relations', *Journal of Interamerican Studies and World Affairs* 42 (2): 63–85.

Giddens, A. (1999) *The Third Way: the Renewal of Social Democracy*, Cambridge: Polity Press.

—— (2007) *Europe in the Global Age*, Cambridge: Polity Press.

Gilson, J. (2005) 'New interregionalism? The EU and East Asia', *European Integration* 27 (3): 307–26.

Habermas, J. and Derrida, J. (2003) 'February 15, or, What binds Europeans together? Plea for a common foreign policy, beginning in core Europe', in D. Levy *et al.* (eds) *Old Europe, New Europe, Core Europe*, London: Verso. Online. Available: http://websites.usu.edu/politicalscience/FileManager/Download.asp?Parent=7389&FilePath=shannon's.pdf (accessed on 28 November 2008).

Holzner, B. (1978) 'The construction of social actors: an essay on social identities', in T. Luckmann (ed.) *Phenomenology and Sociology*, Harmondsworth: Penguin.

JCIE and the University of Helsinki (2006) 'ASEM in its tenth year. Looking back, looking forward: an evaluation of ASEM in its first decade and an exploration of its future possibilities', ASEM, March. Online. Available: www.mofa.go.jp/policy/economy/asem/tenth/report1.pdf (accessed 12 October 2008).

Kaldor, M. (1999) *New and Old Wars: Organised Violence in a Global Era*, Cambridge: Polity Press.

Kantner, C. (2006) 'What is a European identity? The emergence of a shared ethical self-understanding in the EU', EUI Working Papers 2006/28, Fiesole: RSC Istituto Universitario Europeo. Online. Available: www.iue.it/RSCAS/WP-Texts/06_28.pdf (accessed 18 November 2008).

Lincoln, Y. S. and Guba, E. G. (1985) *Naturalistic Inquiry*, Beverly Hills, CA: Sage Publications.

Lucarelli, S. (2007) 'The EU in the eyes of the others: towards filling a gap in the literature', *European Foreign Affairs Review* 12 (3): 249–70.

—— (ed.) (2007) 'Beyond self-perception: the others' view of the European Union', *European Foreign Affairs Review* special issue 12 (3): 1–170.

—— (2008) 'European political identity, foreign policy and the others' image: an under-explored relationship', in F. Cerutti and S. Lucarelli (eds) *The Search for a European Identity: Values, Policies and Legitimacy of the European Union*, London: Routledge.

Olsen, J. P. (2005) 'The political organization of Europe: differentiation and unification', Arena Working Papers WP 05/23, Oslo: Centre for European Studies. Online. Available: www.arena.uio.no/publications/working-papers2005/papers/wp05_23.pdf (accessed 18 November 2008).

—— (2005) 'Unity and diversity: European style', Arena Working Papers WP 05/24, Oslo: Centre for European Studies. Online. Available: www.arena.uio.no/publications/working-papers2005/papers/wp05_24.pdf (accessed 18 November 2008).

Risse, T. and Maier, M. L. (2003) 'Europeanisation, collective identities and public discourses', IDNET Thematic Network Final Report, Fiesole: RSC Istituto Universitario Europeo. Online. Available: www.polsoz.fu-berlin.de/polwiss/forschung/international/atasp/publikationen/artikel_papiere/25/index.html (accessed 18 November 2008).

Sassatelli, M. (2002) 'Imagined Europe: the shaping of a European cultural identity through EU cultural policy', *European Journal of Social Theory* 5 (4): 435–51, London: Sage Publications.

—— (2006) 'Landscape as heritage: negotiating european cultural identity', EUI Working Papers, RSCAS 2005/06, Fiesole: Istituto Universitario Europeo. Online. Available: www.iue.it/RSCAS/WP-Texts/06_05.pdf (accessed 18 November 2008).

Schutz, A. (1970) *Reflections on the Problem of Relevance*, New Haven, CT: Yale University Press.

Slocum, N. and Van Langenhove, L. (2005) 'Identity and regional integration', in M. Farrell (ed.) *Global Politics of Regionalism*, London: Pluto Press.

Smith, K. E. (2003) *European Union Foreign Policy in a Changing World*, Cambridge: Polity Press.

Telò, M. (2006) *Europe: a Civilian Power? European Union, Global Governance, World Order*, Basingstoke and New York: Palgave Macmillan.

TWN (15 October 2005) 'EU seeks aggressive opening of developing countries in exchange for agriculture', TWN Info Service on WTO and Trade Issues, Oct05/9. Online. Available: www.twnside.org.sg/title2/twninfo269.htm (accessed 10 October 2008).

—— (23 January 2007) 'The EU approach to FTA talks with ASEAN, India, Korea', TWN Info Service on WTO and Trade Issues, Jan07/04. Online. Available: www.twnside.org.sg/title2/twninfo490c.htm (accessed 10 October 2008).

—— (31 October 2005) 'EU agriculture proposal shifts burden to South in NAMA service', TWN Info Service on WTO and Trade Issues, Oct05/27. Online. Available: www.twnside.org.sg/title2/twninfo287.htm (accessed 10 October 2008).

TWN web site (12 September 2008) 'Introduction'. Online. Available: www.twnside.org.sg/twnintro.htm (accessed 12 September 2008).

University of Helsinki NES (2006) 'European Background Study. ASEM in its tenth year. Looking back, looking forward: an evaluation of ASEM in its first decade and an exploration of its future possibilities', European Background Study. Online. Available: www.mofa.go.jp/policy/economy/asem/tenth/report3.pdf (accessed 12 October 2008).

Von Busekist, A. (2004) 'Uses and misuses of the concept of identity', *Security Dialogue* 35 (1): 81–98. Online. Available: http://sdi.sagepub.com/cgi/content/abstract/35/1/81 (accessed 10 October 2008).

Wendt, A. (1999), *Social Theory of International Politics*, Cambridge: Cambridge. University Press.

Whitman, R. (2002) 'The Fall, and Rise, of Civilian Power Europe', National Europe Centre paper 16. Online. Available: https://dspace.anu.edu.au:8443/handle/1885/41589 (accessed 18 November 2008).

Part II
Africa

4 African regional integration and the role of the European Union

Ludger Kühnhardt

African regional integration has had a remarkable new beginning since the formal beginning of the African Union (AU) in 2002. Following the Treaty of Abuja, in force since 2004 and envisaging an African Economic Community in six stages by 2028, and following the New Partnership for Africa's Development (NEPAD), since 2002 a mandated initiative of the African Union including NEPAD's unique African Peer Review Mechanism for the measuring of good governance, the African Union has become the frame for a new African regionalism. The new beginning in African integration is impressive, promising and creative. It is not only a rhetoric operation but a substantial recognition of the need to redefine the parameters of political, socio-economic and security developments on the African continent (Bach 2005: 171–86).

Historical evolution: from OAU to AU

The independence of African nation states was accompanied and supported by the Organisation of African Unity (OAU), founded in 1963. The OAU was driven by an anti-colonial impulse and aimed at protecting the national sovereignty of each African state. The economic decline in Africa between the 1970s and 1990s became an almost all-pervasive stereotype that was reinforced by the sad realities of civil wars and failed states, failing regimes and widespread bad governance. For some, Africa was already considered a lost continent (Ferdowsi 2004).

In the midst of the African crisis, a new beginning became inevitable. The term 'African Renaissance', introduced by South Africa's President Thabo Mbeki, became the proud expression of a new vision (Mbeki 1998). When Libya's leader Muammar Gaddafi launched the initiative to replace the Organisation of African Unity by the African Union in 1999, he also had in mind his personal ambition and that of his country. But an objective reality evolved, namely the consensual recognition of real regional integration as the frame for a new beginning in Africa's development. This consensus was based on a notion of African unity that was no longer related to an anti- or postcolonial definition of pan-Africanism. For the century ahead, pan-Africanism was to be achieved by means of regional integration.

The result was almost frantic institution-building in the shortest possible period of time, often without clear focus and more often without a solid understanding of the need for deepening integration if region-building was to make sense and eventually become solid. Africa opted for a territorially inclusive way of coming together. Except for Morocco, all African states joined the African Union. The array of seventeen formal structures of the African Union as outlined in the Constitutive Act of the AU is impressive (African Union 2000). Most noticeable are:

1   The AU's President's Assembly (Article 7), its supreme body, which meets once a year and takes decisions by consensus or two-third majority on substantial matters and by a simple majority on procedural matters.
2   The AU's Executive Council, consisting of the Foreign Ministers of the African Union and deciding on regular matters from foreign trade to communications and foreign policy.
3   The Pan-African Parliament is located in Midrand, composed of representatives from across the continent and active since 2004.
4   The AU Commission is based in Addis Ababa and is composed of ten commissioners (chairman since 2008: Jean Ping of Gabon). Its secretariat is responsible for co-ordinating the activities and meetings of the African Union.
5   The AU Permanent Representatives' Committee (Article 3) is composed of nominated permanent representatives of the member state governments. It prepares the work of the Executive Council.
6   The African Court of Justice has been mandated to primarily rule on human right matters in Africa. Over time, it will merge with the African Court of Human and Peoples' Rights, currently seated in Arusha, whose first eleven judges were elected on 22 January 2006 by the Executive Council of the AU.
7   The AU Peace and Security Council is designed to be responsible for monitoring and intervening in conflicts and is intended to have an AU peacekeeping force at its disposal. The Peace and Security Council was formally launched in Addis Ababa on 25 May 2004 and received initial EU support of €250 million for its peacekeeping facility.
8   The AU Economic, Social and Cultural Council serves in an advisory capacity and is composed of representatives of professions and civil society.
9   The financial institutions of the AU include the African Central Bank, the African Monetary Fund and the African Investment Bank.

In sharp contrast with past experience, Article 30 of the Constitutive Act of the African Union defines the procedure to suspend membership in the AU in clear words: 'Governments which shall come to power through unconstitutional means shall not be allowed to participate in the activities of the Union' (African Union 2000).

In spite of the impressive wording of the Constitutive Act of the African Union and several subsequent documents related to matters of African governance, the normative principles of the factual operations of the African Union remained unclear. Bigger, to this day, is the gap between declared principles and operational procedures on the one hand and means of energetic and coherent implementation of principles and objectives on the other. The biggest uncertainty, however, exists in defining the relationship between the objectives of the African Union and the aspiration of manifold regional integration groupings across the African continent. The overlap of membership looks like an image of the solar system – and it echoes the situation of a map that was drawn before the discovery of how things shown on the map may work.[1]

The multiplication of regional groupings across Africa has not been a new phenomenon. With the NEPAD they have been streamlined, in a way. Currently, eight regional groupings in Africa have been designated as building blocks for the development of an African Economic Community (AEC) by 2028: the Arab Maghreb Union (AMU, headquartered in Rabat), the Economic Community of West African States (ECOWAS, headquartered in Abuja), the Economic Community of Central African States (ECCAS, headquartered in Libreville), the Common Market for East and Southern Africa (COMESA, headquartered in Lusaka), the Southern African Development Community (SADC, headquartered in Gaborone), the Intergovernmental Authority for Development (IGAD, headquartered in Djibouti), the Community of Sahelo-Saharan States (CEN-SAD, headquartered in Tripoli) and the East African Community (EAC, headquartered in Arusha). So far, none of these regional groupings has been able to fully bridge the gap between aspiration and reality.[2]

But it is fair to recognise that Africa has moved to more shared responsibility and to policies of non-indifference about what is going on across the continent. Two trends have become noticeable since the early 1990s:

1   At the regional level, the existing regional integration systems experienced a general overhaul, with strong emphasis on economic development and functional deepening, including in the sphere of security and parliamentary representation.
2   At the continental level, the goal of African unity became more politicised and institutionalised while being broadened through mechanisms of functional deepening; simultaneously the limits of autonomous claims to national sovereignty as the highest goal of statehood were increasingly recognised and the notion of protecting human rights won ground over the stereotyped claim of non-interference in domestic affairs of individual African countries.
3   So far, African leaders have not been able to define a coherent sequencing of the work ahead of the eight regional groupings or of their possible eventual merger with the African Union. As much as regional

integration in its theoretical nature and its comparative dimension, the role of regional groupings in Africa and the issue of overlapping membership on the African continent is underresearched. This fact also reflects the underdeveloped research potential of Africa. African institutions of regional integration lack human resources, and so does the academic sector across Africa. While the European Union is supported by more than 13,000 civil servants, the African Union counts 700 professionals. Their commitment and competence is beyond doubt. But their figure is simply too limited to cope with the rising expectations in any meaningful way. Human capacity-building remains an integral necessity to enhance the quality and breadth of integration-building in Africa. Africa has an enormous need to increase academic training facilities. Together with African partners in Europe, comprehensive programs in tertiary education and further education programs dealing with matters of regional integration need to be launched.

(Stamm 2006)

Value-added of regional integration in Africa

The simplest question, seldom posed in Africa, is: why regional integration at all? The prevailing trend among integration actors and integration analysts tends to focus on the technical question of how to make integration work. How integration may work depends on why integration should take place. Although regional integration, by and large, is a constructivist activity, integration is more than a technical operation. The technicalities of regional integration – including the question of how to measure regional integration progress – are relevant. But they still remain tools and should not be confused with the need to clarify the purpose of integration. In order to achieve integration objectives and to strengthen the legitimacy of region-building, clarity about normative preconditions, political objectives and genuine goals of value added ought to be defined and regularly recalibrated.

The purpose of regional integration in the African context seems to be evident, yet this question does not necessarily find coherent answers (see Agubuzu 2004; Dinka and Kennes 2007; Economic Commission for Africa 2004; Francis 2006; Gottschalk and Schmidt 2004: 138–58). In light of the many failures of African development of the past three to four decades, it sometimes seems as if regional integration may be understood as the panacea to run away from this failed past. The overriding experience however of regional integration is the fact that weak states produce only weak integration. Strong regional integration requires solid, functioning and accountable national structures. Regional integration is no substitute for reforming the nation state across Africa. Successful regional integration requires a solid preparation of each member state of a regional grouping.

First and foremost, region-building is trust-driven. Without trust in the honesty, sincerity and objectives of one's partner, no regional grouping can overcome the point of mutual suspicion. Up to a certain point, co-operation is possible even among adversaries. But genuine and deep trust-based region-building requires the mutual recognition of the regime of governance of all partners in a regional grouping. In order to do so, regime symmetry must be minimal at least and should be solid in order to carry region-building efforts beyond the simple point of functional co-operation without deeper commitment. Because of this precondition for strong and real regional integration, it is no surprise that, to this day, no African regional grouping, the African Union included, has addressed the issue of common legislation. Functioning institutions and working tools of integration are important – but eventually they make sense only as a consequence of regional integration commitment. The recognition of the objective of democratic region-building must define the starting point and the ultimate objective of sincere and sustainable regional integration processes (Waller 1999: 49–54; Grimm 2003: 138–92; M'boge and Gbaydee Doe, 2004: 13–56).

Regional arrangements as building blocs for the continent

More than on any other continent, regional integration in Africa is linked to the development strategy of the continent. With the normative myth of African unity as represented by the Organisation of African Unity, also many of the assumptions of the African development strategy and, more important, of the Africa-specific development tools have been reconsidered. Several insights must be formulated even if they touch taboos or vested interests in Africa and among the friends of Africa elsewhere.

1   Aid-based development has not worked. Since the early 1960s, the African continent has received more than $1,000 billion of public development aid. This amount equals the transfer of public resources from West Germany to East Germany in the first decade after German unification of 1990. Almost a generation later, in East Germany only pockets of sustainable development can maintain competitiveness in the globalised world. Since the opening of China under Deng Tsiao Ping in the late 1970s, the People's Republic of China has received approximately the same amount – $1,000 billion – through an external resource transfer. Unlike in Africa and in Germany, the resource transfer in the Chinese case was not one of public aid. It was a resource transfer of private investment which has triggered remarkable and sustainable economic growth – the key to making a country wealthy. The results have turned China from a basket case into a vibrant and new centre of economic gravity with double digit growth rates for more than a decade, now rising to become an economic world power.

2   Yet the Chinese development model may not serve as a comprehensive model for Africa. Africa does not share with the countries of North East

Asia the strong economic nationalism that, at least up to a point, benefits from competition among the countries in the region. There is no African equivalent of the combination of China, Japan, Korea and the South East Asian tiger countries, at least not at the moment. Africa is different from North East Asian societies as far as the tradition and heritage of formal education and the pursuit of systemic thinking are concerned. Historically, Africa's traditions of education, by and large, were oral. Africa's intuitive, often naturalistic approach to life stands in contrast to the scripture-based sharp discipline and structure of form, function, authority, hierarchy and norms in North East Asia. The entrepreneurial spirit that is often associated with the societies of North East Asia is not an African tradition. The most recent Chinese 'discovery' of Africa provides new insights into the development potential of Africa and the problems of African development (Tull 2005; Fues *et al.* 2006; Sautman 2006). China's assertive investment strategy serves the purposes of the rising Chinese economy. It also serves the African countries that can offer energy sources and raw materials which the Chinese need. It improves their infrastructure and thus provides an important frame for future development activities. It does, however, not serve those African countries that are not on the Chinese radar screen. Applying modes of mutually reinforcing self-interest can be a successful strategy if applied to Africa's development. For Europe this means to go beyond development, aid, guilt and self-interest-driven strategies. For Europe, the lesson of the new Chinese presence in Africa is simply: Get ready to recognise Africa as a partner and equal. Get ready to conceptualise strategies and projects of mutually reinforcing self-interest. It is here that the European (and especially German) tradition of *Ordnungspolitik* (order policy) may come in as a more sophisticated and sustainable development model than the Chinese rush for quick and rather one-dimensional results.

3   It is remarkable that Africa has begun to discover one essential precondition and consequence of the rise of China and the subsequent rise of India: to tap the potential of the African diaspora. Most private investment in China was contributed by overseas Chinese. In the meantime, the more than 20 million overseas Indians have understood the mechanism and effect. They have discovered the investment potential in India. They realised that the reversal of the brain drain must not be to their detriment. In fact, besides capital, they bring experience and inspiration. Africa is well advised to enhance the role of the African diaspora and turn the issue of the brain drain into a matter of brain circulation. This would include a structured policy of (possibly temporary) migration to Europe and North America, but also a structured transfer of technical skills from Europe and North America to Africa.

4   Most important, an updated development concept for Africa needs to include the wretched and poor of Africa as a source of opportunity.

Poverty eradication is the goal, as stated in the UN Millenium Declaration and many fine statements by the African Union, regional groupings in Africa and many donor countries. But poverty eradication is no purpose in itself. It is aimed at empowering the individual in his or her human dignity through the better growth of his or her talent and potential. At the moment, poverty is all too often still considered a burden or an excuse in Africa. If Africa were to learn from the Chinese and, increasingly, the Indian experience Africa would define poverty and poor people as an opportunity. Poor people are an opportunity to invest in their better future and hence into a better future of the whole continent. The future of Africa cannot be based on different strategies as the future of any other modern society: education, urbanisation, possessive individualism and the broadening of the market as an inclusive order of freedom. To make such a sociological development work, the political sector needs to provide the frame but cannot generate the content.

In the course of Western modernisation the rule of law has preceded democracy, sometimes even modern statehood. It cannot be different in Africa. Reliable rule of law is the key to advance domestic stability and regional integration. Accountable participation in the name of democracy will follow suit. Democracy cannot generate social inclusion by itself. It requires a legal frame that protects the weak and predicts life for the strong. Without the primacy of rule of law good governance remains rhetoric. With reliable rule of law in strong states the primacy of regional law can become a logical continuation rather than a limit of individual state action. There is no cultural obstacle or limit to the application of this insight. The application of this law of reliable and sustainable modernisation may take time. There is no reason why eventually it cannot work with the same result in Africa as it has done in Europe or North America. The main reason does not lie in anthropological, cultural and religious factors. The main reason lies in the structure of societal developments under the condition of the homogenising yet incomplete and fragile modern state. Only rule of law is an objective and sustainable glue that holds a state together, makes it strong and ready to open to co-operation and eventual integration with neighbours and partners. Therefore, regional integration too needs to be law-based and empowered with a legislative component gradually shaping a community law.

Interests of the European Union

The EU is promoting regional integration in Africa and elsewhere. During past years its focus in Africa, the Caribbean and the Pacific (ACP) was related to the negotiation of Economic Partnership Agreements. Since 2002 the EU has enticed its ACP partners to engage in these negotiations. The EU claimed that the negotiations would strengthen regional integration in ACP. By replacing preferential trade agreements (that have been in place through subsequent Yaoundé Conventions, Lomé Agreements and the Cotonou Agreement of 2000) by free-trade mechanisms, the EU would comply with World Trade Organisation (WTO) provisions. At the same time, the EU claimed, relations with ACP regions would be put on the basis of equality and a true partnership.

By 2008 interim agreements had been reached with several sub-regions and individual countries or contingent groupings of countries in ACP More than anybody else, EU officials had become doubtful of the multiply potential of Economic Partnership Agreements. The EU was looking for a new rationale in its relations with the countries of ACP (Ferdowsi 1999; European Commission 2006: 7–23; Council of the EU 2006: 61–182; Grimm and Kielwein 2005; Molt 2007: 33–8; Müller-Brandeck-Bouquet *et al.* 2007). On 23 June 2000 a new long-term approach in the relationship between the EU and its ACP partners, including Africa, began: The Cotonou Agreement was signed between the EU and fifteen Caribbean, fourteen Pacific and all forty-eight Sub-Saharan countries. Africa provides 95 per cent of the total ACP population and gets 80 per cent of all support funds defined by the Cotonou Agreement. This agreement replaced the Lomé IV Convention and is intended to last for twenty years. Its main features are the following:

1   The Cotonou Agreement emphasises political dialogue with a strengthened inclusion of civil society.
2   In terms of economic co-operation, it replaced preferential relations with the principle of reciprocity as requested by the WTO but potentially to the disadvantage of several EU partner countries in Africa; until 2008 new regional Economic Partnership Agreements (EPAs) with each of the ACP regions were to be negotiated.
3   The ACP countries are no longer exempted from the WTO Multi-fibre Agreements with their restrictions on textile exports from developing countries to industrialised markets. This is extremely relevant to some African countries: 58 per cent of total exports from Lesotho and 39 per cent of total exports from Mozambique are in textiles.

Several preferential elements of the Lomé Convention favoured agricultural activities in countries producing beef (Botswana, Namibia, Zimbabwe), sugar (Tanzania, Mauritius, Malawi, Swaziland) and the economies of the landlocked African countries. They have been discontinued by the Cotonou Convention (Moreau 2000: 6–10; Schmidt 2000: 29–38; Babarinde and Faber 2004: 27–47).

The main reason for the fundamental shift from preferential trade arrangements to the principle of reciprocity was the ruling of the WTO Dispute Settlement body according to which the provisions of the Lomé Convention were unfair in giving preference to banana exporters in the Caribbean and in other countries with special relations with Europe. The Cotonou Agreement stipulates the principle of reciprocity in free trade. To comply with its logic, the Cotonou Agreement divided the ACP countries into different regional groupings. The subsequent negotiation of Economic Partnership Agreements left it to the African countries to decide under which configuration they wished to negotiate with the EU. Since 2002 the EU has negotiated EPAs with the following groupings in Africa:

1 West Africa: all ECOWAS member states plus Mauritania.
2 Central Africa: all Economic and Monetary Community of Central Africa (CEMAC) member states plus São Tomé and Príncipe and the Democratic Republic of the Congo.
3 Eastern and Southern Africa: all COMESA member states except Angola, the Democratic Republic of the Congo, Egypt, Libya and Swaziland.
4 SADC minus: all Southern Africa Custom Union (SACU) member states, including South Africa as an observer, plus Angola, Mozambique and Tanzania.

In light of the ambivalent experiences with negotiating Economic Partnership Agreements, the EU should reconsider its strategy toward ACP.

First, the preferential trade relationship with Africa and subsequently also with the Caribbean and the Pacific region has accompanied European integration from its very beginning. Since the initial commitment of the Treaties of Rome in 1957, the European relationship with former or current colonies and overseas territories of some of the states members of the European Economic Community (EEC, later European Community (EC) and EU) was based initially on a late colonial and later on a postcolonial relationship. It moved from dependence to co-operation, from colonial dominance to guilt and development aid. It continued to cover special vested interests of some former European colonial powers in some of their former colonies (and continuously existing overseas territories). The EU as a whole has grown as this relationship has matured. EPAs were meant to be a modernising continuation of this policy of five decades. However, they were too narrow, one-dimensional in their economic orientation and almost anti-political. They never had the potential to be a comprehensive strategy for re-designing Europe's relationship with ACP.

Second, the negotiations of EPAs were inherently contradictory as far as the main normative objective of the EU is concerned: promoting regional integration in ACP. While the EU was claiming to promote regional integration, it did not recognise the existing regional groupings as its integral and comprehensive negotiation partner. Instead of negotiating in the Caribbean with the Caribbean Community (CARICOM) the EU 'invented' the Caribbean Forum of African, Caribbean and Pacific States (CARIFORUM) to include Cuba and the Dominican Republic. Neither of these countries is considered to be a helpful engine of Caribbean regional integration by CARICOM, to which they do not belong. Instead of negotiating with the Pacific Islands Forum (PIF), which has established itself in recent years as the nucleus of pan-Pacific regional integration, the EU preferred a different approach of negotiation vis-à-vis Australia and New Zealand on the one hand (both of which are PIF member states), the Melanesian group of PIF countries, Papua New Guinea in particular, on the other hand, while not pursuing a comprehensive negotiation strategy with the PIF as a whole. In Africa, the situation was likewise incoherent. The EU was negotiating with four idiosyncratic groupings and not comprehensively with any of the existing regional groupings. But in order to support regional integration in Africa, the EU needs to recognise regional groupings as they exist, no matter what their substance, no matter how complex and difficult the relationship therefore may be and no matter how comprehensive the EU approach ought to be to accommodate the interests and conditions of all the respective regional partners. Everything else would always remain, at best, lukewarm support of region-building.

Third, the EU needs to develop a comprehensive political strategy for its future relations with the regional groupings in the ACP region. Together, they may well pursue the goal of reciprocal free trade as one tool but they should never elevate reciprocal free trade to be the ultimate and comprehensive goal of a bi-regional relationship. The regional groupings in ACP have matured. They still may be weak, contradictory and insufficient. Yet as they exist they are expressions of a genuine and independent expression of region-building. They have become political processes and ought to be supported as such. They have to be taken seriously by the EU as a political and economic expression of the genuine interest of the respective people, societies and states. The EU can define criteria for the management of bi-regional relationships. These criteria ought to be defined by normative principles inherent in the European integration project, including the promotion of human rights, rule of law, democracy, good governance and market economy. But only a political approach culminating in coherent, comprehensive and multidimensional bi-regional association agreements with the existing regional groupings in Africa, in the Caribbean and in the Pacific region can serve as the basis of a new, mature and equal relationship between the EU and large parts of a world that have outgrown post-colonialism.

The need to recalibrate implementation strategies

In order for the EU to take African regional integration seriously, Africa has to break what Nigeria's former President Olusegun Obasanjo has called the 'over-dependence–underperformance syndrome' (Murithi 2007: 13). In concrete terms, this requires a tangible recalibration of development strategies aimed at moving from aid-driven development to aid-framed and supported private initiative as key to sustainable development. As far as the daunting problem of overlapping membership in different and often idiosyncratic regional groupings is concerned, Africa has to move from efforts to understand the chaotic world of overlapping memberships in regional groupings to an analytical frame that is trying to make sense of region-building in Africa through the prism of concentric circles: applying the concept of subsidiarity and implying the need for a clear ordering of competences, priorities and potentialities, Africa has to redesign its region-building map along the notion of concentric circles:

First circle. African states ought to be considered the prime basis for any integration scheme on the continent. They need to strengthen their ability to provide public goods, protect non-negotiable normative principles (especially human rights, the rule of law, a market economy and good governance) and contribute to the development of supranational levels of governance in Africa. Only strong and capable states can be good partners in integration and engines for region-building.

Second circle. The regional groupings in Africa need to be considered the second layer in the construction of regional integration in Africa. They need to move ahead to become multidimensional structures of governance, vertically covering a broad array of public domains and horizontally reconnecting with the states and societies that are constitutive parts of each regional grouping. Eventually African regional groupings will have to move from the economic agenda to the agenda of peace and governance. They will also need to create some form of supranational authority and a gradually growing common legislation, monitored and, if necessary, advanced by the work of an independent regional judiciary.

Third circle. At the continental level the African Union serves as facilitator and engine for the advancement of regional groupings. The African Union co-ordinates regional activities and should intent to harmonise objectives, instruments and policy formulations. It may remain the embodiment of the quest for African unity. This quest ought to be understood as an expression of a common identity and a shared political culture, supported by efforts of collective security and continent-wide implementation of standards of human rights and governance. But, in the end, most probably the African Union will play more the role of a hybrid of Council of Europe, the Organisation for Security and Co-operation in Europe (OSCE) and the United Nations (UN). Africa's 'European Union' will rest with some of the continents regional groupings.

Fourth circle. Africa might consider an extension of the scope and radius of its continent-wide co-ordination organs by reaching out to a co-operative structure that includes the most important strategic partners of Africa. Such a co-operative association with the EU, the US, China, Russia and the Arab League could serve as an external collective development and security platform aimed at stabilising the genuine African efforts in peace-building and post-conflict management, but also supporting those aspects of global governance in which African issues and global issues are inextricably linked.

Africa has entered a new stage of region-building. The concept to achieve the African Economic Community by 2028 has been achieved at different levels in different regions of Africa. New components have been introduced into the agenda of African regional integration with the need for post-conflict management, the importance to move from petrified pluralism to dynamic pluralism, from static to real rule of law and from formal to deep integration including a legislative component. The core issues at this moment in time are trust, based on symmetrical regime structures and implementation based on clearly defined goals, criteria and timetables. Only some of the many African regional groupings can be expected to achieve the necessary success on this path. For the time being, most likely ECOWAS, SADC and the EAC are the prime candidates for success. They are multidimensional, have gone through the experience of crisis and renewal, are political in nature, and promising in potential and seriousness of their leading actors.

Other regional groupings will probably play a supportive role, either functional or sector-specific, in the context of the overarching leadership of the strongest of the African regional groupings. The African Union will need to distinguish between strong and weak regional groupings according to the normative principles of trust and democracy, rule of law and good governance, potential and capacity to project multidimensional interests and agendas. At the core of deep integration stands the recognition of the primacy of some sort of supranational political authority, usually backed by a supranational legal authority. Only with these mechanisms in place can economic authority grow. Like democratic accountability and the supranational rule of law, economic credibility as a precondition for a genuine AEC which is both sustained and successful.

At this point in time, the question for Africa is not whether maximalist or gradualist concepts of region-building prevail. A smart approach would combines maximalist objectives with gradualist approaches and processes. Gradualist federalism can be a smart and successful way to combine idealism with realism, vision with rational management of daily affairs and contingent obstacles. Such an approach will help to generate a unique and respected form of multi-level governance in Africa (Kambudzi 2008: 13–27).[3] Concentric circles of overlapping policy issues are a better perspective for Africa than the solar system-like and almost unrelated circles of formalistic memberships. A strategy of concentric circles for African region-building requires a clear ordering of political competences between the different levels of governance.[4] Such a strategy could break the circle of pretension and rhetoric integration that is still strongly represented in African region-building.

Preconditions for improved performance in African regional integration

The major question for African region-building is of a strategic nature: how to achieve results-oriented deep integration? How to do things better, more effective and with sustainable effects? How to define the potential of integration from its opportunities instead of being scared or worried about its limits? On paper, the declaratory frame around the actors of African region-building is impressive. The new momentum for regional integration in Africa is a fine opportunity that should not be missed. But it needs strategic focus, honest reassessment of priorities and links between the existing structures and – most important – an optimal use of limited resources in order to achieve visible and lasting early results.

African states, African regional groupings and the AU need to conceptualise their common future toward a functioning multi-level governance system in Africa on the basis of three components:

1 A clear strategy linked to manageable priorities.
2 A clear time frame linked to realistic procedures of work.
3 A clear definition of binding criteria.

The third aspect is probably the most important one to advance African regional integration. Strategies, priorities, even timetables and verbal commitments are cheap currency and in fact they are a rhetoric currency widely available in Africa (as elsewhere). But the need to define clear and binding criteria for the implementation of visions, programmes and projects is key to moving from rhetoric to real integration in Africa.

European integration projects were mostly achieved because of a combination of three different and potentially contradicting factors:

1 The insight of the limits of national actor capacity and the inner strength to recognise that regional solutions will be better.
2 The recognition that a joint will requires compromises which are not always based on a speedy 'return on investment' but need to be understood as a long-term commitment of all partners.
3 The understanding that different interests can be coupled through mutual trust in the overall usefulness of a project in spite of existing differences in motivation and objectives.

Conclusion

Africa has ample room to identify win–win constellations originating in deep and real region-building. Infrastructure measures and basic needs provision, optimising human resources and migration potential, generating employment and sustainable growth, prioritising education and closing the digital divide, preserving the human habitat and providing work conditions in line with human dignity – these are but a few of the basic challenges that should be reconsidered as opportunities for Africa. The wisdom of African leaders will find the right answers and turn strategy into reality. Important is one of Europe's experiences: Africa needs working, efficient and uncompromising institutions, but it should not fall into the trap of mistaking institution-building for region-building. Regional integration is a matter of real issues and concrete results in joint projects. Regional integration is not done by emulating any sort of institutions that one might conceive. Regional integration happens through institutions and policies that work.

Notes

1 See African Union Commission (2007). This important and stimulating study provides options for the rationalisation of the regional economic communities in Africa. The study tends, however, to underestimate the need for firm criteria in order to implement policy decisions and it is focused on economic and technical matters, thus neglecting the political and legal issues discussed in this chapter. All in all, the assumption that integration can be optimised through mechanistic technical processes must arouse scepticism when taking into account the unpredictable political dependency of any integration progress.
2 On the current formal situation of regional economic integration across Africa see ECA (2004: 127–57).
3 Kambudzi's paper is the most stimulating and thoughtful contribution in a remarkable book. The book echoes the 2007 debate among AU heads of state and government about the potential for a unified African government. While, in the end, the majority of Africa's political leaders opted for a gradual path toward continent-wide integration, their debate – and the subsequent echo of it in political circles and among academics in Africa – has advanced the quality and depth of the African discourse on regional integration considerably. Kambudzi, Secretary of the AU Peace and Security Council, must be lauded for advancing the debate and focusing it in a way that combines realism with idealism. His paper is a lasting milestone in the intellectual reflection about African region-building. It will serve as a landmark for the future debate on region-building in Africa. On the Grand Debate among the AU leaders see Lecouture (2008: 45–59).
4 For an initial proposal of how to order competences in an African multi-level governance system see Houghton (2008: 79–89).

References

African Union (11 July 2000) 'The Constitutive Act of the AU'. Online. Available: Africa-union.org/About_AU/AbConstitutive_Act.htm (accessed 29 October 2008).
African Union Commission (2007) 'Rationalization of the Regional Economic Communities (RECs): Review of the Abuja Treaty and Adoption of Minimum Integration Programme', Addis Abeba: African Union.
Agubuzu, L. O. C. (2004) *From the OAU to AU: the Challenges of African Unity and Development in the Twenty-first Century*, Lagos: Nigerian Institute of International Affairs.
Babarinde, O. and Faber, G. (2004) 'From Lomé to Cotonou: business as usual?' *European Foreign Policy Review* 9/2004: 27–47.
Bach, D. (2005) 'The global politics of regionalism: Africa', in M. Farrell *et al.* (eds) *Global Politics of Regionalism: Theory and Practice*, London: Pluto Press.
Cheru, F. (2002) *African Renaissance: Roadmaps to the Challenge of Globalization*, London and New York: Zed Books.

Council of the EU (2006) 'European Union Strategy for Africa: Conclusions by the Heads of State and Government Meeting in the European Council, Brussels, December 15–16, 2005', Compendium on Development Co-operation Strategies, Brussels: European Commission, Directorate General for Development, pp. 61–182. Online. Available: http://ec.europa.eu/development/body/publications/docs/2006/Compendium_EN_2006.pdf#zoom=100 (accessed 12 October 2008).

Dinka, T. and Kennes, W. (2007) 'Africa's Regional Integration Arrangements: History and Challenges', ECDPM Discussion Paper 74, Maastricht: European Centre for Development Policy.

ECA (2004) 'Assessing Regional Integration in Africa', ECA Reports, Addis Ababa: Economic Commission for Africa.

—— (2006) 'Regional economic integration in Africa', in P. de Lombaerde (ed.) *Multilateralism, Regionalism and Bilateralism in Trade and Investment: 2006 World Report on Regional Integration*, Dordrecht: Springer.

European Commission (2006) 'Strategy for Africa: an EU Regional Political Partnership for Peace, Security and Development in the Horn of Africa', Com (2006) 601, Brussels: European Commission. Online. Available: http://ec.europa.eu/development/body/tmp_docs/com2006601_en.pdf (accessed 12 October 2008).

Ferdowsi, M. A. (ed.) (1999) *Vom Enthusiasmus zur Ernüchterung? Die Entwicklungspolitik der Europäischen Union*, Munich: Dritte Welt.

—— (ed.) (2004) *Afrika. Ein verlorener Kontinent?* Munich: Wilhelm Fink.

Francis, D. J. (2006) *Uniting Africa: Building Regional Peace and Security Systems*, Aldershot: Ashgate.

Fues, T., Grimm, S. and Leufer, D. (2006) 'China's Africa Policy: Opportunity and Challenge for European Development Co-operation', Briefing Paper 4. Online. Available: http://asiandrivers.open.ac.uk/Druckfassung%20Briefing%20paper.pdf (accessed 29 October 2008).

Gottschalk, K. and Schmidt, S. (2004) 'The African Union and the new partnership for Africa's development: strong institutions for weak states?', *International Politics and Society* 4 (2004): 138–58.

Grimm, S. (2003) 'Europäische Demokratieförderung in den 1990er Jahren', in S. Grimm (ed.) *Die Afrikapolitik der Europäischen Union. Europas außenpolitische Rolle in einer randständigen Region*, Hamburg: Institut für Afrika-Kunde.

Grimm, S. and Kielwein, N. (2005) 'Die Afrikastrategie der Europäischen Union. Kohärenz gegenüber einem vielschichtigen Kontinent im Wandel', Analysen und Stellungnahmen 9, Bonn: Deutsches Institut für Entwicklungspolitik. Online. Available: www.die-gdi.de/CMS-Homepage/openwebcms3_e.nsf/(ynDK_contentByKey)/ENTR-7BRDNY/$FILE/9%202005%20DE.pdf (accessed 12 October 2008).

Houghton, I. (2008) 'Identifying the domains of competence and the possible impact of the establishment of a Union government on the sovereignty of states', in T. Murithi (ed.) *Towards a Union Government for Africa: Challenges and Opportunities*, Pretoria/Thswane: Institute of Security Studies.

Kambudzi, A. M. (2008) 'Portrayal of a possible path to a single government for Africa', in T. Murithi (ed.) *Towards a Union Government for Africa: Challenges and Responses*, Pretoria/Thswane: Institute of Security Studies.

Lecouture, D. (2008) 'Reflections on the 2007 Grand Debate on a Union government for Africa', in T. Murithi (ed.) *Towards a Union Government for Africa*, Pretoria/Thswane: Institute of Security Studies.

M'boge, F. and Gbaydee Doe, S. (2004) 'Overview of civil society in Africa', in F. M'boge and S. Gbaydee Doe (eds) *African Commitments to Civil Society Engagement: a Review of eight NEPAD Countries*, Nairobi: African Human Security Initiative.

Mbeki, T. (1998) 'The African Renaissance, South Africa and the world', speech at the United Nations University, Tokyo, 9 April. Online. Available: www.unu.edu/unupress/mbeki.html (accessed 29 October 2008).

Molt, P. (2007) 'Zur Afrikastrategie der Europäischen Union', *Politik und Zeitgeschichte* 48 (2007): 33–8.

Moreau, F. (2000) 'The Cotonou Agreement: new orientations', *Courier* 9 (2000): 6–10.

Müller-Brandeck-Bouquet, G., Schmidt, S., Schuhkraft, C., Kessler, U. and Gieg, P. (eds) (2007) *Die Afrikapolitik der Europäischen Union: Neue Ansätze und Perspektiven*, Opladen: Budrich.

Murithi, T. (ed.) (2007) 'Institutionalizing pan-Africanism: transforming African Union values and principles into policy and practice', IIS Paper 143, Pretoria/Thswane: Institute of Security Studies 13.

Sautman, B. V. (2006) 'Friends and interests: China's distinctive links with Africa', Center on China's Transnational Relations Working Paper 12. Online. Available: www.cctr.ust.hk/articles/pdf/WorkingPaper12.pdf (accessed 29 October 2008).

Schmidt, S. (2000) 'Aktuelle Aspekte der EU-Entwicklungspolitik. Aufbruch zu neuen Ufern?' *Aus Politik und Zeitgeschichte*, B 19–20 (2000): 29–38.

Stamm, A. (2006) 'Wissenschaftskooperation. Neue Formen der Zusammenarbeit mit Subsahara-Afrika', in S. Klingebiel (ed.) *Afrika-Agenda 2007. Ansatzpunkte für den deutschen G8-Vorsitz und die EU-Ratspräsidentschaft*, Bonn: Deutsches Institut für Entwicklungspolitik.

Tull, D. M. (2005) *Die Afrikapolitik der Volksrepublik China*, Berlin: Stiftung Wissenschaft und Politik.

Waller, P. P. (1999) 'Demokratische Renaissance in Afrika?' *Internationale Politik* 8 (1999): 49–54. Online. Available: www.internationalepolitik.de/archiv/jahrgang1999/download (accessed 29 October 2008).

5 European military intervention in Congo

Belachew Gebrewold

When the crisis worsened in the Great Lakes area in general, and in the Democratic Republic of Congo (DRC) in particular, after the Rwandan genocide in 1994, the EU sent its Special Representative Aldo Ajello to the region. The EU intervened militarily in DRC; it contributed millions of euros for both civilian and military operations in DRC. Not only in DRC but also in the whole Great Lakes region the EU's financial and diplomatic involvement has been considerable. The EU contributed financially to the African Union to sustain its military operation in Burundi; its contribution to the Demobilisation and Reintegration Programme for the Great Lakes Region was considerable. Similarly, it allocated millions of euros to a disarmament programme in Congo Brazzaville. In the DRC the EU financed the establishment of an Integrated Police Unit (IPU). The EU's Police Mission in Kinshasa (EUPOL Kinshasa) and its successor (as of 1 July 2007) EU Police Mission in Democratic Republic of Congo (EUPOL RD Congo) trained and supported Congolese police. In order to prepare for the elections that took place in 2006, the EU allocated substantial amount of money to establish and implement a strategy of elections security guaranteed by the Police National Congolaise with the assistance of MONUC and EUFOR RD Congo. The military and non-military involvement of the EU in DRC is unprecedented in the EU's involvement in Africa.

Has the EU achieved its goals in the DRC? What factors determine the successes and setbacks of interventions like the EU's in DRC? The thesis of this chapter is that interventions make sense and are successful only if they take into account multi-faceted and multi-level determinants of a durable peace. These include a co-ordinated, coherent and genuine peace policy instead of one based on the short-term interests of those intervening. The regional and global dimensions of a conflict have to be taken into account. Local conflicts have increasingly gained regional and even global profiles through the arms trade, resource exploitation and competition between global players. Hence it is not enough to focus on how well equipped or well manned intervention forces are, one must also consider how these multiple levels of a conflict are addressed.

The broader framework for the EU military intervention in the DR Congo

On 12 December 2003 the EU issued a strategy paper to address security threats such as hunger, malnutrition, AIDS and many other diseases, poverty, conflicts in a number of countries, terrorism, proliferation of weapons of mass destruction, state failure and organised crime. Responses to these threats include co-operation in fighting terrorism, policies against proliferation, dealing with regional conflicts, 'putting failed states back on their feet', acting before a crisis occurs, conflict prevention and co-operating with partners such as Africa through effective multilateral systems leading to a fairer, safer and more united world (Council of the EU 2003). It is hoped this will be achieved through integrating a range of external policies: humanitarian aid, development co-operation, international environmental policy, international police, justice and intelligence co-operation, foreign policy (multilateral diplomacy and the promotion of the values of the EU), the politico-military field (including European Security and Defence Policy, ESDP) and immigration policy. It has become increasingly evident that active prevention of conflict has to be pursued instead of a reactive approach to conflicts. Multilateralism consists of an intricate web of states, regimes, treaties and organisations, i.e. multi-level governance, to improve people's access to peace, security and development. In the case of failed, collapsed or weak states this includes nation-building, preventing and settling conflicts in the EU's neighbourhoods and controlling migration flows (Biscop 2005: 24–40).

As Article 12 of the Cotonou Agreement of 2000 states, the EU has pledged to pursue a coherent policy towards ACP states. Article 11 of the same agreement states that the parties shall pursue an active, comprehensive and integrated policy of peace-building and conflict prevention and resolution within a partnership framework. Based on the Cotonou Agreement (in Articles 5, 13 and 96, for example), the promotion of human rights, the rule of law and good governance are the pillars of the EU's policy towards Africa. The EU earmarked €2.7 billion in the tenth European Development Fund (EDF) as an incentive allocation for countries that pursue governance reforms towards more democracy, human rights and the rule of law. Addressing causes of conflict, preventing conflicts, and post-conflict reconstruction have become increasingly important in EU foreign policy in general and Africa policy in particular. The European Security Strategy of 2003 emphasised this.

The EU's 'effective multilateralism' intends not only to achieve conflict resolution or prevention through global actors or institutions, but also to support both existing and future regional security mechanisms in Africa. The UN Charter (Chapter VIII, Article 52(3)) states that 'The Security Council shall encourage the development of pacific settlement of local disputes through such regional arrangements or by such regional agencies either on the initiative of the states concerned or by reference from the Security Council'. As a consequence the African Union strives to promote security self-reliance within the framework of the Union (Constitutive act of the African Union; African Union 2000: Art. 4(k)). Furthermore, the Union emphasises its right to intervene in a member state pursuant to a decision of the Assembly in respect of grave circumstances, namely war crimes, genocide and crimes against humanity (Constitutive Act of the African Union: Art. 4(h)).

One of the specific objectives of the AU is to 'co-ordinate and harmonise policies between existing and future Regional Economic Communities for the gradual attainment of the objectives of the Union' (Constitutive Act of the African Union: Art. 3.i). The protocol relating to the establishment of the Peace and Security Council of the AU states that it 'wants to co-ordinate and harmonise continental efforts in the prevention and combating of international terrorism in all its aspects (Art. 3d)'. In the Horn of Africa, the Intergovernmental Authority on Development (IGAD) has been playing a central role in the peace process for Somalia and Sudan – Sudan People's Liberation Army/Movement (SPLA/M). In West Africa, the Economic Community of West African States (ECOWAS) has been the main actor in Sierra Leone, Guinea, Liberia, etc. In Southern Africa, the Southern African Development Community (SADC) has been playing an important security role (Lesotho in 1998, the Democratic Republic of Congo, Zimbabwe). The EU has been trying to support these institutions financially, diplomatically and logistically.

The Cairo Declaration of the Africa–Europe Summit in Cairo, 3–4 April 2000, under the aegis of the Organisation of African Unity (OAU) and the EU, reaffirmed a common commitment to settle disputes by peaceful means, and to renounce any recourse to the threat or use of force in any manner inconsistent with the UN Charter, or against the national territory of another state, including the acquisition of territory by force; to facilitate the return to non-violent, stable and self-sustaining situations; to build peace through effective policies and to prevent conflicts.

As a result the EU conducted an EU military operation in the Democratic Republic of Congo in 2003, called Artemis, in accordance with the mandate set out in United Nations Security Council Resolution (UNSCR) 1484, and deployed its forces to operate in accordance with the objectives set out in the 'Framework for EU action in response to the crisis in Bunia' (eastern Democratic Republic of Congo) approved by the Council (Council Joint Action 2003/423/CFSP).

In EU policy towards Africa, peace, security and good governance are emphasised as factors that facilitate economic growth, trade and interconnection to achieve Millennium Development Goals (MDGs). Hence, in this context, the prerequisites for attaining the MDGs:

1 *Peace and security:* tackling the exploitation of natural resources that trigger conflicts; sustaining peace in post-conflict situations; linking relief, rehabilitation and development; security sector reform (SSR),

disarmament, demobilisation, reintegration and reinsertion (DDRR); addressing the proliferation of small arms and light weapons (SALW).

2   *Supporting African peace-support operations:* co-operating in addressing common security threats including non-proliferation of weapons of mass destruction (WMD); combating terrorism.

3   *Good and effective governance:* supporting legitimate and effective governance; addressing crises of legitimacy, i.e. states' weakness (absence of a genuine social contract between state and citizen); ineffectiveness (limited capacity to deliver basic social services).

This can be achieved through reforming the state (building effective and credible central institutions; police and judicial system, public financial management, national parliaments; developing local capacity; reinforcing respect for human rights and democracy; promoting gender equality, fighting corruption and organised crime and promoting good governance in the financial, tax and judicial areas, and mutual monitoring within the framework of the African Peer Review Mechanism (APRM). The EU Strategy for Africa is the framework for future EU–Africa co-operation in security and development related areas. The tenth European Development Fund, whose budget is €22.7 billion for the period 2008–13, intends to allocate 90 per cent of it to Sub-Saharan Africa and the European Neighbourhood and Partnership Instrument for partner countries in North Africa. Hence, Peace and Security play a key role in intercontinental relations. Accordingly, the EU allocated €242 million to the AU mission in Sudan and to support for the operation in the Central African Republic led by the Economic and Monetary Union of Central Africa (Communauté Économique et Monétaire de l'Afrique Centrale, CEMAC). The contested elections of 2005 in the Central African Republic resulted in the killing of numerous civilians, widespread banditry and the displacement of approximately 185,000 people out of a total population of 4.1 million. The neighbouring countries of the CEMAC attempted to stabilise the country with almost 400 peacekeeping soldiers. €3.5 million from the EU's African Peace Facility has been allocated to support the peacekeeping operation led by CEMAC in the Central African Republic (EU 2005).

The EU has pledged to allocate €300 million for the period 2008–10 in order to strengthen African capacities for the prevention, management and resolution of conflicts, Security sector reform and disarmament, demobilisation and reintegration, assistance to the counter-terrorism centre and the African Centre for Study and Research on Terrorism (CAERT), based in Algiers, and stemming the illicit flow of small arms and light weapons. The African states are expected to join to counter terrorism, whereas technical assistance, information and support to the AU Anti-terrorism Centre. Capacity-building includes such things as strengthening the AU's African Standby Force by building on existing activities of member states through training, technical, planning and logistic support, military and civilian, and strengthening of fragile states. The EU member states declare their willingness to adopt the EU Code of Conduct on arms exports, discouraging transfers which contribute to instability, tackling illegal trafficking, border management controls and an international arms trade treaty. Further, the EU conducts its own crisis management missions in Africa, including potential deployment of EU battle groups.

The European Union and Congo

When the crisis exacerbated in Great Lakes region in general and the DRC after the genocide of Rwanda in 1994 in particular the EU sent its Special Representative Aldo Ajello. The military operation Artemis, conducted in summer 2003 in Ituri, DRC, was the peak of the EU's involvement in the region. In Ituri, eastern DRC, in 2003 with 1,500 troops the EU intervened militarily besides support for the transitional national government by providing €2.5 million. The EU contributed €25 million to the African Union to sustain its military operation in Burundi. For the Demobilisation and Reintegration Programme for the Great Lakes Region the EU contributed €20 million, in the same way the EU already financed with €2 million a disarmament programme in Congo Brazzaville. In the DRC by allocating €8 million the EU supported the establishment of an Integrated Police Unit, and this project was carried on with a further budget of €4.4 million for 2005. In order to prepare the elections that took place in 2006 the EU allocated €9 million to establish and implement a strategy of elections security to be implemented by the Police National Congolaise with the assistance of the MONUC (Council of the EU 2005b).

The EU has been active in Congo mainly since the mid-1990s; on 5 February 2002 the EU formally resumed its direct co-operation with the DRC after a ten-year suspension (Kobia 2002: 431). The EU did not want to punish the Congolese population for the failure of its corrupt government, which the EU decided to bypass. It allocated €40 million to €50 million per year for structural work, health, urban development and humanitarian aid, all projects to be funded through NGOs and other institutions. The Congolese state delegated its power as National Authorising Officer (NAO) to the EU as Principal Authorising Officer (PAO) (Kobia 2002: 432).

The eighth EDF programme allocated €120 million for poverty alleviation, transport management, health sectors, urban development and the supply of drinking water, institutional administrative support, refugees and internally displaced persons (IDPs), food security and agricultural production, democratisation, human rights and the rule of law, justice, demobilisation, disarmament, repatriation, reinstallation and reintegration, facilitation of the Inter-Congolese Dialogue, and a rapid reaction mechanism (to intervene quickly and effectively in crisis situations). The long-term engagement of the EU is envisaged as focusing on political dialogue and conflict prevention and supporting trade and regional integration and co-operation to enable countries to participate in both the regional and global economy and to consolidate peace and prevent conflicts.

For security and humanitarian reasons the EU decided to intervene in eastern Congo in 2003, when the conflict between various warring parties, including several militia groups, resulted in humanitarian catastrophe. The relations between Kabila's transitional government and the two main rebel groups, Bemba's Mouvement pour la Libération du Congo (MLC) and Rassemblement Congolais pour la Démocratie (RCD), worsened in 2003. The continual creation of new rebel groups and changes of alliance between these armed groups exacerbated the conflict.

The Lusaka Cease-fire Agreement was signed on 10 July 1999 by the DRC, Angola, Namibia, Rwanda, Uganda, Zimbabwe, and later by the Mouvement pour la Libération du Congo and the Rassemblement Congolais pour la Démocratie. On 30 July 2002 in Pretoria the DRC and Rwanda signed a peace agreement and on 6 September 2002 in Luanda the DRC and Uganda signed their agreement. The Inter-Congolese Dialogue was signed as an Agreement on Transition on 17 December 2002 in Pretoria. On 6 March 2003 the Agreement on the Constitution of the Transition was signed in Pretoria, and on 4 April 2003 the Transitional Constitution of the Democratic Republic of Congo was adopted. On 30 June 2003 the composition of the Government of National Unity and Transition was announced. The Memorandum of 29 June 2003 on Security and the Army paved the way for the establishment of an Integrated Police Unit out of the Congolese National Police.

As a reaction to the ongoing violence, the EU decided to conduct a EU military operation in the Democratic Republic of Congo (Artemis), in accordance with the mandate set out in UNSCR 1484 (2003) (ICG 2003). The Council adopted a Common Position 2003/319/CFSP (based on Article 15 of the Treaty of the EU) on 8 May 2003 to support the implementation of the above peace agreements through rapid implementation of the processes of disarmament, demobilisation, repatriation, reintegration and resettlement (DDRRR). The forces were deployed to operate in accordance with the objectives set out in the 'Framework for EU action in response to the crisis in Bunia' adopted by the Council 5 June 2003 (Council Joint Action 2003/423/CFSP) and launched on 12 June 2003. Artemis lasted from 12 June to 1 September 2003.

The Joint Declaration on UN–EU Co-operation in Crisis Management of 29 September 2003 underpinned the mission's international support. The government of the DRC asked the High Representative of the Common Foreign and Security Policy of the EU (CFSP) for EU assistance in setting up the IPU and on 15 December 2003 the Political and Security Committee of the EU (PSC) agreed to support the establishment of the IPU. On 17 May 2004 the Council adopted Joint Action 2004/494/CFSP to support the process of the consolidation of internal security in the DRC. The IPU was decisive in that.

The IPU was composed of 1,008 police officers from the whole country, and its tasks were the protection of state institutions and the Transitional Government authority and the maintenance of law and order. Its aim was to train 38,000 police. When the Transitional Government of DRC made an official request under UNSCR 1493 of 28 July 2003 the EU agreed to rehabilitate and refurbish a training centre and provide basic equipment, train the IPU and monitor and follow up the implementation of the IPU mandate following the initial training (Löser 2007; ICG 2006).

Based on the Joint Action 2004/847/PESC of 9 December 2004, the Council adopted a decision setting up an EU police mission, EUPOL Kinshasa, which monitored, mentored and advised on the setting up and the initial running of an Integrated Police Unit in Kinshasa. The IPU will contribute to ensuring the protection of state institutions and reinforce the internal security apparatus. The IPU will reform and reorganise the Congolese National Police (CNP), train new police and co-ordinate the various Congolese forces maintaining order during the election period. The mandate of the Special Representative Aldo Ajello was extended by Joint Action 2004/530/CFSP. The Joint Action allocated a maximum amount of €4.37 million to fund the planning phase and operations in 2005.

For this task a thirty-one-strong EU police mission was launched as EUPOL Kinshasa on 12 April 2005, composed of police officers from Belgium, France, Italy, the Netherlands, Portugal, Sweden, Canada and Turkey.

> During its first term, EUPOL Kinshasa, in close liaison with MONUC, contributed *inter alia* to (i) the identification and training of IPU members, (ii) the inspection and verification of equipment and assistance in managing it, (iii) the definition of organizational and functional standards and (iv) the drafting of relevant rules and regulations for the IPU.
>
> (Löser 2007: 165)

With the assistance of EUPOL Kinshasa the IPU became operational in June 2005; the Congolese Transitional government asked the EU to extend the mandate of EUPOL Kinshasa until 31 December 2006 (Löser 2007: 163–6). The three essential missions of EUPOL Kinshasa were:

1 To provide security for some Transition politicians and for dignitaries on official missions, and to guard the buildings housing state institutions.
2 To contribute to the security of the elections by organising prevention and intervention patrols.
3 To constitute a tactical reserve force of 350 men for the purposes of maintaining order (Council of the EU 2006).

On 8 December 2006 the Council adopted a Joint Action, amending and extending Joint Action 2004/847/CFSP on the EU police mission in Kinshasa, regarding the Integrated Police Unit (EUPOL Kinshasa), to remain in force until 30 June 2007. The objective was to help ensure the proper integration of the IPU into the National Congolese Police (PNC) and to strengthen its advisory capacity in relation to the Congolese police with a view to facilitating the security sector reform (SSR) process in the DRC, working with the EU's EUSEC DRC mission which advises the DRC authorities on SSR. Starting from 1 July 2007 EUPOL RD Congo succeeded EUPOL Kinshasa, which was deployed in Kinshasa between February 2005 and June 2007 to secure the parliamentary and presidential elections. The objective of EUPOL RD Congo was to support the Congolese authorities' SSR in the area of policing and its co-operation with justice authorities. EUPOL RD Congo consisted of thirty international agents: police, justice, security and human rights experts; it was initially expected to last until 30 June 2009 (Council of the EU 2006).

France has trained and equipped 2,000 Rapid Intervention Police at a cost of €2 million and provided a senior officer to assist the Rapid Intervention Police commandant for two years, whereas the UK advocated a unified European approach. The United Kingdom has earmarked up to £8 million, besides £4 million which has already been provided, for training and equipping the police to provide election security and supplied £253,000 in radio equipment (ICG 2006).

On 2 May 2005 the Council adopted a Joint Action on the EU mission to provide advice and assistance for security sector reform in the DRC, following an official request from the DRC government six days earlier. The EU then decided to establish EU security sector reform mission in the Democratic Republic of the Congo (EUSEC DRC) to provide advice and assistance for security sector reform, with the aim of contributing to a successful integration of the army in the DRC. The objective was to support the implementation of the Global and Inclusive Agreement signed by the Congolese parties in Pretoria on 17 December 2002 and the Final Act signed in Sun City on 2 April 2003 regarding the transition process and the restructuring of an integrated national army. In June 2005 the EU created a civilian mission for Congo called EUSEC DRC whose establishment was based on UNSCR 1592 (2005) for the security sector reform in Congo (Löser 2007: 166). Its mission extended until 30 June 2009.

The assistance programme of SSR encompasses the development of norms of good practice in the security sector; the control, collection and destruction of small arms; enhancing civilian control over the military; and community-based policing and justice reform; poverty reduction; conflict prevention; post-conflict reconstruction; promotion of human rights and democratisation; the facilitation of the integration of the Congolese army; the support of good governance in the field of security; the provision of logistical support to the modernisation of payment of DRC armed forces and its financial administration (Löser 2007; Helly 2006). The €7 million project was intended to run for twelve months, and EUSEC was to provide forty to forty-five military advisers to check payment flow and information technology and equipment, and to support administrative reform.

As the former colonial power Belgium was keen to play a significant role in the DRC's army reform. Within the framework of EUSEC SSR Belgium spent about €30 million annually starting in 2005 on security sector reform, out of its total Congo funding of about €125 million (ICG 2006). It led a series of workshops which developed practical guidelines for army integration; trained the First Integrated Brigade in Kisangani between January and June 2004; trained 285 Congolese instructors in Belgium and another 250 in Kinshasa; engaged in a joint training programme with the South Africans for the Third Integrated Brigade in Kamina. Belgium agreed to equip three brigades fully and three partially; it offered €500,000 to equip additional brigades; it provided thirty trainers to work with three French trainers; it provided military engineering training to promote the reconstruction of infrastructure.

The EU Commission provided €20 million through the World Bank Multi-country Demobilisation and Reintegration Programme (MDRP). The UK provided some funding to the South African-led integration process, registration support and census process. The UK pledged $25 million over five years to the World Bank's MDRP programme, it provided short training courses in the UK for some Congolese officers, and pledged an additional $5 million of non-combat aid for army integration, conditional upon implementation of the EUSEC plan. The Netherlands provided €5 million to help the South Africans refurbish integration centres in North Kivu and France provided support for officer training (ICG 2006).

The EU's second military operation took place in 2006. Based on the Treaty of the European Union (in particular Article 14, the third sub-paragraph of Article 25 and Article 28.3), the EU expressed its commitment to supporting the transition process in the DRC in the Council Joint Action 2006/319/CFSP of 27 April 2006. This move had been preceded by the Council Joint Action 2006/122/CFSP of 20 February 2006, which extended Aldo Ajello's mandate as the EU Special Representative (EUSR) for the African Great Lakes Region. Furthermore, the United Nations Security Council Resolution 1671 (2006) of 25 April 2006 authorised the EU, acting under Chapter VII of the Charter of the United Nations, to deploy forces (EUFOR RD Congo) in support of MONUC during the election process, with initial funding of €16.7 million for the costs of the EU military operation for a four-month period. Operation EUFOR RD Congo was concluded successfully, at least from the EU's point of view, on 30 November 2006. After the Council meeting on 10 and 11 November 2008 the Council reiterated its support for MONUC and underlined the EU's commitment to work with the International Conference on the Great Lakes Region and the African Union to stabilise the situation in the east of the DRC.

Peace needs coherent and concerted actions

The role of both currently powerful and emerging global actors has to be taken seriously while dealing with the DRC conflict in particular and Africa in general. China's international strategy is to prevent or limit the development of a hegemony which would limit its space within the global system, even as its economic growth is rapid and continuous (Taylor 2006: 1). In 2004 28.7 per cent of China's total crude oil was supplied by Africa; China's trade and investment treaties with Africa are increasing; since the creation of China–Africa Co-operation in 2000 China has forgiven more than US$1 billion in debt (Zweig and Jianhai 2005: 26–30).

Since 2002 Angola has been supplying 15 per cent per cent of China's oil imports and in 2006 Angola overtook Saudi Arabia as the main supplier of oil to China (Alden 2007: 8, 67). In Zambia China focuses on minerals such as copper. China has discovered both market and commercial opportunities in Africa: African consumers are receptive to the inexpensive products that China typically produces, and Africa's rich natural resources (oil and minerals) are ripe for exploitation (Broadman 2007: 10–11; Taylor 2006: 70–1; Rocha 2007: 19). In the Sudan China's National Petroleum Corporation owns 40 per cent of the state oil consortium and thanks to Chinese investment in the Sudanese oil sector (about $15 billion between 1996 and 2006) Sudan has become a leading oil exporter, providing about 10 per cent of Chinese oil demands. Sudan is China's second largest trading partner in Africa and bilateral trade was $2.9 billion in 2006, mainly because China buys 65 per cent of Sudan's oil and is the leading supplier of arms to the Sudanese government (Prunier 2007). Sixty-two per cent of total African exports to China consist of oil, increasing at an annual compound rate of 30 per cent. Angola supplies 47 per cent of Africa's oil exports to China, followed by Sudan, 25 per cent, the DRC, 13 per cent, Equatorial Guinea, 9 per cent, and Nigeria, 3 per cent, whereas 87 per cent of all imports from China and India to Africa comprise textile, apparel, electric machinery, equipment, medicine, cosmetic products and batteries (Broadman 2007: 82–3). Chinese economic strategy includes turning the country's arms industry into a top global player by 2020. This has meant arms sales to war-torn countries like Sudan, Ethiopia, Eritrea, DRC and Sierra Leone. China is increasingly interested in the exploitation of oil in countries such as Angola, Nigeria, Sudan, Equatorial Guinea, etc. It vetoes any intervention by the United Nations in the internal affairs of such 'key' countries under the pretext of human rights violations. African countries bought arms worth $1.3 billion in 2003 from China. China is providing Africa with 6–7 per cent of its arms demands annually for its bloodiest conflicts – in Sudan, Eritrea, Ethiopia, DRC, Chad, Zimbabwe and Sierra Leone.

The rapid increase in Chinese–African bilateral trade from $10 billion in 2000 to $70 billion in 2007 made China Africa's second largest trading partner after the US. Moreover, China's direct investment in Africa increased from $491 million in 2003 to over $2.5 billion in 2006. In October 2007 the Industrial & Commercial Bank of China purchased a 20 per cent stake in South Africa's Standard Bank and in 2007 China granted a $9 billion loan and investment package for the DRC that will be repaid in cobalt and copper. However, Chinese development assistance to Africa since 2000 has been between $1 billion and $2 billion per year, whereas the EU and member countries annually contribute about $18 billion (including debt relief), multilateral institutions $9 billion, and the US about $5 billion.

Secret shipments of arms from countries such as South Africa, Bulgaria, France, Belgium were heading for DRC (Lemarchand 2000: 345). Belgium was accused of becoming 'a hub of international trafficking in arms to Burundi' (*Africa Research Bulletin* 1998a: 13280). Romania, Israel, Belgium, the US and others transferred arms to Rwanda, and through Rwanda to Laurent D. Kabila, in the 1990s before and after the genocide in Rwanda and during the civil and inter-state war in the DRC (*Africa Research Bulletin* 1998b: 13357).

Conclusion

We have seen above the considerable role of the EU in DRC. It has invested a lot; it has trained police. It has played a big role in reforming the security sector; it has contributed greatly to the organisation of a successful transition period and the holding of national elections after the transition period; it has supported MONUC. But that is not enough. It is important to take three factors into account. First, the global dimension of the DRC conflict has to be addressed; second, the member states of the EU have to act in concert comprehensively, not just militarily; third, the stance of the EU member states regarding the countries of the Great Lakes region has to be consistent and coherent.

First, peace in the DRC is essentially dependent on the global constellation. For example, the US was not happy about the EU's actions because the autonomous EU engagement in the Congo (outside the NATO framework) excluded the US from the military decision-making process. The EU attempted to show that it was capable of conducting military operations independently. This makes the US nervous. The Chinese presence in Africa will have decisive impacts on Africa's politics and economies by creating a chain reaction in the international security system.

Second, a huge military and economic intervention by the EU in Africa in general and the DRC in particular cannot solve the problems there. The success of military intervention and financial, logistic and diplomatic aid depends on how the member states co-ordinate their policies and put aside their shortsighted national interests. States such as the UK and France pursue their own foreign policies towards Africa, which do not always reflect the principles of the EU in spite of their joint actions and common positions. Such conflicts of interest and policy divergences have considerable impacts on the economic development and political security of African states.

Third, some undemocratic regimes in Africa have had unconditional allies in some EU member states. France was an unconditional ally of former presidents like Mobutu of Zaire and Habyarimana of Rwanda. The UK has continuously backed the Rwandan and Ugandan regimes despite their negative role in the DRC. Such alliances undermine economic development, political stability, the peace and security of African states and regions, and, in the long run, they threaten the security of Europeans themselves, through illegal migration, terrorism and organised crime. Hence sustainable peace in Africa will not be dependent only on military, financial or logistical support and external interventions, through the EU or similar institutions and powers, but rather on a coherent and genuine peace policy at the intrastate, regional and global levels for the benefit of all.

References

Africa Research Bulletin (1998a) 'Burundi–China', *Africa Research Bulletin* 34 (12): 12950. Online. Available: www3.interscience.wiley.com/cgi-bin/fulltext/119100554/ PDFSTART (accessed 3 September 2008).

—— (1998b) 'Romanian arms sales claim', *Africa Research Bulletin* 35 (2): 13017. Online. Available: www3.interscience.wiley.com/cgi-bin/fulltext/119100563/ PDFSTART (accessed 3 September 2008).

African Union (2000) 'Constitutive Act of the African Union'. Online. Available: www.iss.co.za/AF/RegOrg/unity_to_union/pdfs/oau/treaties/Constit_Act_of_ AU_2000.pdf (last accessed 6 January 2009).

Alden, C. (2007) *China in Africa*, London: Zed Books.

Biscop, S. (2005) *The European Security Strategy*, Aldershot: Ashgate.

Broadman, H. G. (2007) *Africa's Silk Road: China and India's new Economic Frontier*, Washington, DC: World Bank.

Council of the EU (2003) 'A secure Europe in a better world: European Security Strategy', Council document 10881/03, 25 June. Online. Available: http://register.con-silium.europa.eu/pdf/en/03/st10/st10881en03.pdf (accessed 6 January 2009).

—— (2005) 'The EU and Africa: towards a strategic partnership', EU press release, 15961/05 (Presse 367), 19 December. Online. Available: http://ue.eu.int/ueDocs/ cms_Data/docs/pressData/en/er/87673.pdf (accessed 12 December 2008).

—— (2006) 'EUPOL–KINSHASA: the first European police mission in Africa', press document EUPOL. Online. Available: www.consilium.europa.eu/uedocs/ cmsUpload/DocumentPresentationEUPOLOctobre2006EN.pdf (accessed 29 October 2008).

European Union 2005 (2005) 'EU support for peace and security in Africa', European Union News Releases, February 2005. Online. Available: www.eurunion. org/News/press/2005/Africa%20final.pdf (accessed 6 January 2009).

Helly, D. (2006) 'Developing an EU strategy for security sector reform', *European Security Review* 28, February. Online. Available: www.saferworld.org.uk/images/ pubdocs/ESR%20Saferworld%20Developing%20an%20EU%20SSR%20 strategy%20Feb%202006.pdf (accessed 12 July 2008).

ICG (2003) 'Congo Crisis: Military Intervention in Ituri', ICG Africa Report 64, 13 June. Online. Available: www.crisisgroup.org/library/documents/report_archive/ A401005_13062003.pdf (accessed 12 November 2008).

—— (2006) 'Security Sector Reform in the Congo', ICG Africa Report 4, 13 February. Online. Available: www.crisisgroup.org/library/documents/africa/central_africa/104_security_sector_reform_in_the_congo.pdf (accessed 30 October 2008).

Kobia, R. (2002) 'European Union Commission Policy in the DRC', *Review of African Political Economy* 93/945: 431–43.

Lemarchand, R. (2000) 'The crisis in the Great Lakes', in J. W. Harbeson and D. Rothchild (eds) *Africa in World Politics: the African State System in Flux*, Boulder, CO: Westview Press, pp. 324–52.

Löser, B. (2007) 'The EU's Peace and Security Strategy in the DRC', in B. Gebrewold (ed.) *Africa and Fortress Europe: Threats and Opportunities*, Ashgate: Aldershot, pp. 159–70.

Prunier, G. (2007) 'Sudan: genocide in Darfur'. Online. Available: http://mondediplo.com/2007/03/08darfur (accessed 8 March 2008).

Rocha, J. (2007) 'A new frontier in the exploitation of Africa's natural resources: the emergence of China', in F. Manji and S. Marks (eds) *African Perspectives on China in Africa*, Oxford: Fahamu, pp. 15–34.

Taylor, I. (2006) *China and Africa: Engagement and Compromise*, London: Routledge.

United Nations (1945) 'Charter of the UN', UN document. Online. Available: www.un.org/aboutun/charter/index.shtml (accessed 18 October 2008).

Zweig, D. and Jianhai, B. (2005) 'China's global hunt for energy', *Foreign Affairs* 84 (5): 25–38.

6 The migration policy of the European Union, with special focus on Africa

Heinrich Neisser

Migration challenge of the European Union

Migration is a complex and multi-faceted phenomenon. It is difficult to define the term 'migration' including all the relevant criteria and to describe the different types of migration movements:

> A person who goes to another country and remains there for the rest of his life, we say, is a migrant; and one who says a two-hour visit to the nearest town is not. Between these two extremes lies a bewildering array of intermediate instances, which can only be distinguished by more or less arbitrary criteria.
>
> (Peterson 1968: 286)

Migration is the permanent movement of individuals or groups from one place to another. It is a basic fact of human history. Migration has now become an important socio-economic feature of contemporary European society. In this context it is therefore important to assess what migration is, why people migrate and how the process of migration fits within the wider forces of inclusion and exclusion in Europe. There are various reasons for the individuals' movement: prosecution of political reasons, labour migration, and so on. The free migration of labour in the EU is a right of EU citizens. Most migration comes from third countries. The elaboration of a common EU policy is a complicated process, as it touches sensitive areas such as internal security.

The Europeanisation of the migration policy started with the Treaty of Maastricht. Since this treaty the migration policy has been a substantial part of the third pillar (Justice and Home Affairs) based on an intergovernmental co-operation between member states. Under the Treaty of Amsterdam the subjects of asylum and migration were moved from the third pillar to the first pillar. The creation of the migration policy as a community task was a reaction to a situation which changed enormously. In 1990 the Iron Curtain fell and the member states of the EU were faced with a domestic increase in the numbers of asylum seekers from Eastern and Central European states. At the same time the number of asylum seekers from developing countries increased.

Since then the EU authorities are facing various challenges. Governments of the member states are unwilling to lead an open debate on migration solution: they fear to provoke public hostility. Populist parties of the right play a large part in the tightening of immigration rules. They organised largely round the issues of race, immigration, citizenship and cultural assimilation. Answering those problems, public policy must seek to internationalise the problems at the level of the EU but also at a global level (Neisser 2007: 140). Only in this way is it possible to find complex solutions to a complex problem. Migration and asylum are tightly intertwined with issues such as security, labour markets, health and education. Within the EU measures in different fields of policy must be coherent. Coherence is a prerequisite of effectiveness. In the following contribution I would like to explain the goals and procedures of the migration policy established by the EU. Migration not only concerns labour but other categories of the population as well. The motives of the migration are different. The EU has had to cope with this phenomenon both internally and externally. For the EU it was necessary to establish a new area of competence in accordance with the Treaty of Maastricht the third pillar of the Union: justice and home affairs. This main goal of this competence is to ensure an area of freedom, safety and justice. The following chapter shows the importance of migration and asylum policy in shaping this area of freedom, safety and justice. In this regard three perspectives are essential: a common asylum and migration policy, co-operation with third countries and tight border controls.

Legal framework of European migration policy

The legal system of migration policy comprises many types of rules, situated on different levels of the Union's legal system.

The first step towards establish clearer responsibility was made in 1986 by establishing an ad hoc Working Group on Immigration. From this initiative two conventions on immigration policy has been adopted: the Dublin Convention on Asylum in 1990 and the External Frontiers Convention in 1991 (Hix 2005: 353).

The Dublin Convention aimed to prevent multiple asylum applications: all states' asylum regulations are mutually recognised and it was ensured that asylum applications would be processed only by the member state in which an asylum seeker first arrived in the EU. The External Frontiers Convention provided for the mutual recognition of visas for non EU nationals. Third-country nationals residing legally in one member state don't need a visa to travel to another EU state for a period of less than three months. But some countries refused to ratify the Dublin Convention as well as the External Frontiers Convention. The UK and Spain refused to sign the External Frontiers Convention due to their ongoing disagreement over Gibraltar.

The European Council in Tampere on 15–16 October 1999 started the period of the establishment of a Common European Asylum and Migration policy. In Chapter 17 of the presidency conclusions four elements are defined:

1   Partnership with countries of origin (A I): the approach of the EU includes activities in the regions of origin such as combating poverty and conflict, improving living standards, growing job opportunities.
2   Common European Asylum System (A II):

   a   Nobody should be sent back to persecution.
   b   Elements of the system:
      i   A clear, workable determination of the state responsible for the examination of an asylum application.
      ii   Common standards for a fair and efficient asylum procedure.
      iii   Common minimum conditions of reception of asylum seekers.
      iv   The approximation of rules on the recognition and content of the refugee status.
      v   Temporary protection of third-country nationals (Council of the EU 2001).
      vi   Finalisation of the European Dactyloscopie (EURODAC) identification System of asylum seekers. (See EURODAC regulation Dec 2000, automatic fingerprint identification system since 15 January 2003).
   c   Fair treatment of third-country nationals (A III): people who are residing in the EU legally will be granted rights and obligations comparable to those of EU citizens.
   d   Management of migration flows:
      i   Closer co-operation between the member states concerning border control;
      ii   Combating of illegal immigration, including the criminal network involved. The rights of the victims to be guaranteed.

The Hague Programme was adopted at the European Council meeting of 4–5 November 2004, where the Summit discussed an area of Freedom, Security and Justice. The European Council adopted a new multi-annual programme for the next five years. This programme comprised the following activities:

1   A Common European Asylum System with a common procedure and a uniform status for those who are granted asylum or subsidiary protection. The ongoing development of European asylum and migration policy should be based on a common analysis of migratory phenomenon in all their aspects (first phase).
2   In its second phase the Common European Asylum System should be based on the full and inclusive application of Geneva Convention and other relevant treaties, and should be built in a thorough and complete evaluation of the legal instruments that have been adopted in the first phase. This evaluation has been carried out and will be considered in the second phase. The second-phase instruments and measures should be submitted to the Council and the European Parliament 'with a view to their adoption' before the end of 2010.

3 *Integration of third-country nationals.* The European Councils calls for equal opportunities to participate fully in society. Obstacles to integration need to be actively eliminated. A coherent European framework of integration should be established. It compromises the following aspects. Integration:

   a   is a continuous, two-way process involving both legally third-country nationals and the host society.

   b   includes, but goes beyond, anti-discrimination policy.

   c   implies respect for the basic values of the EU and fundamental human rights.

   d   requires basic skills for participation in society.

   e   relies on a frequent interaction and intercultural dialogue between all numbers of society within common forums and activities in order to improve material understanding.

   f   extends to a variety of policy areas, including employment and education.

4 Partnership with third countries to: improve the capacity for migration management and refugee protection; prevent and combat illegal immigration; inform on legal channels for migration; resolve refugee situations by providing better access to durable solutions; build border control capacity; enhance document security and tackle the problem of return.

5 Partnership with countries and region of origin developing EU Regional Protection Programmes in close consultation and co-operation with the United Nations High Commissioner for Refugees (UNHCR).

6 Partnership with countries and regions of transit.

7 An effective removal and repatriation policy against illegal immigrants. This policy must be based 'on common standards for persons to be returned in a humane manner and with full respect for their human rights and dignity'.

8 A better management of migration flows, i.e. border checks and the fight against illegal immigration. It needs solidarity and fair sharing of responsibilities, including its financial implications, between the member states.

9 The Schengen Information System (SIS II) has to become operational in 2007. It involves a database of people who have been issued with arrest warrants and of stolen objects.

10 The European Agency for the Management of Operational Co-operation at the External Borders (established on 1 May 2005) should be evaluated by the end of 2007.

11 Common visa rules: introduction of biometrics in the visa information system.

Apart from these programmes the EU adopted essential parts of the migration and asylum *acquis* (Van Krieken 2004). The treaty of Amsterdam brought immigration and asylum into the EC treaty. Articles 61–9 ('Visas, asylum, immigration and other policies referring to the free movement of persons') commit the Council to adopt a common approach to politics in the following areas:

1   Standards and procedures of checking on persons crossing in the EU's external borders.
2   Rules on visas for a stay of longer than three months, including a single list of countries whose citizens require visas to visit the EU.
3   The conditions under which third-country nationals shall have freedom to travel in the EU for up to three months.
4   Standards and procedures for granting and withdrawing asylum and refugee status, including minimum standards for the reception of asylum seekers and refugees.
5   Minimum standards for the temporary protection of displaced persons (*de facto* refugees rather than asylum seekers).
6   Measures on immigration policy, including common conditions of entry and residence and common rules on illegal immigration and repatriation.
7   Measures defining the rights and conditions under which third-country nationals can work and reside anywhere in the EU.

On the basis of the primary law essential measures on the level of secondary law have been adopted. Frequently in the field of migration and asylum policy directives are applied as the legal instruments. Directives are an instrument for harmonising national law but they also give member states the power to adopt their own rules within the framework of the directives. The following part gives essential information about the legal framework at the level of the secondary law:

1   *Migration.* The existing directives concern the scope of legal immigration:
   a   *Family reunification.* The Council Directive 2003/86/EC of 22 September 2003 on the right to family reunification entered into force on 3 October 2003. Member states' legislation had to comply with this Directive not later than 3 October 2005.
   b   *EU long-term resident status.* The Council Directive 2003/109/EC of 25 November 2003 on a long-term resident status for third-country nationals who have legally resided for five years in the territory of a member state entered into force on 23 January 2004. Member states' legislation had to comply with this directive by 23 January 2006 at the latest.
   c   *Students.* A directive on the conditions of admission of third-country nationals for the purposes of study, pupil exchange, unremunerated training or voluntary service was adopted by the Council on 13 December 2004 (Directive 2004/114). It entered into force on 12

January 2005. Member states' legislation must comply with the directive by 12 January 2007.

d   *Researchers.* A directive on the facilitation of the admission of researchers into the EU was adopted by the Council on 12 October 2005 (Directive 2005/71). Its provisions had to be implemented by member states by 12 October 2007.

2   *Asylum.* The following regulation and directives contain the 'four main legal instruments on asylum'. In the field of responsibility, reception, procedures and qualification the prerequisites for a Common EU Asylum System are already given in the shape of harmonised minimum standards:

a   The Dublin regulation (Council of the EU 18 February 2003).
b   Each member state has a duty to enable asylum applications for third-country nationals within their territory, but it is only one member state that is responsible (Art. 3). The latter is in general that member state where the application for asylum was lodged in the first place (Art. 13). Nevertheless, Chapter III of the Dublin regulation defines some exceptions valid in the given order (Art. 5) in turn. The member state is responsible (even if the first asylum application was not lodged in this respective member state) in cases where:
   i   Family members of unaccompanied minors are legally residing in it (Art. 6).
   ii   Family members of the asylum seeker are residing in it as refugees and that the lodging of an application in this state is wanted (Art. 7).
   iii The asylum seeker is provided with a residence document or a valid visa for it (Art. 9).
   iv   A third-country national enters the respective member state and does not need an entry visa for it (Art. 11).
   v   The application is lodged in the international transit area of an airport situated on its territory (Art. 12).

Finally, a humanitarian clause is incorporated into Chapter IV, Article 15, of the Dublin Regulation: 'Any Member State, even where it is not responsible under the criteria set out in this regulation, may bring together family members, as well as other dependent relatives, on humanitarian grounds based in particular on family or cultural considerations' (Council of the EU, 18 February 2003: 15). The latter might be dependence in the case of pregnancy, a newborn child, serious illness, severe handicap or old age.

1   The Reception Conditions Directive (Council of the EU, 27 January 2003);
a   This directive guarantees access to information within fifteen days of the asylum application (Art. 5), to a refugee status document within three days after the application (Art. 6), to medical screening (Art. 9),

to emergency care and essential treatment of illness (Art. 15), to the education system in the case of minors (Art. 10), to vocational training (Art. 12) and to material reception conditions (Art. 13).

b   Furthermore, free movement within a defined area that allows 'sufficient scope for guaranteeing access to all benefits under this Directive' must be guaranteed (Art. 7).

c   The member state defines the duration of no access to the labour market. This period of time may not be longer than one year in cases where the first-instance decision has not been taken and 'this delay cannot be attributed to the applicant' (Art. 11).

d   Moreover, the directive regulates the power of the member states to reduce or withdraw reception conditions. This is possible if the asylum seeker leaves the accommodation assigned to him, refuses reporting and does not appear for personal interviews (Art. 16).

e   Finally, the directive sets minimum standards for minors (Art. 18), unaccompanied minors (Art. 19) and victims of torture and violence (Art. 20).

2   The Qualification Directive (Council of the EU 2004):

a   Chapter III regulates the prerequisites that need to be fulfilled to qualify as a refugee. The refugee status is granted in the case of certain kinds of persecution (physical/mental violence, etc.) that needs to 'be sufficiently serious [...] as to constitute a severe violation of basic human rights' (Art. 9).

b   Furthermore, the directive defines the conditions for the cessation of refugee status (Art. 11), for exclusion (Art. 12) and for refusal to renew refugee status (Art. 14).

3   The Asylum Procedures Directive (Council of the EU 2005):

a   Guaranteed access to asylum procedures for all adults who have legal capacity and that apply in person at a designated place (Art. 6), to asylum decisions in a written form (Art. 9), to information in an appropriate language and a translation service (Art. 10), to a personal interview (Art. 12) and to legal assistance at their own costs (Art. 15). Furthermore, Article 17 provides specific guarantees for unaccompanied minors (as does the Council Directive on minimum standards for reception).

b   The asylum seekers must not be detained only for the reason of seeking asylum (Art. 18).

c   The UNHCR has the right to contact with the applicants, to information concerning the applications and to publish its opinion (Art. 21).

d   Chapter III regulates the examination procedures, while the procedures to appeal are defined in Chapter V.

e   Chapter IV regulates the procedures for withdrawing refugee status.

The role of the Commission

Within the institutional framework of the EU the Commission is a driving force in many fields of the integration process. It alone has the initiative to make proposals. The power of initiative, which is held by the Commission, is particularly important for the development of common policies. All common policies, all Community legislation, all Community programmes have been adopted by the legislative bodies with Commission initiatives in the form of explanatory communications and proposals of legal Acts (Moussis 2007: 41).

Apart from this monopoly of the right of initiative, the Commission gives a lot of incentives for the further process of the European integration. It presents ideas, programmes and perspectives as far as the migration and asylum policy is concerned the respective Communications are important. A good example is the 'Communication: the Global Approach to Migration one year on: towards a Comprehensive European Migration Policy' (Com (2006) 735 final; see also Neisser 2007: 144). This communication contains a lot of incentives for the future relations of the EU and the African states.

The Schengen process

In 1985 the so called Schengen Group signed a treaty scrapping all frontier controls within the EU. This group comprised initially France, Germany and the Benelux states. In 1990 a second treaty was signed. It was called 'implementation agreement'. This agreement did allow other member states into the Schengen Group but only on the condition that their governments accepted the total package without further negotiations. This agreement concerned concrete measures. As well a reinforcement of the external border controls and closer and effective co-operation between judicial systems, police forces and administrative services of the member states and for common policies on visas, immigration and the right of asylum. The so called Schengen Information System (SIS) established a common central, computerised system. The main goals of this system are:

1   The removal of checks at a common border, replacing them with the external border controls.
2   Co-ordination between administrations on the surveillance of borders.
3   Defining the role of carriers in the fight against illegal immigration.
4   The drawing up of rules on asylum seekers.
5   A common definition of the rules for crossing external borders.

The Schengen *acquis* has been brought by a protocol attached to the Treaty of Amsterdam. The Schengen area is now within the legal and institutional framework of the EU. It entails parliamentary and judicial control.

Migration policy and the Treaty of Lisbon

The European Council held on 16–17 June 2007 adopted a mandate to elaborate a new treaty which should replace the Constitutional treaty which failed in the ratification process by two negative referenda in France and Netherlands. The negotiations of this treaty (the so-called reform treaty, later the Treaty of Lisbon) started on 23 July 2007 in an intergovernmental conference. As far the migration and asylum policy is concerned the text of the treaty formulates a new framework. The main goals of policies on border checks, asylum and immigration are:

1   Ensuring the absence of any controls on persons, whatever their nationality, when crossing internal borders.
2   Carrying out checks on persons and efficient monitoring of the crossing of external borders.
3   The gradual introduction of an integrated management system for external borders (Council of the EU 2007: 77,1).

For these purposes the European Parliament and the Council adopted in an ordinary legislative procedure measures concerning:

1   The common policy on visas and other short-stay residence permits.
2   The checks to which persons crossing external borders are subject.
3   The conditions under which nationals of third countries shall have the freedom to travel within the Union for a short period.
4   Any measure necessary for the gradual establishment of an integrated management system for external borders.
5   The absence of any controls on persons, whatever their nationality, when crossing internal borders.

Developing a common policy on asylum, subsidiary protection and temporary protection with a view to offering appropriate status to any third country national requiring international protection and ensuring compliance with the principle of non refoulement, the measures for a European asylum system comprise:

1   A uniform status of asylum for nationals of third countries, valid throughout the Union.
2   A uniform status of subsidiary protection for nationals of third countries who, without obtaining European asylum, are in need of international protection.
3   A common system of temporary protection for displaced persons in the event of a massive inflow.
4   Common procedures for the granting and withdrawing of uniform asylum or subsidiary protection status.

5   Criteria and mechanisms for determining which member state is responsible for considering an application for asylum or subsidiary protection.
6   Standards concerning the conditions for the reception of applicants for asylum or subsidiary protection.
7   Partnership and co-operation with third countries for the purpose of managing inflows of people applying for asylum or subsidiary or temporary protection (Council of the EU 2007: 78.2).

The aim of a common immigration policy is to ensure the efficient management of migration flows, a fair treatment of third-country nationals residing legally in member states and the prevention of illegal immigration and trafficking in human beings. Aiming that measures in the following areas can be adopted:

1   The conditions of entry and residence, and standards on the issue by member states of long-term visas and residence permits, including those for the purpose of family reunion.
2   The definition of the rights of third-country nationals residing legally in a member state, including the conditions governing freedom of movement and of residence in other member states.
3   Illegal immigration and unauthorised residence, including the removal and repatriation of persons residing without authorisation.
4   Combating trafficking in persons, in particular women and children (Council of the EU 2007: 79,2).

In all these matters of policy the principle of solidarity and fair sharing of responsibility, including its financial implication, between the member states shall be applied (Council of the EU 2007: 80).

The financial resources for migration management within the European Union

The EU needs a better developed system for sharing the burden of refugees. Some of the member states have particular problems with immigrants from the African states. It concerns first of all Spain, Italy and Malta. Therefore it is necessary to establish a system of financial compensation where countries that receive a disproportionate number of immigrants should be first in line for money from a central EU fund (Moraes 2003: 130).

The Commission elaborated a framework programme on 'Solidarity and the Management of Migration Flows'. This programme gives financial support under the financial perspective 2007–13 for the following funds:

1   European Refugee Fund, €699 million.
2   External Borders Fund, €1.820 million.
3   European Return Fund, €676 million.

Moreover an Integration Fund is a financial instrument to provide support and incentives for the member states to develop integration policies for the integration of third-country nationals. These funds are an essential element of the implementation of a common migration policy. They have different objectives and different functions:

European Refugee Fund

Its objective is to promote a balance of efforts between member states in receiving and becoming the consequences of receiving refugees and displaced persons. This fund aims at expressing solidarity at Community level and to alleviate the pressures felt by member states most affected by the reception of refugees and displaced persons in facing the consequences of this reception, which includes reception conditions during the asylum procedure, the integration of recognised refugees and promoting voluntary return solutions for rejected asylum seekers and refugees who wish to return to their country of origin.

European Return Fund

This fund supports member states' efforts to improve the management of the return of illegal third-country nationals in all aspects. The Return Fund will need to work in complementarity with other financial instruments. It will seek to promote the development of an integrated set of return measures aiming at putting an effective programme in place in member states. This should cover all phases of the return process, from the pre-departure phase and the return as such to the reception and reintegration in the country of return, and should be tailored to take account of the specific situations in different countries. At the basis of such a programme should be an analysis of the situation in the member states with respect to the targeted population, a realistic assessment of the potential for return and the co-operation with the countries of return, a planning and evaluation mechanism with respect to the return process of the targeted population and co-operation throughout the process with relevant stakeholders at national, European and international level (for example, the UNHCR).

External Borders Fund

The most relevant policy option is the establishment of a financial solidarity mechanism at Community level to support member states which bear a lasting and heavy financial burden by being responsible for controlling external borders for the benefit of the Union as a whole. Given the uneven division of responsibility between member states for controlling the external borders of the EU, the policy objectives to achieve are particularly to improve the efficiency of controls, to make it easier and faster for authorised travellers to enter the EU in conformity with the Schengen *acquis*, to achieve uniform application of the EU law by member states and to enhance the efficiency of the issuing of visas and the implementation of other pre-frontier checks.

Support from the Fund should be extended to new member states, as their external borders are operational since their accession even if they have undertaken to remove border controls at a later state when they are judged ready to do so. One of the positive impacts of the External Borders Fund would be on administrative systems and infrastructures of member states, which will get more resources and be able to improve co-ordination and exchanges. The financial support under this fund will be developed in complementarity with the work of the European Agency for the Management of Operational Co-operation at External Borders.

The wave of African refugees

The steadily increasing migration pressure from Africa brings a major challenge to the EU. Three member states of the EU are particularly involved in that process: Italy, Spain, Malta.

Tackling this problem, the EU must provide a dialogue between the African countries and the Union and close co-operation between the EU and the African Union. A ministerial conference was held in July 2006 in Rabat as an joint initiative between Morocco, Spain and France. This conference brought together West, Central and North African states with EU member states to discuss common responses to migratory flows along the West Africa route. States committed themselves to developing a close partnership 'to work together, in the framework of a global, balanced, pragmatic and operational approach, with respect for the fundamental rights and dignity of migrants and refugees, on the phenomenon of migratory routes'. This framework should involve countries of origin, transit and destination, this partnership is focusing on the fight against poverty and the promotion of substantial development in African states. An Action Plan has to be elaborated. A second, follow-up ministerial conference in two years is planned.

An important event in 2006 was an EU–Africa Ministerial Conference on Migration and Development held in Tripoli on 22–23 November. The EU and the whole of Africa came together for the first time to make a political commitment to working together on migration. An Action Plan and Declaration on human trafficking, legal and illegal migration and economic development have been adopted. At the same time the EU strengthened its will to work in partnership with the African Union, African countries and regional organisations, such as the Economic Community of West African States (ECOWAS), the Southern African Development Community (SADC) and the Intergovernmental Authority for Development (IGAD).

Another perspective is a dialogue on the basis of Article 13 of the Cotonou Agreement, covering a broad range of issues from institution and capacity-building and effective integration of legal migrants to return and the effective implementation of readmission obligations, in order to establish mutually beneficial co-operation in this field. On the basis of Article 13 of the Cotonou Agreement a dialogue has been initiated with some Sub-Saharan African states. Migration is currently being incorporated into the programming exercise for the tenth European Development Fund.

On the basis of Article 13 of the Cotonou Agreement a bilaterial dialogue on migration was developed between the EU and Senegal, Mali, Cameroon, Ghana, Nigeria, Mauritania and Niger. This has so far proceeded with Mauritania, Senegal and Mali. Three other countries had to be removed from the list due to varying political circumstances; other countries are proposed for adding the list like Ethiopia, Sudan, Eritrea and Somalia (Com (2006) 735 end; see also Neisser 2007: 152).

Migration policy as a part of the external relations of the European Union

The previous chapter showed the increasing relevance of migration policy to the external relations of the EU. One essential element of the migration policy is the securitisation of migration; that means migration is a security issue. Not only bodily security, but also the native European moral values, collective identities and cultural homogeneity are feared to be threatened by the influx of migration from Africa or elsewhere to Europe (Gebrewold 2007: 174). The EU attempts to address the political, social, economic and cultural challenges threatening security. This is the content of the Council's paper of December 2003 'A Secure Europe in a Better World'. The above-mentioned Hague Programme entails one aspect of the securitisation of migration: the 'external dimension' contained in that programme intends to politically, economically, socially and culturally secure African and Asian countries, so that Europe in its turn is secure. Managing migration requires dialogue and close co-operation with third countries. The implementation of the external dimensions of migration and asylum in accordance with the Hague Programme requires partnership with third countries and regions of origin and transit. The European Council has called for such co-operation in the context of the comprehensive policy and, as a first stage, the focus of implementation on Africa. The Commission presented on 16 May 2007 a communication 'On circular migration and mobility partnership between the EU and third countries' responding to the request from the European Council to consider how legal migration opportunities can be incorporated into the Union's external policies with a particular emphasis on ways to facilitate and encourage circular and temporary migration. In practice mobility between the EU and third countries needs to be enhanced and also better adapted to the specific labour market needs of EU member states.

The comprehensive EU migration policy, as defined by the European Council, provides a coherent and efficient response to the challenges and opportunities related to migration. It builds on the conclusions of the Tampere European Council in 1999, the Hague Programme of 2004 and the Global Approach to Migration adopted by the European Councils in 2005 and 2006. This comprehensive approach involves all stages of migration, aims to harness the benefits of legal migration and covers policies to fight illegal migration and trafficking in human beings. It is based on the general principles of subsidiarity, proportionality, solidarity and respect for the different legal systems and traditions of the member states. It is also based on respect for human rights and the fundamental freedoms of migrants, the Geneva Convention and due access to asylum procedures. It requires a genuine partnership with third countries and must be fully integrated into the Union's external policies. In this manner the EU and its member states address the challenges and opportunities of migration for the benefit of all, an area that constitutes one of the major priorities for the EU at the start of the twenty-first century.

Conclusion

The migration policy of the EU is politically very sensitive. Establishing migration policy as a Community task is the right way. But the EU cooperation is confronted with different obstacles. National migration policies can no longer meet their migration challenges, common efforts are necessary. It is essential to speed up the process of the Europeanisation of migration policy.

The main principle for migration and asylum policy has to be the protection of human rights particularly the right of asylum. The Human rights charter of the EU recognises the right of asylum. Article 18 of this charter stipulates: 'The right to asylum shall be guaranteed with due respect for the rules of the Geneva Convention of 28 July 1951 and the Protocol of 31 January 1967 relating to the status of refugees and in accordance with the Treaty establishing the European Community.' Looking to the reality of migration and asylum policy, we can state that this area is a Community task but the political behaviour of member states governments is very determined by a commitment of sovereignty and remained rather intergovernmental.

Let me finish my contribution by addressing a fundamental perspective. The debate about the asylum question has many ethical implications. Gibney is dealing with these questions in his publication 'The Ethics and Politics of Asylum: Liberal Democracy and the Response to Refugees' and gives some examples:

1   Are states justified in privileging the claims of their own citizens over the claims of refugees, asylum seekers or other immigrants in need?

2   Do states have an obligation to allow any outsider entry at all and, if so, from what does this obligation derive?
3   What are the correct criteria by which to decide where anyone is entitled to reside in the contemporary world? (Birth? Need? Citizenship? Preference? Contribution to the maximization of total global utility?) (Gibney 2004: 18).

For the individual states it is difficult to find an adequate answer. States have different views and different answers. In a political community of states which is on one hand an association of sovereign states (intergovernmental co-operation) and on the other side a supranational community, member states must agree on common ethical principles.

Gibney is pleading for humanitarianism as a desirable principle in shaping migration and asylum policy (Gibney 2004: 233) and Walzer, a well known communitarian, argues that while states are generally free to construct entry policies according to their own criteria, in dealing with refugees they are bound by the requirements of humanitarianism which are based on the principles of mutual aid and benefits (Walzer 1983).

References

Council of the EU (20 July 2001) 'Council Directive 2001/55/EC', Brussels.
—— (27 January 2003) 'Council Directive 2003/9/EC', Brussels.
—— (18 February 2003) 'Council Regulation (EC) No. 343/2003', Brussels.
—— (29 April 2004) 'Council Directive 2004/83/EC', Brussels.
—— (1 December 2005) 'Council Directive 2005/85/EC', Brussels.
—— (17 December 2007), 'Treaty of Lisbon', 2007/C 306/01, Brussels.
European Commission (2005) 'Proposal for a decision of the European Parliament and the Council establishing the European Refugee Fund for the period 2008–2013 as part of the General Programme Solidarity and Management of Migration Flows', Commission Proposal COM/2005 0123 final-COD/0046, Brussels.
—— (2006) 'The global approach to migration one year on: towards a comprehensive European migration policy', Communication from the Commission to the Council and the European Parliament, Com (2006) 735 end. Online. Available http: http:// eur-lex.europa.eu/LexUriServ/LexUriServ.do?uri=COM:2006:0735:FIN:EN:PDF (accessed 20 November 2008).
Gebrewold, B. (2007) *Africa and Fortress Europe: Threats and Opportunities*, Aldershot: Ashgate.
Gibney, M. J. (2004) *The Ethics and Politics of Asylum: Liberal Democracy and the Response to Refugees*, Cambridge: Cambridge University Press.
Hix, S. (1999, 2nd edn 2005) *The Political System of the European Union*, New York: Palgrave Macmillan.
Moraes, C. (2003) 'The politics of European Union migration policy', in S. Spencer (ed.) *The Politics of Migration: Managing Opportunity, Conflict and Change*, Oxford: Blackwell.
Moussis, N. (2007) *Guide to European Policies*, Rixensart: European Study Service.

Neisser, H. (2007) 'European Migration Policy', in B. Gebrewold (ed.) *African and Fortress Europe: Threats and Opportunities*, Aldershot: Ashgate.

Peterson, W. (1968) 'Migration', *International Encyclopaedia of the Social Sciences* 13 (1968): 286.

Van Krieken, P. J. (2004) *The Consolidated Asylum and Migration Acquis: the EU Directives in an Expanded Europe*, The Hague: TMC Assei Press.

Walzer, M. (1983) *Spheres of Justice: a Defence of Pluralism and Equality*, Oxford: Martin Robertson.

7 EU–African economic relations

Continuing dominance, traded for aid?

Dirk Kohnert

EU–African economic relations: burning problems and pertinent questions

Soaring oil and other raw commodity prices as well as growing competition of global players to secure access to vital African resources brought promising prospects for growth and prosperity in Sub-Saharan Africa (Berg and Drummond 2008; OECD 2007; UN 2007; IMF 2007b). On average, Africa grew at about 6.5 per cent in 2007, well above the long-term trend for the fifth consecutive year, the longest growth phase for thirty-five years. All in all, Africa is better placed to withstand a deterioration of the global economic environment than in the 1990s and 1980s. However, growth rates show marked differences between oil- exporting countries and oil importers of 7.4 per cent and 4.7 per cent respectively. Nevertheless, even small land-locked countries profited from the newly gained independence in international relations, and increased bargaining power, provided by the quest of Asian super-powers for African resources and emerging markets.

But the International Monetary Fund (IMF) and World Bank and experts alike cautioned that the volatility of commodity prices could continue to make Africa vulnerable to external shocks. Besides, they warned that progress towards the fulfilment of the Millennium Development Goals of halving poverty by 2015 was by far too slow for Africa's poor, which constitute half the extremely poor worldwide.[1] Beyond increased aid and economic growth, to be promoted by neo-liberal formal trade and investment policy reforms, notably the opening up of markets, they held conditionality of aid and 'good governance' to be decisive (Collier 2006: 204–10). Other researchers showed that in some African countries, notably in those with high income inequality, like the former 'settler economies' of Namibia, South Africa and Zimbabwe, even small changes in income distribution (if enforceable politically without civic conflict) could have a significant larger poverty reducing impact than growth (Bigsten and Shimeles 2007: 153–6).

However, many EU politicians and their scholarly advisers applied double standards, which have poisoned EU–African relations.[2] Whereas they maintained the age-old credo of neo-liberalism at home, which cemented the existing unequal social structures in their own countries, they promoted poverty eradication linked with aid conditionality and good governance in Africa. Secondly, the identification and moral evaluation of alleged impediments to African growth, like the supposed conflict, corruption, ethnic fractionalisation, or poor governance traps (Easterly and Levine 1997; Collier 2006: 190–5) disregarded own historic responsibilities of European governments. EU member states contributed significantly to Africa's economic misery, due to the damaging effects of its self-interested external trade policy which persisted since the advent of colonialism, despite its talk about development assistance. Even after independence of their former colonies, European states fostered over decades corrupt and autocratic regimes in Africa with disregard to principles of 'good governance', as in Nigeria, Congo, or Togo. Large amounts of aid to countries with bad policy sustained those poor policies (Bierschenk *et al.* 1993; Devarajan *et al.* 2001). The aftermath of these regimes is still to be felt today (Kohnert 2008). It constitutes one of the underlying factors of Africa's continuing misery and of increasing African migration to Europe. The prevailing perspective of the EU and of its member countries concerning African immigration remains to be focused on security, the foreclosure of its external borders and prevention (Kohnert 2007). Yet well adapted immigration regulations would serve the interest of all parties involved. Last but not least, it could contribute to protect the over-aged population of European member states in the long run against threatening economic decline. However, two fundamental problems remain unsolved. Costs and benefits of immigration are distributed asymmetrically between EU member countries and between social classes within the EU.

On the other hand, Western donor countries and international aid agencies complain about the negative impact of China's and India's mounting economic and political influence on Sub-Saharan Africa. It allegedly counteracted the Western donors' development-oriented foreign and development policy by neo-mercantilist trade strategies, thereby displacing African local production and fostering other 'Dutch disease' implications (Zafar 2007: 4–5, 12–15; Umbach 2007: 1; Broadman 2007). But Chinese aid and foreign trade policy only honoured established international norms of noninterference in internal politics. And with respect to development cooperation, Peking and Delhi rather promoted Smithian ethics, cherished over centuries by European governments, i.e. the growth of the wealth of particular nations, be it in Europe, Asia or Africa, notwithstanding the accumulation of wealth by governing elites to the detriment of the poor.

Therefore African politicians, international non-governmental organisations (NGOs) and critical scholars alike accuse the EU and European governments of double-talk, undermined generosity with respect to aid and external trade policies, and broken promises concerning the Millennium Goals and G-8 commitments *vis-à-vis* Africa (Kebonang 2007; Hurt 2003: 169–70, 174; Melber 2006; Oxfam 2006). They question fashionable calls for 'saving Africa' which allegedly and persistently reflect underlying

Eurocentric attitudes of cultural superiority as well as hidden vested inter-ests. As the Senegalese head of state Abdoulaye Wade put it, Africa is not ill (though many Africans are, because of AIDS, poverty, bad governance, and unfair international trade regimes). It does not need to be healed nor saved. What Africans want is true equitable partnership (Iweala 2007; Kohnert 2008; Oxfam 2006).

Even if Africa's economies advance, the question is, in how far the major-ity of the population will profit from this development, and whether the rest of the world will not advance even more rapidly. Would this perpetuate the exclusion of Africa from the benefits of globalisation? This the more, in view of the EU's continued wanting commitment to assist Africa in its quest for sustainable development? Could African economies, confronted with vested interests of global players, and marred by deep-seated structural economic deficiencies, reasonably expect a take off to self-sustained growth without a 'big push' by the international donor community? Would temporary trade preferences, granted by the EU, combined with the elimination of tariff and non-tariff barriers to African trade on the side of the EU, do a better job than the Economic Partnership Agreements (EPAs), currently negotiated between the EU and regional clusters of the African, Caribbean and Pacific (ACP) group[3] under asymmetrical power relations? How could alternative possible scenarios affect future EU–African economic relationship? These are questions I should like to answer in the following sections.

The new EU Africa Strategy

The new Africa Strategy of the EU, adopted in December 2005, had as primary objective the achievement of the UN Millennium Development Goals (MDGs), among others, by doubling aid to Africa by 2015 (EU 2007: 4; Grimm 2007: 82). It reflected the spirit of the Cairo plan of action, endorsed at the first Summit between Africa and the European Union, held in Cairo in April 2000 and the second summit in Lisbon in December 2007. The new Africa Strategy creates a common vision for the previously sepa-rated three regional treaties: the ACP–EC Partnership Agreement (Cotonou Agreement of 1998), the Mediterranean co-operation programme (MEDA) and the trade, development and co-operation agreement with South Africa. Besides economic growth and regional integration, it emphasised peace, security and good governance as prerequisites for sustainable development in Africa. The strategy departed from the base of assumed comparative advan-tages of the EU concerning its international relations to Africa, relative to other international competitors, and offers itself as Africa's 'natural partner' (Council of the European Union 2006: 11). It was the first time that the EU approved such a comprehensive Africa strategy as guideline, not only for its own programmes but also for bilateral Africa policies of its (now) twenty-seven member states. It wanted to replace the former onesided policy, which accepted African governments at the most as junior partners, by a strategic partnership of equals, with the African Union (AU), its institutions (like the New Partnership for Africa's Development, NEPAD) and sub-regions, on equal footing. In addition, the EU Commission aimed at greater coherence in the policies of the different actors and EU member states involved, notably concerning divergent objectives of development, security and foreign trade policies (EU 2007: 3–6; Grimm 2007: 82; Council of the European Union 2006: 21–32).

The strategy was certainly driven by good intentions. However, the House of Lords EU Select Committee, London, identified already in its fore-word to the first review of the strategy in 2006 broken promises, lack of commitment, basic tensions and shortcomings of implementation within the EU commission, between member states, uncertainty about funding, insufficient specification of policies for different regions of Africa, etc. (cf. Council of the European Union 2006: 6).

The same applies to the 'Everything but Arms' (EBA) initiative, launched by the EU in 2001, which was hailed as most symbolic European trade initiative towards Africa since the first Lomé Convention in 1975. Although it granted formally liberalised access by Africa's least developed countries to European markets, it was so badly flawed already in its conception that it became practically useless (for details see Collier 2007; Faber and Orbie 2007; Wusheng and Jensen 2005). Notably its rules of origin were too restrictive to be able to trigger self-sustained growth in Africa. Furthermore, the small gains which might result from EBA were expected to fade away in consequence of the EU negotiations on EPAs (cf. below) and the compliance with World Trade Organisation (WTO) obligations, resulting in an actually worse-off situation for Africa.

Next to the AU and its sub-organisations there exist different institutional and regional partners of the EU in Africa. The most important is the New Partnership for Africa's Development (NEPAD), adopted in July 2001, including its key element, the African Peer Review Mechanism (APRM). Both were created to guarantee the member countries the ownership of their development programmes. The new institutions displayed the commitment to self-government and agency on the part of African states. The AU as well as the EU considered it to be an important step in the right direction. Yet NEPAD continued to reflect connotations of conditionality (e.g. the 'carrot and stick' policy of the EU), because of the strong influence of the international donor community already on its conception. In addition, the self-assessment structures of the APRM were quite biased in certain countries like Rwanda, and in general still lacked stringency and independence (Manga Fombad and Kebonang 2006: 51; Kanbur 2004: 157; Abrahamsen 2004).

Parallel with the institutional partners, the EU co-operates with five Regional Economic Communities (RECs) in Sub-Saharan Africa[4] and with the Arab Maghreb Union. African regional co-operation and integration are hampered by considerable inter-regional discrepancies in capacity, resources and degree of political organisation. The degree of regional integration is rather low. Just 11 per cent of international African trade is within its own sub-regions. Existing regional trade arrangements in Sub-Saharan Africa suffer from high external trade barriers, small market size, poor transport facilities and low resource complementarity between member states (Yang and Gupta 2007: 399). The growing structural divergences have been intensified by the recent development of world oil markets. Because of these strong and growing structural discrepancies amongst RECs, the EU insists on separate negotiations with each sub-region on the future EPAs. However, their African partners would prefer joint consultations and suspect the EU of a 'divide and rule' policy.

The Cotonou Agreement of 2000, based on successive ACP–EC Agreements (Lomé conventions I to IV), remains formally valid until 2020. However, its institutions and principles, i.e. joint political dialogue on trade, peace building, conflict prevention and resolution, etc., increasingly collided with different orientations provided by the more dynamic new Africa initiatives mentioned above (Grimm 2007: 82–5). In fact, the Cotonou Agreement risks to be made successively redundant, notably by the current negotiations on the new EPAs (Hurt 2003: 173–4).

EU proposals for EPAs: new barriers to poverty reduction?

More than thirty years after the signing of the first Lomé Convention (1975), the ACP still exports basically raw materials to Europe and provides a ready market for European finished goods. Old procedures have not promoted diversification, competitiveness, growth or poverty reduction in any sustainable manner. Although regional integration belonged since decades to the declared aims of both the EU and the ACP's own development strategies, it was applied with little success, notably concerning the eight existing regional communities in Africa.[5] Inter-African trade and investment remained low, mostly because of lack of political consensus and the will to divest national prerogatives and other non-tariff barriers (ECA 2006: 67). New solutions were urgently required. This all the more, as WTO rules on non-discrimination demanded the transformation of unilateral tariff preferences, hitherto granted to the ACP states, into regional trade agreements.

The new trade regime, negotiated between the EU and African states within the framework of EPAs, is running out of time. Brussels repeatedly threatened to increase trade barriers against African imports, in accordance with WTO rules, if the non-reciprocal trade preferences of the Cotonou Agreement are running out. In view of asymmetrical power relations the least developed countries (LDCs), which were already disillusioned with respect to the high expectations associated with the EBAs (cf. above), faced the risk that the available options for EPAs (Bilal and Rampa 2007; Stevens 2007: 3–4; Storey 2006: 338–44) create new barriers to regional integration and poverty reduction, the declared overall aims of both partners. African countries may even be encouraged to reinforce regional trade barriers in response to unfavourable trade regimes enforced by the EU, last but not least because of potentially severe loss of customs revenue, the major government revenue in many African LDCs (Stevens 2006a: 2).

The EU's strategy, to create clusters of separate free-trade areas linking Europe with four regional groupings of African states, threatens to damage regional solidarity among the concerned African countries. This the more so, if aid, for example the negotiations on the programming of the tenth European Development Fund (EDF), which run parallel to EPA negotiations, were used as a 'stick and carrot' tactic to convince African partners to accept unfair trade regimes (Goodison 2007: 147–8; Oxfam 2006).[6]

But why should the new regional agreements work any better than the existing arrangements? There are increasing anxieties among the African partners about the outcome of the current negotiations. During the EU–Africa Summit in Lisbon in December 2007 African statesmen like the Senegalese President Abdoulaye Wade and South African's Thabo Mbeki made it clear that the EU proposals for EPAs were dead, and had to be renegotiated by extending the deadline by a year, up to the end of 2008. In addition, the AU commission president Alpha Oumar Konaré insisted on Africa's right to protect its infant industries. He accused the EU of playing the old divide-and-rule game in Africa, luring more advanced states like Kenya, Côte d'Ivoire and Ghana, which did not profit from the EBA initiative, but would have suffered from especially high EU tariffs on African exports by 2008, in signing stop-gap Interim Economic Partnership Agreements (IEPAs).[7] Thereby the eighteen African states involved temporarily allayed the fear that their export industries would be shut out of EU markets. However, it remained to be seen whether all EU member states harboured a real commitment to trade liberalisation if tangible interests of powerful agricultural lobbies within the EU would be endangered by cheap African imports. In the past, non-tariff barriers, notably biased rules of origin and quality standards, constituted effective barriers to shield the interests of European producers from undue competition.

Thus most burning questions remained unsolved on the negotiating table for the next round of EPA negotiations, scheduled for 2008. The EU has a keen interest in revising the IEPAs in order to become full EPAs, including commitments for liberalisation of services, investment, government procurement, competition and other trade-related issues. This interest is comprehensible in view of the great part of European gross domestic product (GDP) and employment-related to services (some 70 per cent). But already now the IEPAs dealt a potentially fatal blow to the long-standing, though largely unsuccessful, African efforts for more effective economic integration, the panacea for the solution of Africa's economic misery, propagated also by EU development co-operation (Stevens 2006b: 445–7; Lee 2004). The reason for this was that with the IEPAs all African regional economic groupings now included members which developed contradicting interests and trade perspectives, apart from the East African Community, which signed the IEPAs *en bloc*. Hence the non-LDCs within the groupings were obliged to open their domestic markets to EU exports, whereas the LDCs were not. In addition, there existed legitimate concerns on the African side about declining revenues from taxing imports, a major source of government revenue in many countries, as a consequence of the restrictions imposed by the IEPAs.

Last but not least, the IEPAs allowed the EU to apply special trade dispensation or other safeguards more easily than under the old Cotonou Agreement, whereas there was no protection to guarantee food security for African populations, though this was a sensible question in view of the implications of soaring global food prices for the African poor, which could lead to a new humanitarian crisis in Africa, notably in view of the global financial crisis and the impact of the threatening worldwide recession on African markets.[8] In fact, the liberalisation of trade as propagated by the EPAs will set back poverty reduction programmes and strategies in the ACP and thereby further undermine the Cotonou Agreement, last but not least with regard to the promotion of social sector funding (Laryea *et al.* 2004; Hurt 2003: 161, 169). The apparent lack of credibility concerning the broken promises of increased EU development aid for African LDCs could aggravate the fate of Africa's poor and the menacing humanitarian crisis even further.[9]

All in all, the neo-liberal recipes of the Breton Woods institutions concerning trade liberalisation have done more harm than good as far as Sub-Saharan Africa is concerned, mainly because of the following reasons. First, the opening up of markets had negative effects on economic growth in the long run, mainly because it was not accompanied by an improvement in institutions (Borrmann and Busse 2006: 232–3). Second, the continuing reliance on the supposed comparative advantages of the export of agricultural products and other raw materials (apart from oil and diamonds) did not result in net gains as promised by Ricardian theory, which still forms the basis of modern trade theory (reformulated as the Heckscher–Ohlin model), in view of volatile commodity prices, poor infrastructure and political instability which increases transaction costs. Furthermore, high revenues from commodity exports threatened to increase rent-seeking, corruption or sub-optimal allocation of resources ('resource curse', 'Dutch disease') in African countries with serious governance deficits.[10] Therefore, experts and African politicians alike elaborated alternative proposals to EPAs (Bilal and Rampa 2007: Policy Management Report 11, for a summary), however, they have little chance of being implemented due to lack of political backing by the EU and other Western global players.

Africa's new silver bullet: the impact of growing competition from China on EU–Africa economics

For some years now China's presence in Africa hits the headlines. So far, macroeconomic studies of big projects, investments and the general phenomenon of Chinese infiltration into Africa are in the focus of political and economic reports. Depending on one's own point of view, the Chinese are regarded either as development-promoting entrepreneurs, a view which is widespread among the African power elite, or as new colonists, a perspective which prevails among workers employed by Chinese enterprises, e.g. in Zambia, Angola or Senegal, or, at least in a more or less veiled form, by Western competitors and donors. Over the past six years, China has become one of Africa's important partners for trade and economic co-operation. Trade (exports and imports) between Africa and China increased from US$11 billion in 2000 to US$56 billion in 2006 (UNCTAD 2007). Africa's foreign trade with Asia, notably that with China, has surpassed all other regions over the past decade. African exports to Asia increased by 20 per cent during the five years 2000–05. As a share of Africa's total exports, that to Asia rose from 9 per cent in 1990 to 27 per cent in 2005. At the same time exports to traditional markets of the former European colonial powers decreased from about 48 per cent to 32 per cent (and to the US 29 per cent) (Broadman 2007: 66). Africa imported 33 per cent of its total imports from Asia in 2005, second only to the EU. From the perspective of Asian countries, Africa is the second-fastest growing destination of their products after East and Central Europe (ibid.). In the first ten month of 2007 China's exports to Africa rose again by 36 per cent, while imports from Africa surged by 81 per cent.

'Trade, not aid', the universal remedy of neo-liberalism in propagating development, maintaining that the integration of LDCs into the world market would be more effective than any development aid, an ideology which first gained popularity in the West in the mid-1950s, could have been the slogan of growing Chinese presence in Africa too. But even within the realm of development co-operation China outperformed the West, at least in the view of African elder statesmen: in 2007 the Chinese Eximbank pledged US$20 billion in development funds for African infrastructure and trade financing over the next three years, funds that outstripped all Western donor pledges combined, according to the Senegalese head of state Abdoulaye Wade (Wade 2008: 20).[11]

The same holds for China's soaring foreign direct investment (FDI). Singapore, India and Malaysia currently are the top Asian originators of FDI in Africa, with investment stocks of US$3.5 billion (cumulative approved flows from 1996 to 2004), US$2 billion and US$1.9 billion through 2004, respectively, followed by China, the Republic of Korea and the Taiwan Province of China. China's FDI stock in Africa had reached US$1.6 billion by 2005. Chinese companies were present in forty-eight African countries. Until quite recently, only a few African countries had attracted the bulk of China's FDI in Africa: Sudan was the largest recipient (and the ninth largest recipient of Chinese FDI worldwide), followed by Algeria (eighteenth) and Zambia (nineteenth) (UNCTAD 2007). But other resource-rich countries like Nigeria followed suit more recently. In March 2008, for example, Nigeria was offered up to US$50 billion by Sinosure, China's export credit guarantee agency, to assist funding of projects in Nigeria over the next three years. This was the largest overseas commitment by China so far, and designated to encourage a wide range of Chinese private investment in Nigeria, notably concerning improvement of Nigeria's poor infrastructure, e.g. in the railway and the power sector. The facilities were meant as exchange in return for licences in oil exploration blocs.[12] All over Africa, China executes some 800 projects with a total cost of $5.74 billion. By November 2006 China had signed sixteen co-operation agreements worth a total of $1.9 billion, involving twelve Chinese firms and eleven African governments and companies, all in line with President Hu's pledge to provide $5 billion in loans and to double aid by 2009.

Western donors of developing aid to Africa, notably the EU and some of its member states, were quick to complain about the negative impact of China's and India's mounting economic and political influence on Sub-Saharan Africa. China was accused of displacing African local production, notably in the clothing and textile sector (Kaplinsky and Morris 2007: 269–70), and fostering other 'Dutch disease' implications. In addition, it allegedly counteracted the Western donors' development-oriented foreign and development policy by neo-mercantilist trade strategies. While benefiting from the debt relief efforts of Western donors, the latter were concerned about new debt traps of African countries by imprudent Chinese lending, thereby counteracting the Heavily Indebted Poor Countries (HIPC) initiative. Among others, these worries were reflected in the G-8 *Action Plan for Good Financial Governance in Africa*. Results of a scholarly evaluation revealed these claims, notably the 'free rider' thesis, as largely unfounded. The overall situation is much better than 'China bashers' have us believe (Reisen and Ndoye 2008: 9), nevertheless considerable risks concerning debt sustainability in Africa remain, notably in view of the current global financial crisis. Notwithstanding, some EU member states were quick to act in retaliation of the assumed threat. Thus Paris commissioned a report by the Council on Foreign Affairs on the organised or voluntary Chinese penetration of Africa, published in February 2008, which stated that about 70 per cent of Chinese aid to Africa (US$10 billion) was tied, which allegedly contributed to a trade diversion to the detriment of French African exports.[13] Although the authors of the report cautioned against the revival of the infamous French policy of tied aid, they predicted an augmentation of the relative weight of bilateral aid, the only real means of influence on aid and trade relations. The growing competition of Asian global players with the EU for Africa's resources will probably contribute to a revival of economic nationalism also in other EU member states. High-ranking officials of the European Commission already complained about double talk – not just of France, but also of other EU member states (Spain, Italy, Portugal or Poland) – concerning the trade with Africa and the protection of their own interests (Ricard 2007). Under these conditions it is presumably only a question of time that other major EU states will follow suite and accept implicitly a roll-back strategy, comparable with the *Realpolitik* of the Cold War era. This the more, because the mounting competition of European economies with Asian global players allowed Africa countries to apply a seesaw policy between the two competing blocks in order to optimise their economic and political return. Recent political statements of senior African statesmen, like the Senegalese president Abdoulaye Wade (Wade 2008), criticising the double-talk of Western donors vis-à-vis China, are unequivocal in this respect.

However, the official presence triggers also another attendant phenomenon, which hitherto has attracted little attention, either in politics or in academic research, although it is of equal importance to the economic development of African countries: the immigration of hundreds of thousands of Chinese migrants. Who are they, how and why do they migrate? Where do they settle, how do they organise their economic and social activities? These and other questions have only recently found entry into the international research agenda. But it is already visible that the Chinese presence and the soaring imports of Chinese products do exert also adverse spread effects on the nascent industries in least developed African countries, although the growing pressure of Chinese competition is certainly to be felt differently in different sectors of African economies. Some countries consider it rather as complementary to the growth of commerce and industry in their own country, but African entrepreneurs and workers increasingly feel threatened by unfair competition or exploitation 'made in China'. There is a growing cleavage between the official discourse and window-dressing of representatives of China and Africa, on the one hand, and the local perception of concerned African petty traders, peasants or workers on the other. The ambiguous consequences of Chinese economic and political influence on Africa remain disturbing, in particular with respect to African trade, protection of infant industries, social rights and workers' protection, and last but not least concerning the neglect of environmental questions. The implications for EU–Africa relations are open to question. At least European humanitarian aid and pro-poor growth initiatives of the EU might be seen more positively by Africa's poor than by some African statesmen of doubtful democratic credentials who resent any interference in the internal affairsof their country.

Conclusion

Promising growth rates, increased trade, aid and competition of the major global players for African resources all boost development and the bargaining power of Sub-Saharan Africa towards the EU. Progress towards the Millennium Development Goals has been made, but far too slowly. Due to the legacy of Africa's colonial past African LDCs remain vulnerable to external shocks. In addition, unfair EU foreign trade policies still contribute to poverty and unsatisfactory development. Political and economic dominance of African states by the EU and its former colonial powers perpetuates asymmetrical power relations in the new EPAs. Most African governments welcome the growing Chinese influence as counterbalance to the imposition of Western imposition of aid and unfair trade policies of major Western global players. Others regard the take-off of foreign trade relations with China with growing suspicion. Besides, there is a growing cleavage between the official discourse of the representatives of China and Africa and the perception among the local populations which may contribute to a re-evaluation of European humanitarian aid and pro-poor growth initiatives by African states.

Notes

This chapter is a revised version of Kohnert (2008). Thanks for valuable suggestions go to Rolf Hofmeier, Wolfgang Hein, Martin Beck and Valeria Bello.

1 The problem is not one of absolute poverty, as assumed in models of conventional economics, or expressed in (doubtful) figures of poverty indicators of per capita income of less than US$1 per day, as commonly assumed. Poverty is basically a social concept, related to history. What count are relations of inequality, i.e. the gap between the impoverished bottom billion of Africans and the rest of the world, which is accelerating: since the 1980s at a rate of approximately 5 per cent per year (Collier 2007).

2 Concerning double-talk and lack of commitment vis-à-vis Africa, the EU was by no way unique. The same applied to other global players like the US government and Bretton Woods institutions. The independent evaluation office of the IMF published a scathing critique of the IMF's aid policy in Africa (IMF 2007a).

3 The forty-eight African members form by far the largest and most powerful group within the ACP, which comprises at present seventy-eight states, mostly former European colonies.

4 Economic Community of West African States (ECOWAS), including the West African Economic and Monetary Union (WAEMU, in French UEMOA) of francophone West Africa, the Southern African Development Community (SADC), the Economic and Monetary Community of Francophone Central Africa (EMCCA/CEMAC), the East African Community (EAC) and the Common Market for Eastern and Southern Africa (COMESA).

5 The African Union recognises eight regional economic communities in Africa: Arab Maghreb Union (UMA), Community of Sahel-Saharan States (CEN-SAD), Common Market for Eastern and Southern Africa (COMESA), East African Community (EAC), Economic Community of West African States (ECOWAS), Economic Community of Central African States (ECCAS), Intergovernmental Authority on Development (IGAD) and Southern African Development Community (SADC) (ECA 2006).

6 Apparently, the EU used the EPAs–aid linkage as 'stick and carrot' tactic to convince African partners of unfair trade regimes The tenth EDF entails €22 billion in grants, and €2 billion in loan financing. According to Paul Goodison (2007: 147–8), the newly programmed tenth EDF could well become the single largest 'institutional bribe' in the history of development aid. In August 2007 negotiations got stuck because of the proposed linkage between EDF and a timely agree-

ment on EPAs, as proposed by EU Trade Commissioner Mandelson, i.e. the reduction of EDF by 50 per cent, in the event that the EPAs were not concluded in time, or of 25 per cent if they did not correspond to the conditions imposed by the EU. This was considered as insolence and strongly rejected, notably by the Pacific group ACP.

7 Until 20 December 2007 eighteen African countries signed Interim Economic Partnership Agreements (IEPAs). Beside the East African Community, which signed *en bloc*, all other African regional groupings were fractured by the IEPAs. The signatories enjoyed the same preferential access to EU markets as the twenty-six African LDCs which profited already from the EPA preference scheme without reciprocal obligations of the EU. However, it was open to doubt whether all the participants of the IEAPs had the capacity and a genuine commitment to implement the agreement. IEPAs focused on goods-only agreements, i.e. they only addressed access to EU markets, development co-operation and revised rules of origin but included the obligation to negotiate the remaining points of the EU's EPA proposals, i.e. the liberalisation of services and other trade-related issues, like investment, government procurement, competition, etc., in 2008.

8 The Food and Agriculture Organisation (FAO) reported in April 2008 that thirty-six countries were currently facing a food crisis, twenty-one of them in Africa.

9 On 9 April 2008 EU President Barroso condemned EU member states which had promised in 2005 to increase aid to 0.56 per cent by 2010, and to 0.7 per cent by 2015, respectively, whereas an OECD report revealed in early April that the ODA of major EU countries decreased considerably in 2007.

10 On the link between governance and trade policy cf. in addition Goodison (2007), Hugon (2007) and Oxfam (2006).

11 India followed China's path when it announced in April 2008 its intention to double the credit lines to projects in Africa, from US$2.15 billion to $5.4 billion between 2003–04 and 2008–09 (Johnson 2008).

12 In fact, China was in for a $4 billion deal for drilling licences in Nigeria, including grants for economic and technical co-operation in anti-malaria drug and rice production (cf. Green and McGregor 2008). However, the new Nigerian government of Yar'Adua soon realised that the deals with the Chinese agreed upon under the reign of its predecessor Obasanjo in 2006 were questionable, vague and 'over-inflated'. Therefore, on 4 November 2008, it suspended the US$8.3 billion contract with China Railway Construction Corporation to modernise the 1,315 km railway line between Lagos and Kaduna and ordered a review of the contract.

13 One example quoted explicitly in the report was Angola: 'En Angola, une line de crédit chinoise de 5 milliards $ devrait ôter toutes les chances de la France pour la construction de l'aéroport et de 3,000 km de voie ferrée' (cf. rapport du Conseil des affaires étrangères: 'Les intérêts économiques français face à l'irruption de nouveaux acteurs en Afrique', quoted in 'La Lettre du continent' 2008: 3).

References

Abrahamsen, R. (2004) 'The power of partnerships in global governance', *Third World Quarterly* 25 (8): 1453–67.

Berg, A. and Drummond, P. (2008) 'Regional Economic Outlook: sub-Saharan Africa', Africa Department, April 2008, Washington, DC: International Monetary Fund.

Bierschenk, T., Elwert, G. and Kohnert, D. (1993) 'The long-term effects of development aid: empirical studies in rural West Africa', *Economics* 47 (1): 83–111.

Bigsten, A. and Shimeles, A. (2007) 'Can Africa reduce poverty by half by 2015?' *Development Policy Review* 25 (2): 147–66.

Bilal, S. and Rampa, F. (2007) 'Alternative (to) EPAs: possible scenarios for the future of ACP trade relations with the EU', Policy Management Report 11, Maastricht: European Centre for Development Policy Management.

Borrmann, A. and Busse, M. (2006) 'Institutional prerequisites of Economic Partnership Agreements', *Intereconomics* 41 (4): 231–6.

Broadman, H. G. (2007) *Africa's Silk Road: China and India's New Economic Frontier*, Washington, DC: World Bank.

Brown, W. (2000) 'Restructuring north–south relations: ACP–EU development co-operation in a liberal international order', *Review of African Political Economy* 27 (85): 367–83.

Collier, P. (2006) 'African growth: why a big push?' *Journal of African Economies* 15 (2): 188–211.

—— (2007) *The Bottom Billion: Why the Poorest Countries are failing, and What can be Done about it*, Oxford: Oxford University Press.

Council of the European Union (2006) 'The EU and Africa: Towards a Strategic Partnership', vol. 1, Report, Thiirty-fourth Report of Session 2005–06, London: EUC Council of the European Union.

Devarajan, S., Dollar, D. and Holmgren, T. (eds) (2001) *Aid and Reform in Africa: Lessons from ten Case Studies*, Washington DC: World Bank.

Dickle, M. (2008) 'Nigerians halt $8 bn rail deal with Beijing', *Financial Times*, November.

Easterly, W. and Levine, R. (1997) 'Africa's growth tragedy: policies and ethnic divisions', *Quarterly Journal of Economics* 112 (4): 1203–50.

ECA (2006) 'Assessing regional integration in Africa' II 'Rationalising regional economic communities', Economic Commission for Africa, UNECA, Addis Ababa: United Nations Publications.

European Commission (2007) 'From Cairo to Lisbon: the EU–Africa Strategic Partnership', Com (2007) 357 final, 27 July 2007, Brussels: Commission of the European Communities.

Faber, G. and Orbie, J. (eds) (2007) *European Union Trade Politics and Development: Everything but Arms unravelled*, New York: Routledge.

Goodison, P. (2007) 'The future of Africa's trade with Europe: new EU trade policy', *Review of African Political Economy* 34 (111): 139–51.

Green, M. and McGregor, R. (2008) 'China offers Nigeria $50b n credit', *Financial Times*, 2 April 2008.

Grimm, S. (2007) 'The EU–Africa strategy: where we stand', in S. Klingebiel (ed.), *Africa Agenda for 2007: Suggestions for the German G8 and EU Council Presiden*cies, Discussion Paper 4, 2007, Bonn: German Development Institute, 81–85.

Hugon, P. (2007) 'La politique économique de la France en Afrique : la fin des rentes coloniales?' *Politique Africaine* 105: 54–69.

Hurt, S. R. (2003) 'Co-operation and coercion? The Cotonou Agreement between the European Union and ACP states and the end of the Lomé Convention', *Third World Quarterly* 24 (1): 161–76.

IMF (2007a) 'The IMF and aid to sub-Saharan Africa', IMF Report, Washington, DC: Independent Evaluation Office of the IMF.

—— (2007b) 'Regional Economic Outlook: Sub-Saharan Africa', World Economic and Financial Surveys, Washington, DC: International Monetary Fund.

Iweala, U. (2007) 'Stop trying to "save" Africa', *Washington Post*, 15 July 15.

Johnson, J. (2008) 'India follows China's path with Africa overtures', *Financial Times*, 9 April.

Kanbur, R. (2004) 'The African peer review mechanism (APRM): an assessment of concept and design', *Politikon* 31 (2): 157–66.

Kaplinsky, R. and Morris, M. (2007) 'Do the Asian drives undermine export-oriented industrialization in SSA?' *World Development* 36 (1): 254–73.

Kebonang, Z. (2007) 'Generosity undermined: the Cotonou Agreement and the African Growth and Opportunity Act', *Development in Practice* 17 (1): 98–103.

Kohnert, D. (2006) 'Afrikanische Migranten vor der Festung Europa', GIGA Focus Afrika 12, Hamburg: German Institute of Global and Area Studies. Online. Available: http://se2.isn.ch/serviceengine/FileContent?serviceID=10&fileid=83BEF80D-521D-45D4–930A-296EB1E1F5DD&lng=de (accessed on 14 October 2008).

—— (2007) 'African Migration to Europe: Obscured Responsibilities and Common Misconceptions', GIGA Working Paper 49, Hamburg: German Institute of Global and Area Studies. Online. Available: www.giga-hamburg.de/dl/download.php?d=/content/publikationen/pdf/wp49_kohnert.pdf (accessed on 14 October 2008).

—— (2008) 'EU–Africa Economic Relations: Continuing Dominance, traded for Aid?' GIGA Working Paper 82, Hamburg: German Institute of Global and Area Studies. Online. Available: www.giga-hamburg.de/dl/download.php?d=/content/publikationen/pdf/wp82_kohnert.pdf (accessed on 14 October 2008).

'La Lettre du continent' (7 February 2008) 534: 3. Online. Available: www.africain-telligence.fr/LC-/archives/default_archives.asp?num=534&year=2008 (accessed on 14 October 2008).

Laryea, G. *et al.* (eds) (2004) 'New ACP–EU Trade Arrangements: New Barriers to eradicating Poverty?' Brussels: EUROSTEP.

Lee, M. C. (2004) 'The US and EU: undermining regional economic integration in Africa', *News from the Nordic Africa Institute* 2004 (3): 5–8.

Manga Fombad, C. and Kebonang, Z. (2006) 'AU, NEPAD and the APRM: democratisation efforts explored', in H. Melber (ed.), *Current African Issues* 32, Uppsala: Nordic Africa Institute. Online. Availbale: www.styluspub.com/Books/BookDetail.aspx?productID=139376 (accessed 12 October 2008).

Melber, H. (2006) 'The EU and regional integration in Africa: a critical appraisal of the Economic Partnership Agreements', in M. Brüntrup *et al.* (eds) *Africa, Regional Co-operation and the World Market*, Uppsala: Nordic Africa Institute.

OECD (2007) 'African Economic Outlook, 2007', OECD report, Paris: OECD Development Centre and African Development Bank.

OXFAM (2006) 'Unequal partners: how EU–ACP Economic Partnership Agreements (EPAs) could harm the development prospects of many of the world's poorest countries', Oxfam Briefing Notes, London: Oxfam. Online. Available: www.oxfam.org.nz/imgs/whatwedo/mtf/unequal%20partners.pdf (accessed 19 November 2008).

Reisen, H. and Ndoye, S. (2008) 'Prudent versus Imprudent Lending to Africa: from Debt Relief to Emerging Lenders', OECD Working Paper 268, Paris: OECD Development Centre.

Ricard, P. (2007) 'Bruxelles accuse Paris de tenir un double discours sur le commerce avec l'Afrique', *Le Monde*, 15 December.

Stevens, C. (2006a) 'Economic Partnership Agreements (EPAs): Where we are', ODI Briefing Paper 4, June, London: Overseas Development Institute. Online. Available: www.odi.org.uk/resources/odi-publications/briefing-papers/4-economic-partnership-agreements-where-we-are.pdf (accessed 14 November 2008).

—— (2006b) 'The EU, Africa and Economic Partnership Agreements: unintended consequences of policy leverage', *Journal of Modern African Studies* 44 (3): 441–58.

—— (2007) 'Economic Partnership Agreements: What happens in 2008?' ODI Briefing Paper 23, June, London: Overseas Development Institute. Online. Available: www.odi.org.uk/resources/odi-publications/briefing-papers/23-economic-partnership-agreements-2008.pdf (accessed 14 November 2008).

Storey, A. (2006) 'Normative power Europe? Economic Partnership Agreements and Africa', *Journal of Contemporary African Studies* 24 (3): 331–46.

Umbach, F. (2007) 'China's energy and raw material diplomacy and the implications for EU–China relations', *China aktuell/ Journal of Current Chinese Affairs* 1: 39–56.

UN (2007) 'World Economic Situation and Prospects, 2007: Midyear Update', UN report, New York: United Nations.

UNCTAD (2007) 'Asian Foreign Direct Investment in Africa: Towards a New Era of Co-operation among Developing Countries', Current Studies on FDI and Development 3, Paris: UNCTAD.

Wade, A. (2008) 'Time for the West to practise what it preaches', *New African*, March 2008: 20.

Wusheng, Y. and Jensen, T. V. (2005) 'Tariff preferences, WTO negotiations and the LDCs: the case of the "Everything but arms" initiative', *World Economy* 28 (3): 375–405.

Yang, Y. and Gupta, S. (2007) 'Regional trade arrangements in Africa: past performance and the way forward', *African Development Review* 19 (3): 399–431.

Zafar, A. (2007) 'The growing relationship between China and sub-Saharan Africa: macroeconomic, trade, investment, and aid links', *World Bank Research Observer* 22 (1): 103–30.

8 The European Union and its Africa strategy

Case study Ethiopia

Stefan Brüne

> Security problems are a manifestation of underlying political problems.
>
> (Xavier Solana)

For the presidents of the European Commission and the European Parliament it is a breakthrough, and Louis Michel, EU Commissioner for Development and Humanitarian Aid, has referred to it as 'a real turning point' (EU 2005). *The European Union Strategy for Africa* (Commission of the European Communities 2005), submitted to the European Council by the British government during its term of Council presidency and subsequently adopted in December 2005, is indeed a novelty. It envisages a strategic partnership between the EU and the African Union and purportedly offers a comprehensive, common frame for all EU actors in the spheres of foreign and development policy that will shape future measures to support African states. For the first time, a strategy that takes the entire African continent into account is to form the basis for coherent North–South and foreign trade policies pursued by both the EU as a whole and the Union's individual member states. Peace and security, good governance and the acceleration of economic growth are the central aims of the strategy, and this orientation is intended to aid African states in realising ambitious millennium goals.[1] Partnership is a further important element of the new strategy. The adoption of what it is hoped will be a 'comprehensive, integrated, and long-term' strategy marks the end of a consultation process, during which the African Union (created in mid-2002) and the regional economic communities associated with it were called upon to comment on the EU's policy goals and vision of its relations with Africa.

Europe's search for an international profile has been characterised recently by a conspicuous surge of rather remarkable initiatives in the area of foreign policy quite generally and more specifically in the realm of North–South policies. In April 2005 the Commission approved a *Millennium Development Goals Package*, which – complemented in May the same year by a scheme of defined steps to be realised – established a base for the European Council's ambitious self-commitment. According to these plans, funds of European development aid are to be doubled by the year 2015. The fifteen pre-expansion EU member states have agreed to allocate first 0.5 per cent (2010) and later 0.7 per cent (2015) of their gross national income to development spending.[2] As a result, an additional €20 billion will be available by the year 2010; half this sum is earmarked for projects in African countries. Further institutional reforms agreed upon in June 2005 provide for improved co-ordination and more rapid implementation of European aid measures. In July 2005 the Commission submitted a proposal for a common declaration to the European Council and Parliament, *The European Consensus on Development* (Council of the European Union 2005), which was approved in December 2005. Thus, for the first time in European history, a fundamental document now exists that obliges all relevant EU actors in the realm of foreign affairs and development policy to pursue common goals, values, basic principles and procedures.

In this chapter, the significance of this burst of documents on the aims and principles of EU policy towards Africa (the contents of which can only be outlined very briefly here) for practical EU politics will be examined. Those who observe European external relations with respect to the South and in the sphere of foreign trade remain sceptical. They have long been of the opinion that such euphoric pronouncements often are without any binding effect on the actual conduct of politics, defined mainly by the desire to raise the EU's profile in international affairs. According to Olsen (1998) such policy statements mostly fulfil symbolic functions within the process of European integration. Hoebink (2006) has criticised conflicting and self-contradictory objectives, and, based on his analysis of relations with Ghana, Crawford (2005) has concluded that the national interests of the major European donor states remain the decisive factor in determining the Union's relations with other countries.

On the backdrop of such evaluations, and in the face of increasing international criticism of Europe's idealistic self-presentation (Natsios 2006), this contribution offers an assessment of the causes, and consequences, of this widespread lack of coherence by focusing on Ethiopia as a case study. I will argue here that most donors fashion their policies in relative isolation, in keeping with specific national paths that reflect each country's respective national interests.

Ethiopia, the United States and the European Union: the primacy of geopolitics

Situated in North East Africa, Ethiopia is by far the most populous country in the Horn of Africa[3] and for decades has been one of the most important recipients of international aid. As one of the poorest countries on the earth – 90 per cent of the Ethiopian population subsist on less than US$2 per day and the average *per capita* yearly income is $100 – this agrarian country ranks 169 out of 177 countries in the United Nations *Human Development Report* (United Nations Development Programme 2007). For international donors such as the

World Bank and the EU, this multi-ethnic state, which uses development aid money to cover as much as 40 per cent of its state expenses, is the most important recipient country in Africa. In 2005 alone, Ethiopia received US$1 billion in international aid, including US$490 million from the EU.

Ethiopia owes its position as *donor darling* – a position it has held since 1991, for the most part independent of domestic political constellations – to the interaction of several factors. Besides an undisputed high need for development assistance[4] and, moreover, motives related to security policy, the fact that Ethiopia has also successfully instrumentalised historical and cultural factors has also played a significant role. The Ethiopian Empire with its Christian tradition was the only non-colonised African member country of the League of Nations besides Liberia and was perceived by Europe and the United States (US) as a model of stability and cultural kinship in surroundings marked by Islam. Moreover, these good relations were also promoted by the ability of Ethiopian governments to adapt quite flexibly to the changing paradigms of the politically influential international *donor community* without jeopardising their own power basis and, for the most part, despite the changes in political orientation of successive regimes. The Ethiopian actors often proved quite skilful at combining strategically staged political scenery with flexible political realism in the areas of foreign affairs and security policy. For example, the Tigrayan People's Liberation Front (TPLF) – today part of the ruling Ethiopian People's Revolutionary Democratic Front (EPRDF) – successfully linked Marxist rhetoric and organisational forms with pragmatic pro-Western foreign policies. In the run-up to the Iraq War, Ethiopia was one of the four African countries – besides Eritrea, Uganda and Rwanda – that supported the US by granting overflight rights, which were ultimately not made use of. Given its size and exposed position in the Horn of Africa, the country is regarded as a dependable partner with respect to Western security interests and as a key factor in safeguarding stability in the region. In the words of Donald Yamamoto, US Deputy Assistant Secretary of State for African Affairs:

> Ethiopia is a cornerstone for US foreign policy and also for international policy in Africa. It is one of the four cornerstone countries in Africa not only for the US but for the international community, because it is important not only for a strategic position but also because it is a chair for the African Union.
>
> (*Sudan Tribune*, 1 January 2006)

Besides existing bilateral agreements with individual member states, EU relations with Ethiopia are based, in particular, on the Cotonou Agreement. Completed in 2000, the agreement binds seventy-eight African, Pacific and Caribbean States (referred to as the ACP states) to the EU; the signatory states have pledged that they will respect human rights and promote democracy. Article 9 states that:

The Parties undertake to promote and protect all fundamental freedoms and human rights, be they civil and political, or economic, social and cultural. [...] The Parties reaffirm that democratization, development, and the protection of fundamental freedoms and human rights are inter-related and mutually reinforcing. Democratic principles are universally recognized principles underpinning the organization of the State to ensure the legitimacy of its authority, the legality of its actions reflected in its constitutional, legislative and regulatory system, and the existence of participatory mechanisms. On the basis of universally recognized principles, each country develops its democratic culture.[5]

(ACP–EC Council of Ministers 2000: art. 9)

In relations between Europe and Ethiopia, foreign trade and natural resources do not play a significant role. Although the EU is Ethiopia's most important trade partner, the country has no known deposits of internationally traded natural resources. The country's main export product is coffee.

From rising star to embarrassing partner: the recent Ethiopian crisis and the European Union

When the Soviet-supported regime of Colonel Mengistu Haile Mariam ended in Addis Ababa in May 1991, the US as well as the EU fostered new hope of a fundamental new beginning in Ethiopia. Advised by international specialists, the new TPLF-dominated government soon drafted a new federal constitution. The constitution adopted in December 1994 marked the end of authoritarian and centralistic development planning and provided for the transition to a multi-party democracy under parliamentary control and with a division of the legislative, executive and judiciary branches and guarantees of fundamental freedoms. The constitution of the Federal Democratic Republic of Ethiopia was considered to be one of the most modern in the world; it even provided the right to secession, albeit only under conditions that could hardly be fulfilled in practice.

Despite these changes, which occurred under the benevolent gaze of Western donors, Ethiopian political culture failed to liberate itself from its authoritarian traditions. The most striking characteristic of Ethiopian politics was the persistence of semi-clandestine decision-making structures, the core of which was dominated by the TPLF's Central Committee, which employed Marxist justification strategies in the tradition of Ethiopian student move-ments. The Federal Republic of Ethiopia features the contradictions of a federal constitutional state under centralised control of a single party with a partially liberalised economy that is dominated by quasi-party-controlled companies. To date, no national concept for the promotion of democracy and good governance has been drawn up. Instead, a strategy paper in Amharic (its title translates roughly as 'The Development Lines of Revolutionary Demo-cracy'), apparently co-authored by Prime Minister Meles Zenawi, has been circulating that formulated basic considerations on the relationship between the state and the economy (Zenawi 1992 Ethiopian Calendar, ETC). At first, the contradiction between democratic facade and authoritarian practice – purportedly a structural characteristic of African states in transitional phases – seemed to be relatively less significant when it came to redesigning European and American commitments to support Ethiopia. Since the TPLF defined itself as a 'liberation movement that had come into power', a 'culture of political cadres' was regarded as a tolerable historical relict that was part of the framework of domestic development. Within this cadre culture, internally legitimated decision-making processes were all the democracy that had been familiar so far (even whoever belonged to the TPLF's Central Committee was unknown to the public for a long time) and conflicts were generally resolved by authoritarian and, in many cases, violent means. Disregard for compromise, ideological convictions and the proudly asserted attachment of former fighters to 'the people' were all factors that interacted to strengthen this regime. TPLF supporters from rural areas regarded urban life styles as foreign and suspicious, and incentive systems based on economic benefits rather than political power were virtually unknown. Pride in 'our own' was further reinforced by the traditional 'culture of secrecy' characteristic of the country's northern regions. For a long time, Ethiopian political culture has been marked by a lack of public debate and openly expressed controversy – a deficit that often proved useful in maintaining political power in the past (Brüne 2001).

From a European perspective, the fact that the TPLF, as an ethno-regional organisation, could claim to represent only 8 per cent of the entire Ethiopian population seemed to represent an opportunity. The hope that the TPLF would rely on policies that reflected federal and decentralised structures in the interests of the party's power was perceived as an important starting point for the democratisation efforts promoted by Europe. But such hopes, cultivated especially by experts in development policy, soon proved to be unrealistic, as the expected processes of decentralisation and democratisation fostered by federal structures failed to emerge. Instead, the party alliance controlled by the TPLF succeeded in controlling and dominating the governmental and administrative organs of the newly established states by means of intimidation and by establishing satellite parties. As a result of political interventions by the central government in 2002, regional governments in the newly established regions Somalia and Oromia and in the southern province lost power.

In the period that followed, European countries oriented their policies to the demands of their relation with the US and 'extended' security concerns increasingly gained the upper hand over classic security policy.[6] In this process, the central government made use of the fact that it could point to ongoing operations by armed opposition groups. Particularly in the Oromia and Somalia regions – the violent genesis of the Ethiopian state in a process that involved the suppression and marginalisation of communities in the south remains taboo – skirmishes between government forces, on the one hand, and the Oromo Liberation Front and the National Ogaden Liberation Front, on the other, repeatedly occurred. This revaluation of military options within security policy was further promoted by the events of 11 September 2001, in the wake of which military co-operation between the US and Ethiopia intensified markedly. American Special Forces were especially active in the south-east of the country.

Moreover, Western donors increasingly realised that, in authoritarian, neopatrimonially governed Third World states, 'change agents' can be identified only under very favourable conditions. Although representatives of the EU continued to voice official criticism of the human rights policy of the EPRDF, the role of *democracy promoters* took a back seat to that of *international security agent*. The argument that there was no real alternative to the EPRDF regime in terms of power politics played an important role in this shift.[7]

The period that followed was marked by a wave of public protests, which were often brutally squelched by security forces with no consequences forthcoming for those who mishandled demonstrators. Student protests at Addis Ababa University in April 2001 left a toll of thirty-one people dead and thousands of students temporarily arrested. After a case brought before the court in Tepi because of alleged election fraud was dropped in March 2002, security forces and demonstrators clashed and more than 100 people died. News about these events did not spread until an EU delegation was sent to the crisis region and demanded an investigation of the incident. Soon after, in May 2002, local security forces in Awassa shot dozens of demonstrators who had protested peacefully against plans to restructure the region administratively.

15 May 2005: democratic founding elections?

Since the first multi-party elections were boycotted (1995) and criticised (2000) by the country's feuding opposition, who charged that their campaign activities had been interfered with by the government, the elections of 15 May 2005 were generally regarded as democratic 'founding elections'. One week before the poll, 1 million people demonstrated in Addis Ababa against the politics of the EPRDF. So the outcome – substantial gains for the opposition – was hardly surprising. The oppositional Coalition for Unity and Democracy (CUD) won all twenty-three seats in Addis Ababa.[8] When the opposition called on the public to protest because of alleged election fraud, Meles Zenawi declared a state of emergency, placed the police and security forces under his personal control, and imposed a one-month ban on demonstrations in and around Addis Ababa. Two weeks later, protests again occurred on the campus of Addis Ababa University, this time with numerous taxi drivers and shop owners joining in. Members of special security units of the Agazi recruited in Tigray reacted to stone-throwing by demonstrators with great brutality. In the resulting wave of violent confrontations that lasted until 13 June 2005, forty-two people died, several hundred demonstrators were injured and 5,000 were arrested.[9]

In this situation, it was only thanks to the intensive mediation of international election observers, particularly the EU Election Observation Mission (EUEOM) and the EU mission in Addis Abeba, that the government and opposition finally agreed on an orderly investigation of the 299 election fraud complaints filed and appealed to their respective supporters to return to order and refrain from further violence. On 27 August, Ana Gomes, head of the EUEOM (numbering some 200 people) submitted a preliminary report that proved to be more critical than expected. The reaction of the Ethiopian government was unusually sharp. In a statement that included personal attacks on Ms Gomes and was published in the state-controlled newspaper *Ethiopian Herald*, Meles Zenawi rejected the report as 'garbage' and a 'lie' (Zenawi, 28 August 2005, ETC).

Announcement of the official election results on 5 September – with the EPRDF winning nearly 70 per cent of the seats in the federal parliament – again triggered bloody unrest. In the course of conflicts, with honking taxi drivers being arrested and young demonstrators building barricades, again several dozen people died; the opposition CUD counted thirty-three dead, including two policemen. More than 150 demonstrators were injured, numerous opposition leaders were arrested, and several thousand people – some sources have referred to tens of thousands[10] – were brought to huge prisons outside the capital. Amnesty International criticised 'the excessive use of force by the police and the arbitrary detention of members and suspected members of the Coalition for Unity and Democracy (CUD) ... prisoners of conscience, arrested solely for non-violent expression of political beliefs' (AI 2005).

On 4 November 2005, Ana Gomes had appealed to the EU Commission and the governments of the EU member states.

> As I write to you, EU ambassadors are unable to leave the compound where we are meeting, random shooting is heard in the streets of Addis Ababa. This follows bloody incidents yesterday, where security forces killed people spontaneously protesting against Prime Minister (PM) Meles' government and EPRDF, the ruling party. The new parliament has been boycotted by the opposition forces, contesting official results and the anti-democratic behavior of the ruling party. ...
>
> Despite those ominous incidents, the conclusions of the EUEOM [EU Election Observation Mission 2005] publicised on August 25, and two critical European Parliament resolutions adopted since then [...] European Governments, also verbally standing by EUEOM conclusions, in practice have been acting as if it was 'business as usual' with Mr. Meles. In the last weeks congratulations for PM Meles' 're-election' have been pouring in from Europe, including the British Presidency and the Presidency of the European Commission. Earlier on, just after the June

killings and arrests, Mr. Meles was invited to rub shoulders with G-8 and 'Africa Commission' leaders in Scotland. ...

Most ironic is that Europe counts in Ethiopia, a country which depends on European aid, the largest recipient in Africa. Europe could definitely make the difference for democracy in Ethiopia. Instead, current European leaders are choosing to fail it. In doing so, they are not just failing Ethiopians. They are also failing Europe. ...

Best regards
Ana Gomes, MEP
(Gomes 2005)

The *Neue Zürcher Zeitung* commented:

Despite this bloody repression, Ethiopia remains for the present the favourite child of foreign development aid workers. Until now, nobody has significantly reduced aid to Ethiopia. The donor states are apparently not adhering to their own principles, according to which only those who strive for democracy and good governance deserve aid.[11]

(*Neue Zürcher Zeitung*, 2 November 2005)

According to information provided by the Ethiopian government, it released a total of 6,274 prisoners on 9 and 10 November. On 15 November 2005, Jan Smith, a Republican and member of the US House of Representatives from New Jersey, proposed a Bill that emphasised that 'Ethiopia's stability was vital to United States interests in East Africa and the Middle East' and then called on the US President 'to suspend all joint security activities of the Government of the United States with the Government of Ethiopia, including activities through the US East Africa Counterterrorism Initiative' (Smith 2005).

On the same day, Tim Clarke, the European Commission's Head of Delegation in Addis Ababa, was interviewed by the Ethiopian newspaper *Capital*. Referring to a joint EU–US statement (EU/US 2005), he called on the government to release all political prisoners and to utilise the mechanisms for dialogue spelled out in Article 8 of the Cotonou Agreement. In answer to a question about the statement of the EU Election Observation Mission, he stated that this was an independent report that did not commit the Commission or the EU in any way. In an editorial published on 27 November 2005 the *New York Times* called for a suspension of aid to Ethiopia. And the Development Assistance Group, that brings together seventeen donors and is co-chaired by UNDP and the World Bank, stated that reconsideration of aid commitments in Ethiopia had become unavoidable. Meanwhile, Meles Zenawi confirmed that some 3,000 young people were being detained in prison.

This brief survey reveals that the European Parliament and the EU Election Observation Mission were most active in publicising the human rights violations and repressive measures of the Ethiopian government. For the European Commission, as well as most of the European embassies in the Ethiopian capital, the focus was on maintaining the *status quo* of the current balance of power. The latter hoped to contribute to securing 'structural stability' as neutral mediators who implemented a policy of proactive crisis management. It was not until the spiral of violence began to escalate that the fragmentary policies of regional stability maintenance and the pursuit of national interests coalesced into some semblance of 'coherence' that also decried democracy deficits – and even then, not all EU states fell into line at the same time.

It was primarily Tony Blair who was forced to deal with difficult decisions made unavoidable by the events taking shape in Europe. Seeking ways to redeem his image tarnished by the disappointments of the Iraq War, the British Prime Minister had invited Meles Zenawi to join the Commission for Africa he called into being shortly before the British EU presidency began to put the search for African solutions to African problems on the international agenda. It was therefore no accident that the centre of Europe-wide protests on December 2005 against human rights abuses perpetrated by the EPRDF government was in London.

> The reason we have chosen London as a center of protest is the realiza-tion that the brutal government of Meles Zenawi is being sustained by the all around support it receives from the government of the United Kingdom. We know that Britain, as a major player in the EU, and your Excellency, as the current president of the EU commission, have signi-ficant power to right the wrongs committed against our people by Meles Zenawi.
>
> (Debteraw, 13 December 2005)

Once the Human Rights Commission of the African Union – following initial hesitancy – joined the chorus of international critics protesting at Zenawi's policies, the Ethiopian Premier made a surprise visit to European Development Commissioner Louis Michel on 4 February 2006 (or, at least, a visit not scheduled on Michel's official agenda). Also attending the meeting were the head of the EU delegation in Addis Ababa, Tim Clarke, and the Ethiopian ambassador to Brussels, Berhane Gebre-Christos. According to reports, Meles failed to realise his main objective, which was the continua-tion of aid payments (originally, some €461 million were to flow from 2002 to 2007). Instead, Louis Michel stated that the current situation ran counter to the interests of all parties involved. The prerequisite for resumption of political dialogue, he asserted, was the treatment of the political opposition in a manner that was in keeping with common practices in democratic states. 'We did not want to discuss aid. It is not on the agenda. We will discuss it when the political dialogue has resumed' (Ethiopia Hagere, 10 February 2006).

On 22 February 2006 the British government also declared that it had suspended some $88 million in aid previously earmarked for Ethiopian state agencies and planned to redirect these funds to grass-roots organisations in the country committed to promoting human rights. This step can be characterised as a belated reaction to the dramatic developments; faced with the massive protests in Ethiopia and abroad, the British government finally had no choice but to make a pragmatic decision in favour of more 'coherence'.

Broker or human rights advocate? The dual role of the European Union in Meles Zenawi's Ethiopia

In retrospective – and from a theoretical perspective – the behaviour of the European actors involved raises a number of fundamental questions. 'The first is whether the West was really ignorant of Ethiopia's internal problems. In other words can the United State's post-Mengistu policy towards Ethiopia be better explained by information void (as regards bad governance) or [...] is it a result of advancing its own interest?' (Negash 2006: 28). One might also rephrase the issue as follows. Why did attempts to promote publicly announced goals of good governance fail? Were there alternatives? What were the motives of the European actors in pursuing a policy, the effects of which caught them quite unawares? Could the European Community have acted with more foresight and in a more united fashion and thus perhaps also more effectively?

For a long period, European relations with Ethiopia in the post-Mengistu era were marked by the hope that concerns for the promotion of democratisation processes and respect for human rights could be tied to the classic aim of pursuing national as well as common European interests. Rather than deliberately calculated demonstrations of power, international co-operation and the patient encouragement of reform processes were the mainstays of a strategy that was to create the necessary preconditions for long-term democratisation and capacity building. Acting in the name of humanity without losing sight of power-driven state relations, the EU and its member states made use of their status as bilateral and multilateral donors and major trade partners of Ethiopia. What is more, it seemed that none of the individual EU states had economic and political interests linked with relations with Ethiopia that were so distinctive or significant that they might have provoked conflicts with Europe's role as an interested but rather neutral mediator. The EU attempted to act on the basis of ideals without setting aside the most essential rule of *Realpolitik*. It brought normative pressure to bear and at the same time felt obliged to maintain the regional power balance that promised to secure political stability.

One of the characteristics of this European engagement in Ethiopia,[12] which was only loosely co-ordinated in 2005, was that primarily security concerns, rather than democracy deficits or key economic interests, led to a process in which the EU's role as international security agent ultimately became more significant than its self-assigned task as a promoter of democracy. When, in the wake of 11 September 2001, the entire Horn of Africa was included in the anti-terror campaign,[13] the question of the internal legitimacy of African partners was pushed even further on to the back burner (and from the perspective of international geopolitics it had been a low priority at any rate). The EU avoided any action that might have destabilised its state partners.

It was in keeping with these interests that European embassy reports on the political situation in Ethiopia assumed that there was no alternative to the 'stability' of the EPRDF regime. The shock that was triggered by the EPRDF regime's massive loss of votes in the 2005 election in parts of the diplomatic community (one high-ranking European diplomat labelled the outcome of the elections in an internal assessment as a disaster) was only partly due to the unforeseen dramatic escalation of events that followed. Such reactions highlight the weakness of perceptions that focus on the state as the most relevant political actor and tend to disregard the significance of public disillusionment and motives for action that have developed historically in a specific context. To be more explicit: Africa will not become more democratic by embracing the normative agendas of external actors. Instead, democracy will be promoted due to the rising influence of local actors – despite the fact that these actors might be discredited internationally and that the processes they unleash take the shape of catalytic crises – because the domestic and international publics are reminded of smouldering and unresolved problems that have all too often been ignored for reasons of political expediency.

Conclusion

The Ethiopian example again shows that external aid may support democratisation and good governance but cannot force societies to realise them. It is also apparent that the use of force by states and the repression of political expression are by no means guarantees for stability. The resulting dilemma of reconciling democratisation and stability will continue to accompany the EU's relations with Ethiopia and Africa as a whole. The assumption that democratisation politics constitutes a form of anticipatory security policy can be considered to be true only if relevant social groups are willing to commit themselves to adopting a catalogue of acceptable reactions as part of a credible process of dialogue. In Ethiopia, the uncompromising attitude of the regime precluded such an agreement and Europe's tacit acceptance of that regime's political grandstanding for representatives of donor countries only aggravated the situation. The EU ignored the obvious fact that the Ethiopian government had acquired impressive professional skills in dealing with international donors and that it had rather successfully exploited inner European and international co-ordination deficits to further and to stabilise its own power.

In this respect, the new EU Africa strategy appears to be primarily an instrument used to clarify European self-understanding. Its function as an operative strategy for realising the EU's self-set goals would seem to be of secondary importance. This attempt to reduce conflicting policy goals and promote a coherent and comprehensive policy for European foreign relations and trade with Africa makes sense from the perspective of European policies and the integration of immigrants in the countries of the EU. However, as long as the EU lacks an effective, integrated common foreign and security policy, the strategy offers little more than a general framework for reference and orientation.

Notes

1 The Millennium Development Goals agreed upon at the end of 2000 stipulate that the number of people who live in absolute poverty should be halved by 2015. According to British Finance Minister Brown at that time, the international community will in fact meet this goal about 135 years later. See also Hausmann (2005).
2 In 2004 each EU country spent an average of 0.36 per cent of its gross national income on development aid; Germany's spending amounted to 0.28 per cent.
3 Ethiopia had eighteen million inhabitants in 1950; today it is believed to have eighty-two million (80 per cent of whom live in rural areas). Estimates are that the country will have 169 million inhabitants by 2050.
4 According to a study published by the Institute of Development Studies, University of Sussex, international aid programmes in Ethiopia were 'bigger than the capacity to manage' them (Maxwell 1996). Donor policies that have allowed international food aid to become a fixed component of Ethiopian budgetary planning is also problematic. There is talk in Addis Ababa of a 'famine industry' that benefits foreign relief organisations as well as the ruling party, which has vested interests in the transport sector.
5 The Cotonou Agreement is in so far unique, as it constitutes a mixture of, on the one hand, written agreements that are not binding according to international law and, on the other, binding agreements on the commitment to negotiate about the interpretation of the first category of agreement.
6 Günter Maihold (2005) has pointed out that attempts to understand development politics as an advanced form of security politics lead to circular statements ('no security without development, no development without security') that are of little use in actual practice.
7 According to Minga Negash (2006: 28) the specific interests of individual institutions within the American administration are in part responsible for the renaissance of classic perceptions of threats to international security.
8 A total of 547 members of the federal House of Representatives as well as all members of the state parliaments were up for election.
9 Some opposition politicians were put under house arrest, others were imprisoned. Work permits were rescinded for journalists reporting for the German broadcasting company Deutsche Welle and for Voice of America for alleged 'biased reporting'.
10 It is now confirmed that during the urban violence in 2005 at least 193 people

died and hundreds of others were injured. By most estimates, tens of thousands were detained and many released without charge after some months. Most credible reports estimate about 30,000 people arrested. It is unknown how many are still detained of facing charges (Smith 2007:7). The British television station Channel 4 had reported that 43,000 people were held in Dedessa Valley alone. According to unconfirmed information from the oppositional groups (SOS Ethiopia), arrests totalled 30,000 in Bir Sheleqo, 18,000 in Ziway, 8,000 in Denkoro Chaka, and 9,000 in Shoa Robit.

11 Translation of the author.

12 Marked improvements in the co-ordination of donors within Europe, with a view to the focus on 'democracy, civil society, and public administration', was a long time in coming. At first, British and German development policy-makers disagreed on whether budgetary aid was a useful measure. The French embassy prided itself on its good bilateral contacts to Meles. For France, combating poverty as an element of development aid was a novelty. Moreover, in part because of the French military stationed in neighbouring Djibouti, France chose to limit itself to pursuing its own interests in the spheres of trade and cultural affairs. Efforts made by the Netherlands and Ireland to promote proactive conflict management have met with little success so far.

13 In Djibouti, where France maintains a permanent military base with some 2,900 soldiers, there are also about 2,000 US soldiers. A further 250 German soldiers (reduced from 1,270 in 2002) are charged with monitoring the seaways in the region.

References

ACP–EC Council of Ministers (2000) 'Cotonou Agreement', EU *Official Journal* L 317. Online. Available: http://eur-lex.europa.eu/LexUriServ/LexUriServ.do?uri=C ELEX:22000A1215(01):EN:HTML (accessed 17 November 2008).

AI (2005) 'Possible Prisoners of Conscience', appeal AFR 25/017/2005. Online. Available http: www.amnesty.org/en/library/asset/AFR25/017/2005/en/dom-AFR250172005en.pdf (accessed 17 November 2008).

Badie, B. (2002) *La Diplomatie des droits de l'homme. Entre éthique et volonté de puissance*, Paris: Fayard.

Bagayoko-Penone, N. (2004) *Afrique. Les stratégies française et américaine*, Paris: Harmattan.

Basedau, M. (2005) *Erfolgsbedingungen von Demokratie im subsaharischen Afrika*, Wiesbaden: VS-Verlag für Sozialwissenschaften.

Bassewitz, N. and Hess, H. (2005) *Zehn Jahre ethnischer Föderalismus in Äthiopien. Zwischen nationaler Selbstbestimmung und Balkanisierung*, Bonn: Friedrich Ebert Stiftung.

Brüne, S. (2001) 'Wachs und Gold. Äthiopiens erprobte Kultur des Versteckens', in U. Caumanns and M. Niendorf (eds) *Verschwörungstheorien. Anthropologische Konstanten. Historische Varianten*, Osnabrück: Fibre Verlag.

—— (2003) *Möglichkeiten und Grenzen der Förderung von Demokratie und Good Governance in Angola, Äthiopien, Guatemala und Kambodscha, Länderbericht Äthiopien*, Bonn: Bundesministerium für Wirtschaftliche Zusammenarbeit und Entwicklung.

—— (2005) *Europas Aussenbeziehungen und die Zukunft der Entwicklungspolitik*, Wiesbaden: VS-Verlag für Sozialwissenschaften.

—— (2008) 'Das alte oder schon das neue Europa? Die autonomen Militärmission der EU in Afrika. Eine erste Bilanz', in H. G. Justenhoven and H. G. Ehrhart (eds) *Intervention im Kongo. Eine kritische Analyse der Befriedungspolitik von UN und EU*, Stuttgart: Kohlhammer.

Brüne, S. and Scholler, H. (eds) (2006) *Auf dem Weg zum modernen Äthiopien. Festschrift für Bairu Tafla*, Münster: Lit-Verlag.

Burnell, P. (2003) 'How to Democratise Authoritarian Regimes?' Paper presented at the Friedrich-Ebert-Stiftung International Workshop on Promotion of Democracy: Current Problems and Policies, Berlin, 10 December 2003.

Capital (15 November 2005) 'Interview with Tim Clarke. Too many people have died'. Online. Available: www.capitalethiopia.com/archive/2005/nov/week2/Interview%20with%20Tim%20Clarke.htm (accessed 17 November 2008).

Carothers, T. (1999) *Aiding Democracy Abroad: the Learning Curve*, Washington, DC: Brookings Institution Press.

Commission of the European Communities (2005) 'EU Strategy for Africa: Towards a Euro–African Pact to accelerate African's development', Communication from the Commission to the Council, 12 October, Com (2005) 489 final, Brussels. Online. Available: http://ec.europa.eu/development/icenter/repository/04_eu_strategy_for_africa_12_10_2005_en.pdf (accessed 3 September 2008).

Council of the European Union (2005) 'The European Consensus on Development', Joint Statement on European Development Policy, 22 November 2005, 14820 (05), Brussels: General Secretariat. Online. Available: http://ec.europa.eu/development/icenter/repository/eu_consensus_en.pdf (accessed 28 November 2008).

Crawford, G. (2005) 'The European Union and democracy promotion in Africa: the case of Ghana', *European Journal of Development Research* 4: 571–600.

Debteraw (13 December 2005) 'Ethiopians again appeal to Tony Blair over crimes in Ethiopia'. Online. Available: www.debteraw.com/Article-82.htm (accessed 18 November 2008).

Ethiopia Hagere (10 February 2006) 'A discreet visit to Brussels', press release. Online. Available: http://ethiopiahagere.objectis.net/discretvisit (accessed 28 November 2008).

EU Election Observer Mission (2005) 'Final Report on the Legislative Elections'. Online. Available: http://ec.europa.eu/external_relations/human_rights/eu_election_ass_observ/ethiopia/2005_final_report.pdf (accessed 27 June 2008).

European Convention (2005) 'Final Report of Group VII on External Action', Brussels, 16 December 2002, CONV 459/02. Online. Available: http://register.consilium.eu.int/pdf/en/02/cv00/00459en2.pdf (accessed 25 November 2008).

European Parliament (2005) 'European Parliament Resolution on the Situation in Ethiopia and the new Border Conflict', Resolution 15 December 2005, Brussels. Online. Available: www.europarl.europa.eu/sides/getDoc.do?type=TA&language=EN&reference=P6-TA-2005–0535 (accessed 15 June 2008).

European Union (2005) 'Council adoption of the EU Strategy for Africa marks new era in Euro–African relations', press release IP/05/1571, Brussels, 12 December. Online. Available: http://europa.eu/rapid/pressReleasesAction.do?reference=IP/05/1571&format=HTML&aged=0&language=EN&guiLanguage=en (accessed 25 July 2008).

European Union/United States (2005) 'Joint Statement of the European Union and the United States on Ethiopia', Brussels, 13 July. Online. Available: www.consilium.europa.eu/ueDocs/cms_Data/docs/pressData/en/cfsp/85699.pdf (accessed 23 November 2008).

Ghebrezghi, S. and Tetzlaff, R. (2005) 'Äthiopiens Parlamentswahlen vom 15. Mai 2005. Liberalisierung wider Willen?' *Afrika im Blickpunkt* 2005 (3): 1–9.

Gomes, A. (2005) 'Urgent appeal. Call on EU governments and the Commission to act', Addis Ababa, 4 November. Online. Available: www.mediaethiopia.com/Election2005/MP_AnaGomes_UrgentAppeal_Nov05.htm (accessed 27 September 2008).

Grimm, S. and Kielwein, N. (2005) 'Die Afrika-Strategie der Europäischen Union. Kohärenz gegenüber einem vielschichtigen Kontinent im Wandel?' Analysen und Stellungnahmen 9/2005, Bonn: Deutsches Institut für Entwicklungspolitik. Online. Available http: www.die-gdi.de/CMS-Homepage/openwebcms3_e.nsf/(ynDK_contentByKey)/ENTR-7BRDNY?Open&nav=expand:Publications;active :Publications\ENTR-7BRDNY (accessed 3 October 2008).

Hausmann, H. (2005) 'Millenniumsziele noch in weiter Ferne. Unionsländer sollen mehr Geld für Entwicklungshilfe bereitstellen', *Das Parlament* 17: 25 April 2005.

Helly, D. and Petiteville, F. (eds) (2005) *L'Union Européenne, acteur international*, Paris: Harmattan.

Hill, C. (1993) 'The capability–expectations gap, or, Conceptualizing Europe's International Role', *Journal of Common Market Studies* 31: 305–29.

Hoebink, P. (2006) 'The Coherence of EU Policies: Perspectives from the North and the South', commissioned study, EU's poverty reduction effectiveness programme. Online. Available: www.heindehaas.com/Publications/Hoebink%202005%20(1)%20Coherence%20of%20EU%20policies%20Report.pdf (accessed 12 February 2007).

Kapstein, E. B. (2004) 'The Politics of Policy Coherence', working paper presented at the OECD Policy Workshop 'Institutional Approaches to Policy Coherence for Development', Paris, 18–19 May 2004. Online. Available: www.ethankapstein.com/articles/politics_coherence.pdf (accessed 28 September 2008).

Klingebiel, S. (2005) 'How Much Weight for Military Capabilities? Africa's New Peace and Security Architecture and the Role of External Actors', Discussion Paper 2, 2005, German Development Institute. Online. Available http: www.die-gdi.de/CMS-Homepage/openwebcms3.nsf/(ynDK_contentByKey)/ADMR-7BSCPX/$FILE/2-2005.pdf (accessed 21 August 2008).

Krause, A. (2001) 'Mehr als ein Papiertiger? Die Konfliktbearbeitungspolitik der GASP in Afrika', HSFK Report 9, 2001. Online. Available: www.buchhandel.de/detailansicht.aspx?isbn=978-3-933293-53-4 (accessed 24 September 2008).

Maihold, G. (2005) 'Die sicherheitspolitische Wendung der Entwicklungspolitik. Ein Kritik des neuen Profils', *Internationale Politik und Gesellschaft* 4: 30–48.

Matthies, V. (2005) *Kriege am Horn von Afrika*, Berlin: Köster.

Maxwell, S. (1996) 'Does European Aid Work? An Ethiopian Case Study', IDS Working Papers 46. Online. Available: www.ids.ac.uk/ids/bookshop/wp/wp46.pdf (accessed 24 September 2008).

Natsios, A. S. (2006) 'Five debates on international development: the US perspective', *Development Policy Review* 2: 131–9.

Negash, M. (2006) 'Ethiopia's Post-election Crisis: Institutional Failure and the Role of Mediation', unpublished manuscript, Johannesburg, January.

Neue Zürcher Zeitung (Zurich), 2 November 2005.

OECD/DAC (2003) *Harmonising Donor Practices for Effective Aid Delivery*, vols 1–3, Paris: OECD.

Olsen, G. R. (1998) 'Europe and the promotion of democracy in post-Cold War Africa: how serious is Europe and for what reason?' *African Affairs*, 388: 343–67.

—— (2002) 'The European Union: an *ad hoc* policy with a low priority', in P. J. Schraeder (ed.) *Exporting Democracy: Rhetoric vs. Reality*, Boulder, CO: Lynne Rienner.

Smidt, W. G. C. (2005) 'Parlamentswahlen in Äthiopien', *Afrika Spectrum* 2: 319–30.

Smith, J. (2005) 'Ethiopia Consolidation Act of 2005', House of Representatives, 15 November. Online. Available: www.govtrack.us/congress/billtext.xpd?bill=h109 –4423 (accessed 23 September 2008).

Smith, L. (2007) 'Political Violence and Democratic Uncertainty in Ethiopia', United States Institute of Peace, Special Report 192, Washington, DC. Online. Available: www.usip.org/pubs/specialreports/sr192.pdf (accessed 12 October 2008).

Solana, J. (2005) 'Contribution by the EU High Representative Javier Solana to the EU Strategy for Africa', S377/05, Brussels, 21 November. Online. Available: http://ue.eu.int/ueDocs/cms_Data/docs/pressdata/EN/reports/87088.pdf (accessed 12 October 2008).

Sudan Tribune (1 January 2006) 'Slam Ethiopia's Zenawi with sanctions'. Online. Available: www.sudantribune.com/spip.php?page=imprimable&id_article=13315 (accessed 17 November 2008).

United Nations Development Programme (2007) *Human Development Report 2007/2008*, UNDP Reports, New York: Palgrave.

Villalón, L. and Von Doepp, P. (eds) (2005) *The Fate of Africa's Democratic Experiences: Elites and Institutions*, Bloomington, IN: Indiana University Press.

Youngs, R. (2002) *The European Union and the Promotion of Democracy*, Oxford: Oxford University Press.

Zenawi, M. (1992, ETC) 'The Development Lines of Revolutionary Democracy', Addis Ababa.

—— (28 August 2005), 'Letter by Prime Minister Meles Zenawi to the Editor of the Ethiopian Herald'. Online. Available http: www.ethioembassy.org.uk/ Facts%20About%20Ethiopia/Elections/Letter%20by%20Prime%20 Minister%20Meles%20Zenawi%20to%20the%20Editor%20of%20the%20Ethiopian%20Herald.htm (accessed 17 November 2008).

Part III
Asia

9 Regional integration

Comparing European and Asian transformations

Philomena Murray

This chapter examines the transformative role of integration in Europe and East Asia, particularly the transformation wrought by regionalism. It scrutinises the European Union (EU)'s regional integration in its own policy spheres and internationally and the transformation of member states, in comparative perspective with East Asia. It examines external transformations that are either sought or effected by the EU, such as the promotion of regional integration in Asia. It seeks to illustrate that regionalism in each region has been prompted by external transformative developments and that regionalism, in turn, has brought about transformations of the structure and architecture of the two regions.

The European Union's transformation

The EU has wrought considerable change in its member states and governance structure. The transformation of the EU since the 1950s, in the aftermath of war and devastation, has seen the EU become the most advanced form of institutionalised regional integration in the world. This integration has been evident in economic, political and social spheres. It has been contested both analytically and in its policy development. It is distinctive in origins and style of negotiations. The study of the EU's integration has been largely concerned with its EU's internal process and conflicts, and the tensions between those who advocate that the state has a central role and those who advocate a new type of governance. In the international context, the study of the EU as an international actor has been dominated by trade and development assistance policies.

Much of the analysis of the EU's international role has tended to examine bilateral linkages with individual countries. However the EU has also been an advocate of regional integration in other parts of the world, such as the Association of South East Asian Nations (ASEAN).

The EU therefore projects itself as an integration exporter and, in some cases, as a norms exporter. This is in keeping with its controversial attempts to be soft power and normative power in international relations (Hyde-Price 2006; Manners 2002, 2006; Sjursen 2006), although this role is not promoted in a coherent manner in the rest of the world. Neither is this aspect of the EU's international *persona* understood in many parts of the world. Many analyses of the EU in its engagement with East Asia, for example, illustrate that the EU is regarded primarily as an economic entity, and not as a dynamic normative entity, either within its own boundaries or outside of them.

Indeed, the fact that the EU has been the site of considerable changes in polity, society and economy is not fully comprehended within the EU member states themselves. There is considerable lack of knowledge in other parts of the world – including East Asia – about the transformative nature of the EU in political or normative terms. This has been recognised by Jachtenfuchs (2001: 256) who suggests that 'the most exciting and most important aspect of European integration – namely the transformation of traditional nation states into constituent units of a new transnational political system that is not going to become a state – is largely overlooked from the outside'.

This does not mean that the EU's transformation has been overlooked by all observers in Asia. For example, a Chinese observer has commented on the 'inspiring' success of the EU (Pan 2004: 1) and the ASEAN Eminent Persons' Group (ASEAN EPG 2006) produced a report in late 2006 relating the ASEAN experience to the EU one, drawing on their meetings with EU officials in Brussels in July 2006, with a generally positive assessment of the EU experience. The report stated, of that visit:

> The study visit afforded EPG Members a better understanding of these issues as ASEAN contemplates its own integration. The EPG considered many ideas. In making its final recommendations, the EPG has emphasized proposals that will be practical to implement.
>
> (ASEAN EPG 2006: 3)

In addition, the official Chinese government paper on the EU is aware of many facets of the EU's roles – trade, aid, foreign policy, the euro – (Chinese Ministry of Foreign Affairs 2003: 3) in international public policy and diplomacy and seeks to develop relations with the EU on three main fronts: political relations; economic and trade co-operation and cultural and people-to-people exchanges.

Transformation in Europe and Asia compared

The EU and East Asia have been sites of considerable conflict in the twentieth century, including the Second World War and the Cold War. They have adopted different approaches to post-war recovery and the development of inter-state relations. Both have had dominant states whose power was radically transformed, yet here the comparisons end, as the reconciliation of Western Europe is not paralleled in the countries of East Asia. Memory plays distinctive roles in each context. Territorial disputes no longer dominate in Europe, although they remain key reasons for conflict in Asia (Calder and Fukuyama 2008: 4). Sovereignty has not been transformed in East Asia as it has in Europe. Nor have Asian nation states been radically transformed as a result of regional integration. Rather, East Asian pathways to integration have been markedly different from those adopted in Western Europe and later the larger EU of twenty-seven member states.

The EU is characterised – and contested in terms of the transformation it has brought about – by the gradual but continued expansion of its membership, the increase in the scope of its activities, the nature of its objectives, the design of its institutional architecture, the expansion of its policy concerns and, finally, the desire by its leaders to define, increase and project its international impact (Green Cowles *et al.* 2001; Radaelli 2004). This transformation is not directly comparable with other regions such as East Asia, for reasons that are discussed in this chapter. This transformation has meant that dealing with the EU is not the same for interlocutors as is dealing with individual states (Elgström and Strömvik 2005).

European Union exceptionalism and the ASEAN experience

The EU is the exception in patterns of regional integration. The contrast is striking, at first glance. The East Asian region has a long history of war, inter-state conflict and domination, territorial disputes and strife. It is common to refer to the East Asian region as very heterogeneous, in terms of race, ethnicity, language and religion (Murray 2008a: 4–6; Pempel 2005: 1).

The historical experience in different parts of East Asia ranges from colonisation by European powers, on the one hand, to domination by one Asian power over another, with concomitant unresolved issues of memory. The diversity of Asia rests as much on the fact that, politically, democracy exists alongside authoritarianism and communism as the fact that, economically, there are different varieties of capitalism and state control of the market. The economic development of this region is also very diverse, ranging from some of the poorest countries in the world to highly developed capitalist success stories. An EU document (EC 2008: 5) points out that 'Asia is home to two-thirds of the world's poorest people – 80 million of them live on less than one dollar a day'. Radical transformation might thus conceivably involve the alleviation of poverty rather than any interest in post-Westphalian forms of governance. The region has, with some exceptions, far lower standards of living than the EU. Unlike the EU, there is relatively little mobility of the factors of production and there is no single market. There is no 'Easyjet' factor of ease of mobility and leisure travel as in Europe, a pattern described by Timothy Garton-Ash, who noted:

> A British student can travel to Rome with *EasyJet* for £4.99. The bars and cafés of London are full of young Poles, working their way. These things are only possible because we have a European Union.
>
> (Garton-Ash 2005: 2)

While this may not necessarily constitute a form of European identity, there is certainly fluidity of movement among parts of the European population. Despite debate on the existence of an Asian identity (Levine 2007) it has been argued that there is no clear Asian identity and there are no Asian values (Pempel 2005). Pempel (2005: 1) argues that many Asian countries are internally divided on ethnic, linguistic or religious lines and that the region lacks agreement on national – and region-wide – cultural norms.

Yet one norm that appears to be pan-Asian, at least at the elite level, is the adherence to sovereignty. This is manifested in the non-interference principle and the long-held belief that informal approaches to consensus in ASEAN were the most appropriate to regional integration initiatives. There was little interest in the creation of supranational institutions. Arguably, in some Asian countries, state-building remains more important and pressing than the pooling of sovereignty.

The EU experience of integration is based on conflict transformation, bargaining and consensus, formal rules of negotiation and the creation and consolidation of new institutions and decision-making processes, binding legislation and the participation of actors above the nation state. There has been a pooling of sovereignty and a process known as Europeanisation. Green Cowles and Risse define Europeanisation as involving the 'evolutions of new layers of politics that interact with older ones' (2001: 217). This may refer to the transformation of the nation state and of policy domains, and, as such, Europeanisation can be juxtaposed with globalisation as a transforming influence on the state. This experience has been studied as a distinctively European experience for some, while others have sought to establish it as a yardstick against which to measure other forms of regional integration (Acharya 2006: 313), with evidence of a form of Eurocentricism.

The ASEAN process has been characterised by what came to be know as the ASEAN way, based on informality, broad consensus and the lack of binding regulation. Co-operation is based on consensus, the state remains the paramount actor and there is a reluctance to embrace supranational institutions. There is no pooling of sovereignty. There is a largely informal method of decision-making. Within the EU context, the transformations wrought by supranationalism, transnationalism and interdependence have been increasingly analysed in the context of Europeanisation, a process that finds relatively little resonance in East Asia, although patterns of dialogue and collaboration have been established over more than forty years. The embedded nature of EU institutions and of law above the state has been accompanied by the transformation of competences, authority and public policy agency in and among the major actors – the EU and the states. There are also changed policy domains and an increase in policy domains that are managed at an EU level, in contrast with ASEAN, whose EPG report presents this assessment of the ASEAN way, and the importance of increased interdependence and transformation:

Recent events such as the Asian Financial Crisis, the SARS epidemic and the Asian tsunami disaster of 2004 remind ASEAN Member States that their well-being and future are now more intertwined. This will require ASEAN Member States to calibrate their traditional approach of non-interference in areas where the common interest dictates closer co-operation. More effective decision-making processes are also necessary to deal with less sensitive issues as well as to respond to urgent crises. To build the ASEAN Community, Member States require strong political will and work together in advancing the common interest.

(ASEAN EPG 2006: 7)

Domestic and international adaptation to the European Union's transformative impact

The EU system is currently characterised by over fifty years of interstate co-operation and bargaining, with the fact that the EU affects more policies than ever before, as exclusive and mixed competences, and that it influences policy over which there is no direct EU competence. There have been improvements in the EU decision-making system, with increased efficiency and effectiveness and the spread of the use of qualified majority voting. There has been a Europeanisation of domestic politics and public administration.

There has also been a form of transnational Europeanisation, where the practices or norms of one or several member states effect and influence those of other member states. Internationally, the EU has transformed aspects of domestic adaptation to its regulations, its stances and its norms, in national government Ministries. Most of the EU's interlocutors have had to adapt to European regulations on a multilateral scale too, as government Ministries adapt to the requirements regarding exporting to the EU. They also need to adapt to the EU's negotiating style in international fora (Elgström and Strömvik 2005; Murray 2005: 92–5, 239–70).

The response of third countries, such as in Asia, to Europeanisation and to EU external relations policies remain relatively under-researched. This external aspect of Europeanisation becomes an important aspect of regional integration itself, when we see that the EU regards itself as an inter-regional actor, promoting integration in Asia, for example. Third countries are increasingly obliged to shift focus from exclusively state-to-state relations to regional bilateralism – relating to the EU as a united entity of twenty-seven member states, to representation in trade and other issues by the Commission or a presidency. They must also adapt to the EU as a negotiator in a multilateral context. The dominance of the EU as a regionally integrated bloc is in sharp contrast to the comparative disadvantage of some third countries' non-membership of a bloc. Some countries engage with the EU as a bloc as members of a regional entity, such as ASEAN, or ASEAN plus Three, as seen in the Asia–Europe Meeting (ASEM) process. They are also involved in their own process of regionalism, the subject of the next section.

Chaban *et al.* (2006)'s analysis of non-EU attitudes to the EU concludes that the EU is regarded as a key player, with a decisive impact upon negotiated outcomes, in negotiations in the economic sphere, and in environmental and aid-related arenas. Their results reveal that, in the field of security, the EU is considered to be a comparatively unimportant actor. Further, where the EU is perceived as significant, it is not necessarily characterised as a leader, due in part to perceptions of divisions and serious rifts within the EU. Their research among East Asian countries brings to light some inconsistencies among EU policies, and this inconsistency serves to diminish the EU's leadership potential.

Asian regionalism

Security concerns and the desire for peace are often as much at the basis of regional integration initiatives as the desire to increase inter-state trade and confront interdependence. This is the case with ASEAN. The Association consists of ten member states – Brunei Darussalam, Indonesia, Malaysia, the Philippines, Singapore, Thailand, Vietnam, Laos, Burma Myanmar and Cambodia. Founded in 1967 (by Indonesia, Malaysia, Singapore, the Philippines, Thailand) in response to a perceived military threat from Vietnam, in a Cold War context of fear both of communism and of domination by a neighbour, ASEAN's members had in common a mutual desire for support and for solidarity, as well as to accelerate economic growth and social progress and to bring about cultural development in region. Its chief hallmarks were its intergovernmental format and its strict adherence to the principle of non-interference in the affairs of another state.

There have been sustained criticisms that the ASEAN format was too loose and informal to deal with the challenges of globalisation and global competitiveness. This came to a height in the aftermath of the Asian Financial Crisis, when ASEAN was found wanting as a leading protagonist on behalf of the countries in difficulty (Hidetaka 2005: 212). It was at this time that there was an enlargement of co-operation, although still on a relatively informal level, to comprehend China, South Korea and Japan in the ASEAN plus Three format. Boisseau de Rocher (2006: 230) points to concerns that ASEAN had not been productive in 'initiating collective responses to the need for reform and the implementation of efficient regional mechanisms'. There was also another development that led ASEAN, Korea and Japan, to reassess their regional relationships and a possible need to engage more closely – the rise of China as an economic regional power and its 'emerging diplomatic assertiveness' (Boisseau de Rocher 2006: 230).

The ASEAN Charter (2008), which was signed by all ASEAN states, seeks to consolidate and formalise some existing practices and to bring about some level of institutionalisation that bears some resemblance to the European structure, although it is regarded as distinctively Asian in focus.

The features of institutional architecture that are worthy of note are the decision to have the ASEAN Summit meet twice yearly – it has been annual hitherto. In addition, the decision was made that the ASEAN Foreign Ministers were to serve as the ASEAN Co-ordinating Council, not unlike the EU. The Charter also provides for a 'Single Chairmanship for key high-level ASEAN bodies'. A further development is the decision to form a type of ASEAN COREPER, with the appointment of member states' Permanent Representatives to ASEAN. This Committee of Permanent Representatives is to be based in Jakarta (ASEAN 2008: Article 12). Consensus and consultation remain the key feature of the ASEAN Charter's work, as seen in the provisions regarding decision-making as follows:

1   As a basic principle, decision-making in ASEAN shall be based on consultation and consensus.
2   Where consensus cannot be achieved, the ASEAN Summit may decide how a specific decision can be made.
3   Nothing in paragraphs 1 and 2 of this Article shall affect the modes of decision-making as contained in the relevant ASEAN legal instruments.
4   In the case of a serious breach of the Charter or non-compliance, the matter shall be referred to the ASEAN Summit for decision.

(ASEAN 2008: Article 20, Chapter VII)

These developments and the reaction to the Asian Financial Crisis were closely monitored by the Europeans. The EU had responded to the rise of the Asian Tigers and to the need to address the European trade deficit with Asia with its first Asia Strategy of 1994 (CEC 1994). It had responded positively to the Singaporean initiative for an ASEM (Yeo 2008: 105–6). It also, by 2001, had developed a further Asia Strategy (EC 2001). Its engagement was based on economic imperatives primarily (Murray 2008b: 188) and on the desire to promote regionalism in East Asia.

The experience of regionalism in Europe and East Asia

It is common in much of the scholarly literature on comparative regional integration, and in particular in EU rhetoric, to refer to the EU experience as the most advanced form of regional integration in the world. The centrality of the EU as a reference point has meant that the EU has cast a long and hegemonic shadow in both integration studies and in empirical analysis. It is not unusual to find references to ASEAN's 'organisational gap' (Calder and Fukuyama 2008: 1; Calder 2008: 15) when discussing ASEAN. The observation that other regional entities – such as ASEAN – have not reached a similar stage of development to that of the EU leads to an EU dominance in some analysis. While there is no doubting the important – and distinctive – achievements of the EU, it is important to avoid comparisons that emulate one set of experiences. As Hale corrects asserts,

As Asia moves towards greater economic integration, it is tempting to make comparisons with Europe or North America, but such comparisons are of limited value because of profound historical differences.

(Hale 2008: 59)

Many scholars are aware of the difficulty of building regional co-operation. For example, Acharya suggests that:

Asia has a long way to go in developing a shared political milieu marked by shared open and transparent polities of the kind that obtain in Europe, but the trend towards openness is already evident.

(Acharya 2006: 313)

In addition there have been agreements among the ASEAN members since 1967 which reflect the nature of East Asian regional concerns and the distinctiveness of the Asian experience. These include the Zone of Peace, Freedom and Neutrality, signed in 1971 in Kuala Lumpur, which commits all ASEAN members to 'exert efforts to secure the recognition of and respect for South East Asia as a Zone of Peace, Freedom and Neutrality, free from any manner of interference by outside powers' and to 'make concerted efforts to broaden the areas of co-operation, which would contribute to their strength, solidarity and closer relationship' (ASEAN 1971: Statements 1 and 2). It is, however, careful to recognise 'the right of every state, large or small, to lead its national existence free from outside interference in its internal affairs as this interference will adversely affect its freedom, independence and integrity'. The Declaration of ASEAN Concord has a clear political component, as it clearly stated for the first time that the member countries would expand political co-operation. The concord also enunciated principles for regional stability and a programme of action for political co-operation. The ASEAN Concord of 1976 commits its members to hold summits, to settle intraregional disputes 'by peaceful means', to extradition agreements; to the promotion of the harmonisation of views and positions; and the taking of common action (ASEAN, 24 February 1976a). The Treaty of Amity and Co-operation (TAC) in South East Asia was signed in Kuala Lumpur, to which other countries could accede, enshrines four important principles: mutual respect for one another's sovereignty; non-interference in each others' internal affairs; the peaceful settlement of intraregional disputes and, finally, end effective co-operation. It also provides for a code of conduct for the peaceful settlement of disputes and mandates the establishment of a High Council made up of ministerial representatives from the parties as a dispute settlement mechanism (ASEAN, 24 February 1976b). The TAC remains the only specifically East Asian regional diplomatic instrument providing a mechanism and processes for the peaceful settlement of disputes.

In a survey[1] conducted by the author with European and Asia Pacific specialists on the EU and East Asia, scholars commented on a number of important factors relating to the Asian experience. They enumerated the lack of regional leader(s) with a mandate to generate sustainable regionalisation; the very different historical experience and different pathways to regional integration and the different circumstances in the two regions. In relation to East Asia, it was proposed by one specialist who was surveyed that the countries in East Asia 'are too disparate in political interaction and constitution'. Respondents noted that the EU's 'top-down approach', its political incentives and the important role of the 'core countries' could not replicated in Asia. There was reference to the 'uniqueness of the EU experience; differences in culture, institutions, levels of development'. One survey respondent commented that:

> European integration and the EU in particular are extremely useful as laboratories, i.e. as a means to observe processes and learn from mistakes as well as successes. However, the EU is not very successful in the generation of common values that are not shared with other Western countries at anything other than a superficial level.
>
> (Extract from survey response to author's survey on EU–Asia relations)

In comparing regionalism in East Asia and Europe, it is evident that European perceptions of Asian regionalism are not coherent. Nor is there a united view within the European Commission as to the nature and possible future development of Asian regionalism. Further, Asian views of EU integration do not necessarily comprehend the policy domain and scope, but only the economic perspective (Chaban *et al.* 2006). From an Asian perspective, the EU experience can come across as that of relative homogeneity, in terms of religion, race and historical experiences, for example (Dai 02003; Peruzzi *et al.* 2007; Tanaka 2008; von Hofmann 2007; Wong 2008; Zyla 2008). The many differences among EU member states may seem somewhat minor when perceived from Singapore, Laos or China. A further comparative element is that of the European adherence to democratic systems and to the rule of law, as well as relatively high levels of economic and social development. Finally, the EU's institutional architecture of supranational institutions based on a pooling of sovereignty also involves constant bargaining among states, often in an uneasy tension of national and European interests.

In East Asia, there is considerable heterogeneity with regard to race, ethnicity and religion. The region is also characterised by different historical experiences in different parts of East Asia, such as European colonialism or Japanese imperialism or the US role in Korea and Vietnam. These historical experiences are marked by a different discourse of memory than exists in Europe. There is no founding moment of an Asian region. There is no historic moment of reconciliation between former enemies as in Europe. There is no Schuman Declaration and no Jean Monnet. There remain territorial disputes among the nation states of East Asia. The discourse of memory (Joerges 2005) is not easily discarded, when one reflects on the power of memory on reconciliation and its justification. The fact that there remain considerable enmities, tensions and territorial disputes means that the EU approach is not as pertinent at present as some have anticipated (Pempel 2005: 1). The nation state – with its essentially Westphalian imagery even in an Asian context – remains far more important for members of ASEAN than is the sharing of sovereignty. Unlike the EU, many ASEAN nations have divested the state of Western colonialism with more recent experience of postcolonial construction and consolidation of the nation state and its institutions and legal system. The role of memory is as potent in East Asia as it is in Europe – it simply takes a different form. Camroux refers to the fact that this can also have an effect on the development on regionalism and how it is perceived:

> The brutal experience, for many at least, of Japanese-inspired Pan-Asianism's geopolitical transformation into the Greater East Asia Co-prosperity Sphere led the whole of the concept [of regionalism and regionalization] into disrepute.
>
> (Camroux 2007: 555)

A further historically important event was 11 September 2001. Responses have varied in Asia and Europe (Acharya 2006: 317) in terms of security co-operation perceptions and the role of the US as the external hegemon and hard power in the Asian region.

While historically the EU is in favour of multilateralism due to its commitment to the UN and the WTO and the promotion of its norm in those *fora*, Asia's advocacy of multilateralism is also based on its historical experience and concerns, such as a desire to preserve the existing rules of international relations, especially those that relate to sovereignty (Acharya 2006: 318). A further aspect is the historical development of Asia – its heterogeneity of religions, economies, polities and norms, in contrast with what some Asians regard as the relative homogeneity of Europe (Murray 2008a: 4–6).

Both Europe and Asia have undergone considerable transformation – and each experience has been distinctive. The Asian case, unlike the EU one elaborated above, consists of systems of democracy alongside authoritarianism and communism. There are varying levels of development, from high to extremely poor countries, and in general, the ASEAN countries are characterised by lower standards of living than Japan, Europe or the US. The philosophical, normative and ideological settings differ. In Asia, there is no common economic ideology, but rather communism and forms of capitalism. Sovereignty remains very important; there are no supranational institutions and in many cases state-building is still in progress.

The role of the state

Perhaps the most important comparative feature remains the value accorded to the state, and especially state sovereignty. The aftermath of several EU Treaties, and especially the referendums in France and the Netherlands on the Constitutional Treaty in 2005 and the more recent Irish referendum, in 2008, on the Lisbon Treaty, all point to a tenacity of national concerns about the EU. There is no widespread commitment among the EU population – nor among its leaders – to sharing of sovereignty, which is often perceived as an erosion of sovereignty. Yet it is the uneasy tension between the European interest and the nation that maintains the EU's robust and dynamic nature. While characterised by national concerns, there have been no efforts to undermine bargaining and inter-state compromise. One Asian observer has commented that 'members of the European Union seem to have been more energetic internally to defend sovereignty in each of their own countries in the process of integration' while presenting the case that sovereignty is obsolete (Pan 2004).

Historically, both ASEAN and the EU were founded at times of crisis and innovative leadership. Recently the Secretary General of ASEAN commented in terms that are not unlike those used about the EU:

> The birth of ASEAN took place on this day forty-one years ago when five wise men of ASEAN [. . .] gathered in a small village [. . .]. They had a dream – the dream of a stable, secure and prosperous South East Asia. Our five wise men gave us a path to the future. [. . .] ASEAN is essentially a Tapestry of Hope. We are all engaged in weaving it into a robust architecture that will reflect our aspirations for the future of our region and a better life for our posterity.
>
> (Pitsuwan 2008)

Rhetoric such as this indicates a level of myth-building about ASEAN that is common in nation formation, and has also been seen in the EU.

The main historical aspect of the development of regional integration in the two regions relates to the role of hegemons – the role of an external state with significant influence on the development of integration. Unlike Asia, the EU had the support of the US for its integration project. A US-focused hub-and-spoke approach still pertains in contemporary Asia – effectively a major brake on potential region co-operation (Beeson 2005: 977).

Interregionalism of Europe and East Asia

The EU does not punch at or above its weight in East Asia, despite its economic clout and weight there (Murray *et al.* 2008). Apart from the economic context, the EU exerts relatively limited influence in that region, in terms of norms and governance. It is, arguably, hampered in achieving a more coherent approach by the very factors of transformation that render it an effective regional actor within its own region – namely the multi-actor nature of the EU process; the multi-level processes of governance and policy-making and the internal variations among the EU policy communities. The first Asia Strategy of the EU (CEC 1994) was motivated by an EU interest in dealing with regional units such as ASEAN; to redress its trade deficit with Asia and to increase its global presence in terms of foreign policy, trade and the euro. There was a desire to engage with and develop closer links with Asia in economic, political dialogue, security, human rights and educational co-operation. This strategy's drive towards a 'partnership of equals' was revised throughout the 1990s, due to a number of factors. These include the EU's continuing lack of economic visibility; the rise of China; the implications of the end of the Cold War and new opportunities for increased trade, particularly in the light of the East Asian rapid economic growth. There was concern that the EU was not perceived as a global actor in Asia and an interest in improving relations with ASEAN and to deal with the evolving, post-Cold War strategic situation, geopolitical alliances and the aftermath of the 1997 Asian Financial crisis. The 2001 Asia Strategy (EC 2001) was designed to strengthen the EU's presence in Asia and to reflect the enlarged EU's growing global weight. The key dimensions of this approach were, first, to strengthen the EU's political and security engagement; second, to strengthen two-way trade, investment relations; third to reduce poverty; fourth, to promote democracy, good governance, rule of law; fifth, to build global partnerships with key partners and, finally, to promote further awareness between the two regions. Recent assessments of this strategy (Cameron 2008; Murray 2008c) have concluded that the strategy has not been fully effective or successful. Cameron concludes that:

> While Asia has succeeded in making some headway with regional co-operation, the EU has been struggling to adapt its approach. [...] It has not really clarified its interests in the region, how they should be prioritized and what means the EU should use to promote them. Overall there is an absence of a strategic vision for the region as a whole. There has also been little attempt to assess the effectiveness of particular policies, whether sanctions against Myanmar, or conditionality and development assistance.
>
> (Cameron 2008: 19–20)

Cameron (2008: 20) has suggested that 'a new overarching Asia strategy could be an indispensable instrument to enhance policy coherence, promote the image of the EU as a strategic player in the entire region, and ensure its own interests and expectations are clearly defined'. The relationship of the two regions require further analysis and examination by the EU and Asian actors and scholars alike.

Conclusion

This chapter has examined the role of transformation in regional integration. It has illustrated that the ASEAN charter, like the Asian Financial Crisis and the rise of the Asian economies in 1990s all constitute transformation, both within the Asian region and among the member states, as they have increased co-operation and even signed the ASEAN Charter. Like Europe, Asia had been confronted with challenges, although of a different kind from those in Europe, such as the Financial Crisis, the SARS epidemic and the devastation of the tsunami – all considerable challenges of hardship. The East Asian region is being transformed even as it is transforming its structures and means of co-operation – and so too is the EU. This is a very exciting time for both regions, which also need to consider the challenges ahead, whether in multilateralism or regional catastrophes or constitutional and legitimacy problems. This chapter suggests that there remains a need to understand the responses to transformation and to each others' problems, as well as the transformation of the state and its actors.

There is little doubt about the transformative role of integration in both Europe and East Asia. Regionalism in each region has been spurred by external transformative developments and by distinctive events. Regionalism, in turn, has brought about transformations of the structure and architecture of the two regions. The future development of both regions will be one that features a key element of interregionalism, as each comes to terms with the other. It is not simply sovereignty or the role of the state that will be the focus of future research, but also the development and transformation of societal norms and values, the sharing of benefits and the social, economic and political interaction of states and their populace.

Note

1 A survey questionnaire designed to gather information on how academic experts perceive the EU–Asia relationship was administered in 2006–07 to academic experts in Europe and the Asia Pacific (based in East Asia, Australia and New Zealand). The survey constitutes an attempt to redress the lack of data on elite perceptions regarding EU–East Asia relations.

References

Acharya, A. (2006) 'Europe and Asia: reflections on a tale of two regionalisms', in B. Fort and D. Webber (eds) *Regional Integration in East Asia and Europe: Convergence or Divergence?* London and New York: Routledge.

ASEAN (27 November 1971) 'Zone of Peace, Freedom and Neutrality Declaration', Malaysia. Online. Available: www.aseansec.org/1215.htm (accessed 12 September 2008).

—— (24 February 1976a) 'Declaration of ASEAN Concord', Indonesia. Online. Available: www.aseansec.org/1216.htm (accessed 12 September 2008).

—— (24 February 1976b) 'Treaty of Amity and Co-operation in South East Asia', Bali. Online. Available: www.aseansec.org/TAC-KnowledgeKit.pdf (accessed 19 December 2008).

—— (January 2008) 'The ASEAN Charter', Jakarta: ASEAN Secretariat. Online. Available: www.aseansec.org/ASEAN-Charter.pdf (accessed 19 December 2008).

ASEAN EPG (December 2006) 'Report of the Eminent Persons Group on the ASEAN Charter'. Online. Available: www.aseansec.org/19247.pdf (accessed 19 December 2008).

Beeson, M. (2005) 'Rethinking regionalism: Europe and East Asia in comparative perspective', *Journal of European Public Policy* 12 (5): 969–85.

Boisseau du Rocher, S. (2006) 'ASEAN and Northeast Asia: stakes and implications for the European Union–ASEAN partnership', *Europe Asia Journal* 4: 229–49.

Calder, K. E. (2008) 'Critical junctures and the contours of Northeast Asian regionalism', in K. E. Calder and F. Fukuyama (eds) *East Asian Multilateralism: Prospects for Regional Stability*, Baltimore, MD: Johns Hopkins University Press.

Calder, K. E. and Fukuyama, F. (2008) 'Introduction', in K. E. Calder and F. Fukuyama (eds) *East Asian Multilateralism: Prospects for Regional Stability*, Baltimore, MD: Johns Hopkins University Press.

Cameron, F. (2008) 'The EU and Asia: an Assessment of EU Policy since 2001', paper presented to International Conference on 'EU–Asia Relations: a Critical Review' at the Contemporary Europe Research Centre, University of Melbourne, 27–28 March. Online. Available: www.cerc.unimelb.edu.au/jean-monnet/EAR-Abstracts-Bios.pdf (accessed 12 September 2008).

Camroux, D. (2007) 'Asia ... whose Asia? A "return to the future" of a Sino-Indic Asian community', *Pacific Review* 20 (4): 551–75.

CEC (1994) 'Towards a New Asia Strategy: Communication of the Commission to the Council', Com (94) 314 final, 13 July 1994, Brussels.

Chaban, N., Elgström, O. and Holland, M. (2006) 'The European Union as others see it', *European Foreign Affairs Review* 11: 245–62.

Chinese Ministry of Foreign Affairs (2003) 'China's EU Policy Paper', October. Online. Available: www.mfa.gov.cn/eng/zxxx/t27708.htm (accessed 19 August 2008).

Cowles, M. and Risse, T. (2001) *Transforming Europe: Europeanization and Domestic Change*, Ithaca, NY: Cornell University Press.

Dai, B. (2003) 'EU's role in the post-Cold War period and future of Asia–Europe relations: an Asian perspective', *Asia-Pacific Journal of EU Studies* 1 (1): 83–100.

Elgström, O. and Strömvik, M. (2005) 'The European Union as an international negotiator', in O. Elgström and C. Jönsson (eds), *European Union Negotiations: Processes, Networks and Institutions*, New York: Routledge.

European Commission (2001) 'Europe and Asia: a Strategic Framework for Enhanced Partnerships. Communication from the Commission', Com (2001) 469 Final, Brussels, 4 September. Online. Available: http://eur-lex.europa.eu/LexUriServ/LexUriServ.do?uri=COM:2001:0469:FIN:EN:PDF (accessed 17 November 2006).

—— (2008) 'European Regional Programmes in Asia', Brussels: EuropeAid. Online. Available: www.delvnm.ec.europa.eu/eu_vn_relations/development_co-o/booklet_asia_2008.pdf (accessed 12 September 2008).

Garton-Ash, T. (2005) 'The birth of Europe: our challenge to the anti-Europeans is: where's your story of the future?' *Guardian*, 17 March. Online Available: http://politics.guardian.co.uk/eu/comment/0,9236,1439705,00.html (accessed 15 May 2005).

Green Cowles, M., Caporaso, J. and Risse, T. (eds) (2001) *Transforming Europe*, Ithaca, NY and London: Cornell University Press.

Green Cowles, M. and Risse, T. (2001) 'Transforming Europe: conclusions', in M. Green Cowles, J. Caporaso and T. Risse (eds) *Transforming Europe*, Ithaca, NY and London: Cornell University Press.

Hale, D. (2008) 'The outlook for economic integration in East Asia', in K. E. Calder and F. Fukuyama (eds) *East Asian Multilateralism: Prospects for Regional Stability*, Baltimore, MD: Johns Hopkins University Press.

Hidetaka, Y. (2005) 'Political leadership, informality, and regional integration in East Asia: the evolution of ASEAN Plus Three', *European Journal of East Asian Studies* 4 (2): 205–32.

Hyde-Price, A. (2006) 'Normative power Europe: a realist critique', *Journal of European Public Policy* 13 (2): 217–34.

Jachtenfuchs, M. (2001) 'The governance approach to European integration', *Journal of Common Market Studies* 39 (2): 245–64.

Joerges, C. (2005) 'Introduction to the special issue. Confronting memories: European "bitter experiences" and the constitutionalization process', *German Law Journal* 6 (2): 245–54.

Levine, S. (2007) 'Asian values and the Asia Pacific Community: shared interests and common concerns', *Politics and Policy* 3 (1): 102–35.

Manners, I. (2002) 'Normative power Europe: a contradiction in terms?', *Journal of Common Market Studies*, 40, 2: 235–259.

—— (2006) 'Normative power Europe reconsidered: beyond the crossroads', *Journal of European Public Policy* 13 (2): 182–99.

Murray, P. (2005) *Australia and the European Superpower: Engaging with the European Union*, Melbourne: Melbourne University Press.

—— (2008a) 'Introduction. Europe and Asia: two regions in flux?' in P. Murray (ed.) *Europe and Asia: Regions in Flux*, Basingstoke: Palgrave.

—— (2008b) 'Contemporary European perspectives on East Asia and EU–Asia relations', in P. Murray (ed.) *Europe and Asia: Regions in Flux*, Basingstoke: Palgrave.

—— (2008c) 'How Europe looks at Asia: between Expectations and Capabilities', paper presented to the international conference on 'EU–Asia Relations: a Critical Review' at the Contemporary Europe Research Centre, University of Melbourne, 27–28 March. Online. Available: www.cerc.unimelb.edu.au/jean-monnet/EAR-Abstracts-Bios.pdf (accessed 12 September 2008).

Murray, P., Berryman, A. and Matera, M. (2008) 'Coherence, Effectiveness and Recognition in EU–East Asia Relations', paper presented to 'EU–Asia Relations: a Policy Review Workshop', jointly hosted by the Contemporary Europe Research Centre, University of Melbourne, and the European Institute of Asian Studies, Brussels, 10 July. Online. Available: www.cerc.unimelb.edu.au/jean-monnet/EAR-Brussels-Wkshop-Prog-4July08.pdf (accessed 12 September 2008).

Pan, Z. (2004) 'What can the Asia–Pacific learn from the European integration?' Konrad-Adenauer Stiftung Online Info-Service, vol. 4/2004. Online. Available: http:/www.kas.de/proj/home/pub/37/2/year-2004/document_id-512 (accessed 27 June 2008).

Pempel, T. J. (2005) 'Emerging webs of regional connectedness', in T. J. Pempel (ed.) *Remapping East Asia: the Construction of a Region*, Ithaca, NY: Cornell University Press, pp. 1–28.

Peruzzi, P., Poletti, A. and Zhang, S. (2007) 'China's view of Europe: a maturing partnership', *European Foreign Affairs Review* 12 (3): 311–30.

Pitsuwan, S. (8 August 2008) 'Speech at the Flag Hoisting Ceremony to Commemorate ASEAN 41st Anniversary', ASEAN Secretariat. Online. Available: www. asean.org/21846.htm (accessed 12 September 2008).

Radaelli, C. M. (2004) 'Europeanisation: Solution or problem?' European Integration online Papers (EIoP), 8 (16). Online. Available: http://eiop.or.at/eiop/texte/2004–016a.htm (accessed 12 September 2008).

Sjursen, H. (2006) 'The EU as a normative power: how can this be?' *Journal of European Public Policy* 13 (2): 235–51.

Tanaka, T. (2008) 'Asian perspectives on European integration', in P. Murray (ed.) *Europe and Asia: Regions in Flux*, Basingstoke: Palgrave.

Von Hofmann, N. (2007) 'How do Asians evaluate Europe's strategic involvement in East Asia?' *Asia Europe Journal* 5 (2): 187–92.

Wong, R. (2008) 'Towards a common European policy on China? Economic, diplomatic and human rights trends since 1985', *Current Politics and Economics of Asia* 17 (1): 155–82.

Yeo, L. H. (2008) 'The origins and development of ASEM and EU–East Asia relations', in P. Murray (ed.) *Europe and Asia: Regions in Flux*, Basingstoke: Palgrave.

Zyla, B. (2008) 'Riding the Asian tiger? How the EU engaged China since the end of the Cold War', *Current Politics and Economics of Asia* 17 (1): 83–105.

10 European energy security

Central Asia and the Caspian region

Martin Malek

Energy security, in terms of secure supply and stable prices, is increasingly related to geopolitics and international relations. This has to be taken into consideration by the European Union (EU) with the world's second largest energy market, with 500 million consumers, as crucial players like the Organisation of the Petroleum Exporting Countries (OPEC), the US, Russia, China, India and others are more or less determined by geopolitical reasons.

The European Commission addressed energy security in its first Green book of November 2000, but in the EU's security strategy of 2003, 'A Secure Europe in a Better World', only a brief paragraph is devoted to this topic. The energy disputes of early January 2006, when Russia cut off gas supplies to Ukraine (which is the main transit country for Russian gas heading for Europe), of early 2007 with Belarus due to a price and transit fee conflict and of January 2009, when Moscow halted gas deliveries to Ukraine and then even shut down the gas pipeline through that country, demonstrated Europe's vulnerability in its dependence on Russian gas to the broader public. These incidents have illustrated the EU's diminishing power as consumer amid high energy and resource prices and especially its weakness in view of an increasingly assertive Russia. Its role has to be scrutinised in this article for two reasons. Firstly, it is the main actor which the EU has to deal with on the rules of the game in the Central Asia and the Caspian Region (CACR), meaning the post-Soviet republics Georgia, Armenia, Azerbaijan, Kazakhstan, Turkmenistan, Uzbekistan, Kyrgyzstan and Tajikistan. And, secondly, most of the projections of energy consumption indicate that one of the most important energy security challenges facing the EU over the next two decades will be its ability to diversify the sources and modes of transit of its energy imports.

Although the EU's twenty-seven member states have ceded some national sovereignty (or competence) to EU institutions in a variety of areas, including economic and trade policy, energy policy remains primarily the responsibility of the member states. However, a fragmented and fractured regional energy market is – and will also be in the future – the best playing field for Russia to 'divide and rule' the individual EU member states and their energy companies. As a German energy expert puts it, 'the still existing lack of coherence of the EU's external energy policy enables Russia to continue the "bilateralisation" of energy partnerships'. According to him, Russia 'is in a powerful position to play off individual European states and their national energy champions against each other' (Umbach 2008). Thus several member states have pursued bilateral energy deals with Russia which will increase their and EU's dependence on Moscow for many years to come. Examples are the North European Gas Pipeline on the sea bed between Vyborg, Russia, and Greifswald, Germany, and the oil pipeline from Bulgaria's Black Sea port of Burgas to Alexandropolis in northern Greece (therefore, entirely on EU territory).

From 1999 (accidentally the year of Vladimir Putin's unexpected rise to power in Russia) oil and gas prices rose steadily until mid-2008. That way Russia acquired a strong position to dictate many conditions to its European consumers, not only in terms of pricing issues for natural gas, but also its interest in acquiring distribution networks and downstream assets. In 2007 Gazprom, Russia's monopoly supplier of natural gas, already had a presence in seventeen EU countries in various forms, either as joint ventures or subsidiaries.

The European Union's present and future oil and gas import dependence

Some general assumptions

In 2005 the EU-27 faced a total energy dependence of 52.3 per cent (1995, 43.3 per cent), which meant that more than a half EU energy consumption was imported. Cyprus, Malta, Luxembourg, Ireland, Portugal, Italy, and Spain face especially high (more than 80 per cent) dependence. There is no serious research denying that EU's total energy economy will become increasingly reliant on energy imports, reaching 64 per cent in 2020 and 67 per cent in 2030 in business as usual projections. The EU Commission has proved its awareness that the interdependence of EU member states in energy is increasing, as is the risk of supply failures and vulnerability.

In 2005 oil and gas together accounted for 56.4 per cent of the EU's total energy mix (solid fuels 17.6, nuclear 14.2 and renewables 6.6 per cent) (Belkin 2008: 6). Due to the environmental obligations of the Kyoto Protocol, the phasing-out nuclear energy programmes in several important EU member states and increasing depletion of oil and gas fields in the North Sea until 2020 (when even the Netherlands will turn into a net gas importer) the EU will become much more dependent on oil and particularly gas imports from outside Europe – mostly from unstable countries in the Middle East, Central Asia and Africa.

The situation is getting even more complicated since the EU, as the European Commission's Green Paper from November 2000 puts it, has 'very limited scope' to influence energy supply conditions. This especially applies

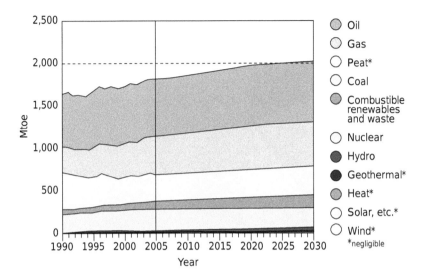

Figure 10.1 Total primary energy supplies of the EU, 1990–2030 (toe million). *Mtoe* million toe; *toe* tonne of oil equivalent, or 107 kcal, or 41.86 GJ (source: International Energy Agency (2008: 19). Reproduced by permission of the OECD/IEA).

to Russia. Notwithstanding official declarations, there is no real 'strategic partnership' between Brussels and Moscow in the sphere of energy politics. *De facto* the EU is powerless to persuade Russia to bend to treaty-backed disciplines Moscow sees as detrimental to its national interests. This has been displayed on numerous occasions. One of them is the fate of the Energy Charter Declaration, an initiative intended to promote energy co-operation and diversify Europe's energy supply. Moscow has not ratified the Energy Charter Treaty, because it would entail the obligation to implement the principles of freedom of transit without distinction of the origin, destination or ownership of the energy, and of non-discriminatory pricing. Another initiative, the Energy Dialogue EU–Russia (launched in October 2000) has so far not produced any tangible results. And the Interstate Oil and Gas Transport to Europe (INOGATE) initiative, whose purpose is to tie the resources of the CACR to European markets, has been joined by all countries of this region while being boycotted by Moscow.

Oil supplies

In 2005 the EU's energy dependence rate for oil amounted to 82.2 per cent (compared with 74.4 in 1995). In 2006, oil and petroleum products covered 37 per cent of the EU-27 primary energy demand of 1.825 million toe. As of the end 2007, EU countries possessed only 0.5 per cent of the proved

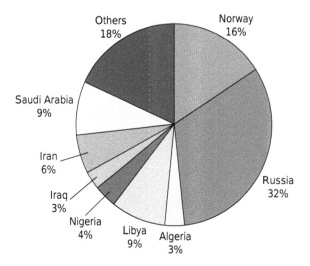

Figure 10.2 EU-27 imports of crude oil, 2006 (%) (source: Commission of the European Communities (2008: 5)).

world oil reserves. Therefore, the Union is highly dependent on imported oil. And given business as usual the EU's reliance on imports of oil will rise to 93 per cent in 2030.

Gas supplies

As of the end 2007, EU countries had only 1.6 per cent of the proved world gas reserves at their disposal. The UK and the Netherlands together account for three-quarters of total EU gas production. But output from both countries is decreasing, and this is driving a general decline in indigenous EU production. Considerable gas discoveries are sometimes made in the EU, but given the projected increase in gas consumption, it is not likely that they will affect the fundamental position of increasing gas dependence of the EU in the foreseeable future.

Over the past four decades, EU's natural gas consumption has grown much faster than primary energy consumption. In 2005 the EU-27 energy dependence rate for natural gas was 57.7 per cent (an increase of 14.1 points compared with 1995). In 2007 the EU imported 300 billion m^3 of gas, accounting for 60 per cent of the consumption. In 2006, the EU 27 imported 42 per cent of its gas (about 130 billion m^3, exclusively through pipelines) from Russia, 24.2 per cent from Norway, and 18.2 per cent from Algeria.

In the western EU markets are large but diversified. In the eastern parts of the Union the markets are smaller but much more dependent on Russia – sometimes close to 100 per cent. Six of the ten new member states in Central

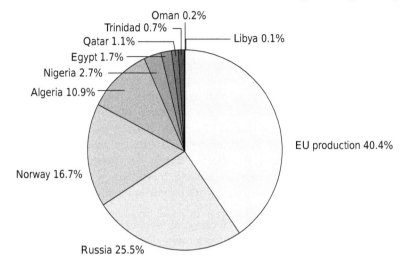

Figure 10.3 Structure of EU gas supplies, 2006 (%) (source: Noël (2008: 4). Reproduced with the permission of the European Council of Foreign Relations).

and Eastern Europe import more than 80 per cent of their gas supply from Russia. The 'old' fifteen member states (EU-15) account for 86 per cent of EU gas consumption. The size of the western European markets means that slightly more than two-thirds of Russian gas consumed in Europe is imported by the EU-15, despite their lesser dependence on Moscow.

EU's reliance on gas imports could increase to 84 per cent by 2030, and the European Commission estimates that the Russian share will climb to 60 per cent of total import. In absolute numbers, the forecast level of Russian gas exports to European countries in 2030 ranges between 210 and 225 billion m^3 per annum. Some sources are even afraid of a risk for the EU becoming so dependent on supplies of energy from Moscow that it constrains EU head of states from criticising any failings in the development of Russian democracy, human rights and freedom of the press.

Foundations of Russia's 'energy foreign policy'

In the 1990s Russia generally emphasised its intention not to deteriorate to the level of a 'raw material appendage to the West'. Then, however – and especially in Putin's second term in office (i.e. since 2004) – Russia has begun to make a virtue of necessity. According to the will of the leadership in Moscow, Russia's new claims of being a superpower and global player should not only rely on ostentatiously drawing attention to the military potential, but also on the – unofficial – concept of an 'energy superpower': Russia wants to turn as many nations as possible inside and outside the Commonwealth of Independent States (CIS) into customers of its oil and gas industry, buy shares of companies supplying energy inside and outside the CIS and control the supply chain up to the end users. Other CIS republics rich in natural resources, such as Azerbaijan, Turkmenistan, Kazakhstan and Uzbekistan, should, according to Moscow's wishes, export their energy exclusively via pipelines running across Russian territory. This entails transit charges and makes both supplier as well as importing countries dependent on the Kremlin, which could easily cut off these pipelines (or at least threaten to do so) whenever required. Another driving force of Moscow's 'pipeline policy' is the desire to decrease dependence on transit states like Ukraine, Belarus, Poland and the Baltic states. All these measures are designed to make as many countries as possible dependent on Russian energy suppliers, which under particular framework conditions could be turned into political dependencies.

The repeated claims of numerous Russian as well as Western politicians, media and pundits that Russia is an 'extremely reliable supplier of energy' are debatable for other reasons as well. According to the Defence Research Agency in Stockholm, there have been at least fifty-five cases (cut-offs, explicit threats, coercive price policy and certain take-overs) when Moscow actively used the 'energy tool' against other states between 1991 and 2006. Only eleven occurred without any political underpinning (Larsson 2007: 80–1). Moscow has obviously long since begun making policy not only with the *prices* of gas and oil but also with the *supply* of these energy sources *as such*. Senior officials (starting with Putin) warned Brussels of alternatives to Russian suppliers as well as of creating alleged or real barriers to Russian companies trying to expand in European markets, which could prompt Russia to orient itself towards East Asian markets. European media outlets quoted Gazprom chief executive officer Alexei Miller saying that 'attempts' to limit his company's 'activities in the European market and to politicise questions of gas supplies, which are in fact entirely within the economic sphere, will not produce good results' (BBC 2006).

Not only former German Chancellor Gerhard Schroeder but also many other influential voices in Western Europe turned against even cautious criticism by European politicians as well as European media of Putin's increasingly nationalistic rule or his war in Chechnya, as it would be counterproductive, given the necessity of being supplied with Russian energy sources. At the same time – and occasionally the same voices – deny a 'unilateral dependence' of the EU on Russia and claim 'mutual dependence', as Moscow is said to depend on its revenues from exports to the EU and rerouting the oil and gas flow to East Asia would be impossible at short notice, due to insufficient pipeline capacities. Though the latter is undeniable, it does not answer the question why the Kremlin's self-confidence seemed to be steadily rising with the gas prices, while the EU heads of states and governments – also and especially at meetings with Putin – gave the impression of being undecided, intimidated or, at any rate, divided. The truth is that there is no symmetrical 'mutual dependence' between the EU and Russia: The EU is, of course, an important customer for Moscow, but 'while Russia could easily shut down its pipelines to Europe for a few days, [...] Europe cannot do without Russian energy even in the very short-run' (Erixon 2008: 8).

What some European Foreign Ministries are striving for, namely a 'rapprochement through entwinement' (*Annäherung durch Verflechtung*, as the German Foreign Ministry puts it), also and particularly with regard to energy, implies a logic which is far removed from the present behaviour and mentality of Russia's elite and, furthermore, ignores the principle question about the desirability of an 'entwinement' of a union of democratic states (as the EU claims to be) and Russia, a country ruled by an increasingly authoritarian regime and whose economy is listed in international ratings as highly corrupt.

As mentioned above, Russia's strategic goals in the sphere of energy policy are also geopolitically motivated. Foreign Minister Sergei Lavrov drew a connection between Russia's energy policy and the creation of a 'multipolar world': 'The emergence of new, global centres of influence and growth and a more even distribution of resources for the development and control of natural resources form the material basis for a multipolar world order' (Lavrov 2007). This is why Gazprom, one of the world's largest energy companies, plays a key role in Russia's 'new energy foreign policy' (Lindner 2007: 1), also beyond the borders of the former Soviet Union. Russian media outlets sometimes compare the international importance of Gazprom with Russia's nuclear weapons arsenal. As a matter of fact, Gazprom and Rosneft, Russia's leading oil extraction and refinement company, are no independent market-oriented suppliers but political actors in the hands of the Kremlin. High prices for crude oil and natural gas not only help the Russian budget, which in 2006, according to the Ministry of Finance, got 52.2 per cent of its revenues from export of these two energy sources, but also those pro-Kremlin business elites which produce and sell them.

Gazprom's export potential

Gazprom holds 25 per cent of the global gas reserves and produces 94 per cent of Russia's gas and 16 per cent of the global output. Production from the three 'super-giant' west Siberian gas fields (Urengoy, Yamburg and Medvezhe) in the Nadym–Pur–Taz region (NPTR), which account for the bulk of Gazprom's output, is now in decline, while the fourth giant field, Zapolyarnoe, is at its peak. The company's ability to maintain, let alone increase, production in the coming decades depends on the development of a new generation of truly gigantic fields – Yamal in north-western Siberia or the offshore Shtokman. Either is likely to cost something like $50 billion, and the development will take about a decade. Gazprom's official line initially was that Yamal will come on stream in 2011. But independent analysts and most of the European gas industry analysts consider this highly unlikely. Some mention 2015 as a more realistic date for Yamal's completion. And Shtokman is now generally expected to start commercial production after 2015 (possibly nearer 2020), instead of 2013 as initially declared. If Russia's future gas production hinges on either of these fields, it is likely to decline after 2010. Moreover, the required investment is so large that Gazprom might be forced to choose one of the two projects, probably Yamal, as it is technologically easier. To the extent that Gazprom does not move towards rapid, large-scale development of the Yamal Peninsula, it has to consider other options, among them increased imports from Central Asian countries. Therefore Gazprom has aggressively sought to channel as much gas as possible from this region through its transit systems. But nevertheless, Gazprom's production is already insufficient to meet all the company's commitments, and it is still quite clear that Russia alone cannot meet the forecasted EU's natural gas demand until 2030.

Russia and oil and gas cartels

There are some signs of a Russian rapprochement with OPEC. In September 2008 Moscow stepped up its contacts with the cartel when Deputy Prime Minister Igor Sechin, a political hard-liner who is also chairman of Rosneft's

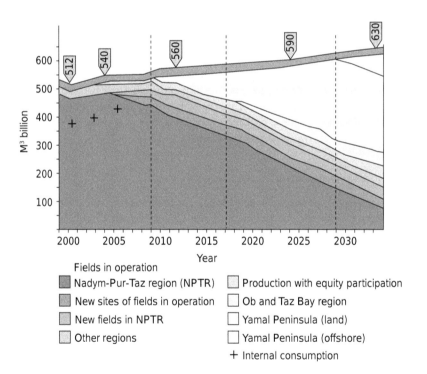

Figure 10.4 Gazprom's gas output, 2000–35 (m³ billion) (source: Noël (2008: 6). Reproduced with the permission of the European Council of Foreign Relations).

board of directors, led a delegation of government Ministers and oil company chief executive officers to the hundred and forty-ninth meeting of OPEC in the Austrian capital, Vienna. And later that month Energy Minister Sergei Shmatko said that Russia will work to influence global oil prices, meaning, obviously, that it will do anything it can to push them as high as possible.

The Kremlin is also seeking greater influence over alternative gas supplies to Europe from Algeria and Libya. And Russia's emerging co-operation with Iran (which has the world's second largest gas reserves but is a relatively minor exporter so far) and Qatar, which together account for about 57 per cent of the world's natural gas reserves, indicates how Moscow strives to control also south-eastern gas inlets to Europe. On 21 October 2008, the three countries agreed to the creation of a semi-cartel known as the 'Gas Troika'.

In Russia, the likelihood of establishing a genuine gas cartel is judged in various ways, but one thing was largely agreed upon, namely that a possible 'gas OPEC' would have great (global) political weight. Such a cartel would, from Moscow's point of view, strengthen Russia's geopolitical position *vis-à-vis* the EU as well as 'refractory' CIS states such as Ukraine and Georgia.

The oil and gas resources of the CACR

From EU's perspective, the oil and gas resources of the CACR have the advantage that they are neither Arabic nor Iranian, Russian or OPEC. Most of the estimates of the CACR's proven oil reserves range between forty and fifty billion barrels. Production levels in 2005 were estimated to be around two million barrels per day. In terms of natural gas, Turkmenistan holds the most significant deposits, but Kazakhstan and Azerbaijan (mainly oil producing countries) and Uzbekistan have some reserves as well. So the importance of the CACR for an energy thirsty world and Europe in particular is hard to overestimate.

Table 10.1 Oil and gas in the CACR

Country	Oil (billion barrels)		Natural Gas (trillion ft³)	
	BP statistical review, year-end 2007	Oil and Gas Journal, 1 January 2008	BP statistical review, year-end 2007	Oil and Gas Journal, 1 January 2008
Russia	79.432	60.000	1,576.753	1,680.000
Azerbaijan	7.000	7.000	45.132	30.000
Kazakhstan	39.828	30.000	67. 203	100.000
Turkmenistan	0.6	0.6	94.216	100.000
Uzbekistan	0.594	0.594	61.603	65.000
World	1,237.876	1,331.698	6,257.780	6,185.694

Source: Energy Information Administration 2008.

European and Russian interests in energy corridors and pipeline routes

Viewpoint and interests of the European Union

The bulk of the world's energy resources, located in Russia, the CACR, the Middle East and North Africa, are all well within geographical reach of the EU: 80 per cent of world natural gas supplies are located within a radius of 4,500 km from Central Europe. The CACR's massive potential as an energy supplier is mirrored by the document 'The EU and Central Asia: Strategy for a New Partnership', adopted in 2007: 'The development of resources in oil and gas has significantly increased the role of Central Asian states as energy producers and transit countries. Increasing oil and gas exploitation will contribute to better world market supplies and will be conducive to diversification. Gas deliveries from the region are of special importance to the EU' (Council of the EU 2007).

However, nearly two decades after the collapse of the Soviet Union there are still only a few routes for bringing energy resources from the region to Europe. EU documents point to the facts that, 'due to the landlocked nature of the Caspian areas, its reserves are not easily accessible and transportation of crude to the international market will require construction of new oil pipeline(s) as the Turkish straits and the Baku–Tbilisi–Ceyhan will not be able to transit the future additional oil. If such pipelines are not built, Caspian oil-producing countries will look for alternatives oil routes, for example towards eastern markets' (Commission of the EU 2008b: 15). In November 2008 the European Commission unveiled a long-term, multidimensional programme for energy security, which includes the 'development of a Southern Gas Corridor for supply from Caspian and Middle Eastern sources and possibly other countries in the longer term, improving security of supply' (Commission of the EU 2008a).

Viewpoint and interests of Russia

Numerous statements by Russian officials as well as Moscow's actions do not leave any doubt that it aspires to expand its political, economic, and military presence in the strategically vital CACR. One of the most important objectives of the Kremlin in the CACR is the exclusion of the US, NATO and the EU to the highest possible extent. For this and other purposes, Russia tried to capitalise on the numerous conflicts on the southern periphery of the former Soviet Union, especially in Moldova (Dnestr region), Georgia (Abkhazia, South Ossetia), Azerbaijan (Nagorno-Karabakh), and Tajikistan (civil war 1992–97) in order to retain its influence. The EU's passive stance played into Moscow's hands (Malek 2008).

While the Central Asian states are continuously being underpaid for their gas, Europe is forced to pay a price far above what would be the case if energy was imported directly from the region. For instance, in the early 2000s Russia bought gas from Turkmenistan at the price of $57 per 1,000 m^3. This gas was then consumed domestically while Russian gas was exported to Europe at a price of $250 per 1,000 m^3. Therefore 'it is no wonder that Russia uses all means necessary to block Europe from engaging directly with the Central Asian states, primarily Kazakhstan and Turkmenistan' (Norling 2007: 10).

Pipelines and transport corridors bypassing Russia

The Baku–Tbilisi–Ceyhan (BTC) oil pipeline would never have happened without strong US support, because the EU did not actively lobby for it (obviously, in order not to 'offend' Russia). Since 2006 it has connected Azerbaijan's capital Baku and the Turkish Mediterranean deep-water port of Ceyhan, from where tankers carry light Azerbaijani crude oil to European refineries. It avoids Russian as well as Iranian territory and the congestion in the Bosporus and therefore provides greater and easier access to world energy markets. Moscow tried for several years to thwart the construction of BTC, anticipating that it would lead to the loss of its monopoly on the transportation of west Caspian oil.

Today, Kazakh oil is primarily exported via a pipeline from the Tengiz oilfield to the Russian Black Sea port of Novorissiysk, which was opened in 2001. In December 2007 Russia, Kazakhstan and Turkmenistan signed an agreement to build a natural gas pipeline along the Caspian Sea coast that would strengthen Moscow's monopoly of energy exports from the region. This was a heavy blow to Western hopes of securing alternative energy export routes. Therefore it was not astonishing that Russian politicians, businessmen and media trumpeted an 'important victory against the West' in what they consider a 'New Great game' over CACR's energy resources.

However, two transportation lines for Kazakh oil bypassing Russian territory are already operational. Both start at the port of Aktau, from where the oil is shipped by small-capacity tankers to Azerbaijan. Azerbaijani and Georgian railroads carry it to the terminals of Batumi, Poti and Kulevi on the Black Sea coast. And since the last week of October 2008 Kazakh crude oil has been injected into the BTC pipeline at the Sangachal terminal near Baku (Guliyev and Akhrarkhodjaeva 2008).

But a better alternative to the current Russian-controlled pipelines would be a trans-Caspian pipeline link, which would inaugurate the possibility of connecting Kazakh and Turkmen oil and/or gas directly to European and world markets. Improved access to the BTC would provide Kazakhstan with a much needed new export route, which would be of special importance in the light of Astana's plans to triple its oil production by the year 2030. This additional Kazakh oil could contribute to the diversification of the global and EU oil supply portfolio avoiding excessive dependence on a restricted number of suppliers.

For everybody but Moscow it would be advantageous to build a trans-Caspian pipeline. Due to fierce Russian resistance this is more a political than a technical challenge. The EU would benefit in a threefold way from such a direct pipeline link to Central Asian gas exporters. First, it would be able to buy gas at a lower price than the levels currently set by Russia. In any case, gas can be brought through new pipelines from Turkmenistan across the Caspian Sea at a lower cost than new Russian fields in Siberia or in the Arctic. Secondly, by diversifying its sources and transit routes, the EU would reduce its dependence on Russian energy. And finally, the Union 'would break the neo-colonial dependency situation to Gazprom that Central Asian producers are locked into' (Cornell *et al.* 2006: 21–2).

As far as Azerbaijan is concerned, Russia's monopoly over gas exports is threatened by the South Caucasus Gas Pipeline (SCGP) or Baku–Tbilisi–Erzurum (BTE) pipeline, which flows in parallel to the BTC pipeline as far as the Turkish town Erzurum and since 2006 delivers gas from the Azerbaijani Shah–Deniz field to Turkey. In a longer perspective, the SCGP could supply Europe with Caspian natural gas through the planned Nabucco, Turkey–Greece and Greece–Italy pipelines.

The EU's flagship project with regard to the CACR is the Nabucco gas pipeline, which could bring gas from the Georgian–Turkish and/or Iranian–Turkish border respectively to the Austrian gas hub in Baumgarten without passing through Russia. Estimated investment costs amount to approximately €8 billion. Azerbaijan's gas reserves, even if supplemented by the planned expansion of the Shah–Deniz field, will not be sufficient to keep Nabucco in business. Other countries in the region will have to supply most of the thirty-one billion m^3 of gas Nabucco is expected to carry by 2020. Iranian gas has been regarded as a possible option to fill Nabucco second to Azerbaijan, but Tehran currently has only little export capacity as a result of high domestic consumption. Owing to its enormous export potential, Turkmenistan is another candidate, but has yet to decide whether to invest in a Trans-Caspian pipeline linking it with Azerbaijan. Gazprom, naturally, does its best to derail Nabucco. An important initiative in this context is the South Stream gas pipeline, intended to transport gas from the CACR to Europe via an almost identical route as Nabucco.

The impact of Russia's military intervention in Georgia

Georgia lacks any significant petroleum reserves, but it became a relevant transit route for Central Asian oil and gas – a 'friendly corridor' between Russia to the north and Iran to the south. BTC and SCGP give Tbilisi a certain role to play in energy markets, but they also served as a lightning rod for Russia's military campaign in August 2008 which led to the occupation of parts of Georgia's territory. Many analysts suspect that a key Russian motive for invading Georgia was to expose the region's instability and to forestall any new pipeline projects there. The Russians fired several times at the BTC, but missed it. So, Moscow's intervention did not inflict major or long-term damage to the transport corridor for Caspian oil through Georgia.

Conclusion

First of all, the EU should make use of all feasible options of energy saving and diversification of energy sources, with special emphasis on an increase in the share of renewable energy (hydro, wind, solar, and bio-mass). But, without a significant technology breakthrough, electricity generation will be heavily dependent on gas, and oil will continue to dominate transport even in 2030. Therefore, security of supply of these fuels will continue to be paramount to the EU's economy. The Union and its member states have to take this into account on several levels. As an EU document put it, 'Energy must become a central part of all external EU relations; it is crucial to geopolitical security, economic stability, social development and international efforts to combat climate change' (Commission of the EU 2007: 18).

The 'Russia first' policy pursued by the EU for many years was obviously not sufficient and very likely even counterproductive for its energy security. Although Russia depends on the EU as its largest oil and gas customer, currently Moscow and not Brussels sets the rules of the game. Gazprom aspires to dominance over natural gas supply and distribution networks in Europe. By obtaining control over the infrastructure in transit countries, Russia limits access to markets for other potential suppliers. Without resolute action, the EU could find its energy security largely under Russian control long before 2030, which would give Moscow an undue and possibly dangerous amount of political influence over European decision-making. A 'depoliticisation' of the EU–Russian gas relationship is as desirable as, at least in the foreseeable future, it seems unlikely.

The Kremlin has shown no willingness to agree to multilaterally binding treaties and agreements. Instead, it prefers a strongly self-interest based energy policy oriented to penetrate and dominate the wider European, Black Sea and CACR energy markets. But the untapped reserves held by the CACR might offer the EU an opportunity to move away from increased dependence on Russian energy sources. Development of CACR's oil and gas reserves via Georgia and Turkey, bypassing Russia and Iran, would enhance EU's energy security. Moscow is well aware of this fact and sets itself the goal of obstructing all export routes bringing gas from the CACR to the EU while bypassing Russia. Moscow tries to acquire as much control as possible over Kazakh and Turkmen gas and the entire natural gas pipeline network of the region. And Russia's efforts to team up with other oil and gas producers (OPEC, 'Gas OPEC') should be another incentive for the EU to push its claims for access to CACR's resources.

References

BBC (2006) 'Gazprom warns EU to let it grow', BBC News, 20 April. Online. Available: http://news.bbc.co.uk/2/hi/business/4925682.stm (accessed 25 November 2008).

Belkin, P. (2008) 'The European Union's Energy Security Challenges', Congressional Research Service (CRS), Report for Congress, Washington, DC.

Commission of the EU (2007) 'Communication from the Commission to the European Council and the European Parliament. An Energy Policy for Europe', Com (2007) 1 final, Brussels, 10 January. Online. Available: http://eur-lex.europa.eu/LexUriServ/LexUriServ.do?uri=CELEX:52007DC0001:EN:NOT (accessed 23 November 2008).

—— (13 November 2008a) 'EU Energy Security and Solidarity Action Plan: Second Strategic Energy Review', press release EC08-233EN, Brussels. Online. Available: www.europa-eu-un.org/articles/en/article_8300_en.htm (accessed 25 November 2008).

—— (13 November 2008b) 'Commission staff working document accompanying the Green Paper: towards a secure, sustainable and competitive European energy network. Oil infrastructures. An assessment of the existing and planned oil infrastructures within and towards the EU', Working Document SEC/2008/2869, Brussels. Online. Available: http://eur-lex.europa.eu/LexUriServ/LexUriServ.do?uri=CELEX:DKEY=483107:EN:NOT (accessed 5 December 2008).

Cornell, S. *et al.* (2006) 'The Wider Black Sea Region: an Emerging Hub in European Security', Silk Road Paper, Baltimore: Central Asia Caucas Institute, Johns Hopkins University. Online. Available: www.silkroadstudies.org/new/docs/Silkroadpapers/0612Blacksea_P.pdf (accessed 24 November 2008).

Council of the European Union (2007) 'The EU and Central Asia: Strategy for a New Partnership', 10113/07, Brussels. Online. Available: http://register.consilium.europa.eu/pdf/en/07/st10/st10113.en07.pdf (accessed 5 December 2008).

Energy Information Administration (2008) 'World Proved Reserves of Oil and Natural Gas: Most Recent Estimates'. Online. Available: www.eia.doe.gov/emeu/international/reserves.html (accessed 18 November 2008).

Erixon, Fredrik (2008) 'Europe's energy dependency and Russia's commercial assertiveness', Policy Briefs 7, Brussels: European Centre for International Political Economy (ECIPE). Online. Available: www.ecipe.org/europe2019s-energy-dependency-and-russia2019s-commercial-assertiveness-what-should-the-eu-do/PDF (accessed 3 February 2009).

Guliyev, F. and Akhrarkhodjaeva, N. (2008) 'Transportation of Kazakhstani Oil via the Caspian Sea (TKOC). Arrangements, Actors and Interests', RussCasp Working Paper, Bremen: School of Humanities and Social Sciences, Jacobs University. Online. Available: www.fni.no/russcasp/Kazakh_Azeri_%20oil_transport_RussCasp_Working_Paper.pdf (accessed 3 February 2009).

International Energy Agency (2008) 'IEA Energy Policies Review: the European Union 2008', Paris: IEA.

Larsson, R. L. (2007) 'Nord Stream, Sweden and Baltic Sea Security', Stockholm: Defence Research Agency.

Lavrov, S. (2007) 'Vneshnepoliticheskaya samostoyatelnost Rossii: bezuslovnyy Imperative'. Moskovskie novosti 1. Online. Available: www.mn.ru/issue.php?2007-1-56 (accessed 19 January 2007).

Lindner, R. (2007) 'Blockaden der "Freundschaft"'. SWP-Aktuell, 2007/A 03. Online. Available: www.swp-berlin.org/common/get_document. php?asset_ id=3613 (accessed 3 February 2009).

Malek, M (2008) 'The European Union and the "frozen conflicts" in the South Caucasus', *World of Diplomacy* 18–19: 72–80.

Noël, P. (2008) *Beyond Dependence: How to Deal with Russian Gas*, London: European Council on Foreign Relations.

Norling, N. (2007) 'Gazprom's Monopoly and Nabucco's Potentials: Strategic Decisions for Europe', Silk Road Paper, November, Baltimore, MD:Central Asia– Caucasus Institute and Silk Road Studies Program, Online. Available: www.isdp. eu/files/publications/srp/07/0711Nabucco.pdf (accessed 3 February 2009).

Umbach, F. (2008) 'Europe's Energy Dependence in Mid-term Perspective', Baltimore, MD: American Institute for Contemporary German Studies, Johns Hopkins University. Online. Available: www.aicgs.org/documents/advisor/umbach.gmf. pdf (accessed 26 November 2008).

11 The role of the European Union in fighting nuclear proliferation in the greater Middle East

The case of Iran

Paolo Foradori

This chapter analyses the EU's non-proliferation policy, assessing the strengths and weaknesses of the EU 'distinctive approach' to this delicate policy sector. The chapter is divided into three parts. The first looks at the origins of the EU non-proliferation policy and discusses in detail the 'Strategy against the Proliferation of Weapons of Mass Destruction' adopted in 2003. The second part examines the EU contribution to non-proliferation in seeking to resolve the Iranian nuclear controversy, which represents a fundamental test case of the EU's efficacy. In the light of the analysis conducted, the third concluding part argues that the EU's ambitions to become a more effective global actor in non-proliferation and arms control have not been fully realised. As the Iranian case shows, despite some important assets at its disposal and the undoubted value of its 'comprehensive engagement' approach, Europe as a 'civilian power' has to overcome major constraints which significantly restrict its capacity to play a major role.

The European Union's non-proliferation strategy

For decades, the 'high politics' of foreign and security affairs have been dealt with either at the national level or within the North Atlantic alliance system, remaining off the EC/EU agenda. This has been particularly true in the field of non-proliferation and arms control, which was monopolised by the bilateral relations between the United States (US) and the Union of Soviet Socialist Republics (USSR) superpowers (and, although to a lesser extent, discussed within the NATO framework). Only in the 1980s did the EC/EU begin dealing with issues of nuclear proliferation in some earnest, with the establishment of a 'Working Group on Nuclear Non-proliferation' within the European Political Co-operation framework.

The changed security environment of the post-Cold War era and its progress in the integration process of the early 1990s gave the EU a strong impetus to further co-operation in foreign affairs.[1] This process culminated in the establishment of the Common Foreign and Security Policy (CFSP) at Maastricht in 1993, with the clear objective of enhancing the role of the EU on the global stage. Given its new international ambitions – and as soon as France finally signed the Nuclear Non-Proliferation Treaty (NPT) – a more structured and coherent EU non-proliferation policy could then start taking shape. Since then, the EU has become increasingly involved in several non-proliferation initiatives, although with different degrees of engagement and success.[2] It is worth mentioning the EU's key involvement in promoting the indefinite extension of the NPT at the 1995 Review Conference; its role in the North Korean nuclear controversy and its participation in the Korean Energy Development Organisation (KEDO) in 1995; the establishment of a common regime in the field of control of double-use nuclear material; its involvement in a series of 'co-operative threat reduction' (CTR) initiatives, especially in the Russian Federation and in former USSR countries; the adoption of a Common Position in 1999 advocating the entry into force of the Comprehensive Test Ban Treaty (CTBT); the EU's positive contribution to the proliferation crisis in Ukraine.

A significant breakthrough in the development of a more credible EU non-proliferation 'actorness' was achieved in 2003 with the adoption of a series of key non-proliferation documents of which the EU 'Strategy against proliferation of Weapons of Mass Destruction' (hereafter Strategy) adopted in 2003 (European Council 2003), represents the most advanced and structured reflection elaborated by the EU in this sector.[3]

According to Alyson J. K. Bailes (2005: 1), four main reasons explain the EU's increased determination to become a more influential player in nuclear diplomacy.

1   9/11 pushed proliferation high up the international agenda, both in connection with so-called 'rogue states' (especially the 'axis of evil' composed of Iran, Iraq and North Korea) and the risk of nuclear terrorism;[4]
2   the Iraq crisis showed the risks and costs involved in dealing with these issues in the way apparently preferred by the US, that is, ostracism, coercion and the use of military force;
3   the EU needed the therapy of work on future, more constructive and consensus-based policies precisely to mend the transatlantic split caused by the Iraqi war;
4   the EU was ready to take up its own security responsibilities and became more aware of its own potential, as part of its dynamic of evolution and not least in response to imminent enlargement (more space to look after, more national policies to harmonize, more partners to draw on).

(Bailes 2005: 1)

The Strategy deserves special attention since it not only informs the Union's actual action in addressing the nuclear threat, but it also illustrates in a systematic and comprehensive fashion the specific 'European approach' to the issue. The main purpose of the Strategy was to draft a coherent EU non-proliferation 'concept' to systematise and give consistency to the Union's action in the field and to 'make it a little more difficult for member states to depart from the course of action they had committed themselves to follow and would, in a sense, "lock them in" politically' (Ahlström 2005: 32).

The Introduction highlights the risks of nuclear proliferation – which is deemed 'a growing threat to international peace and security'[5] (para. 1) – and the resolve of the EU to contribute to eliminating a threat that can originate both from state and non-state actors (namely terrorist groups). The EU non-proliferation policy is a 'central element' (para. 2) of its foreign policy and calls upon the Union to 'act with resolve, using all instruments and policies at its disposal. Our objective is to prevent, deter, halt and, where possible, eliminate proliferation programmes of concern worldwide' (para. 2).

The more interesting and original part of the Strategy is where it explains how and by what means the EU intends to address the nuclear threat. The distinctive character of EU intervention is its holistic and 'broad approach covering a wide spectrum of actions' (para. 14). According to the document, the EU has 'a wide range of instruments available: multilateral treaties and verification mechanisms; national and internationally co-ordinated export controls; co-operative threat reduction programmes; political and economic levers (including trade and development policies); interdiction of illegal procurement activities and, as a last resort, coercive measures in accordance with the UN Charter. While all are necessary, none is sufficient in itself' (para. 29).

The factors that guide the European 'approach' are presented in Chapter II. The cornerstone of the strategy is the concept of 'effective multilateralism'. A multilateral approach 'provides the best way to maintain international order' (para. 14) and consequently the EU is committed to 'uphold, implement and strengthen the multilateral disarmament and non-proliferation treaties and agreements' (ibid.), which provide the legal and normative basis of all non-proliferation efforts. The main objective of EU engagement is thus to pursue the 'universalisation' of the existing disarmament and non-proliferation norms, starting from the NPT, which underpin the non-proliferation regime. The co-ordinated effort undertaken by the EU for the indefinite extension of the NPT is the best example of the European commitment to this end.[6] Indeed, acting within the context of multilateral fora – where decisions are taken on pre-agreed agendas – gives the EU a good opportunity to better co-ordinate the different perspectives of the member states and to find a common position to put forward (Portela 2004: 6).

The pledge to 'mainstream' (ibid.) proliferation in all its policies, drawing upon all resources and instrument available to the Union, has the same goal. The decision to introduce a 'non-proliferation clause' in agreements with third countries is in line with this: a 'carrot and stick' approach designed to elicit better behaviour from partner countries who want to do business with the wealthy European 'club'.

A second key element of the strategy is conflict prevention. This tenet reflects the distinctive international identity of the EU as a 'civilian power'.[7] The strategy states clearly that 'the EU is determined to play a part in addressing the problems of regional instability and insecurity and the situations of conflict which lie behind many weapon programmes, recognising that instability does not occur in a vacuum. *The best solution to the problem of proliferation of WMD is that countries should no longer feel they need them'* (para. 20; emphasis added). And again: 'The more secure countries feel, the more likely they are to abandon programmes: disarmament measures can lead to a virtuous circle just as weapon programmes can lead to an arms race' (ibid.).

While the document acknowledges that it will be not easy to find solutions to the security dilemmas that trigger conflicts (para. 22), the EU has several means at its disposal to address the 'root causes' of instability, including 'through pursuing and enhancing its efforts in the areas of political conflicts, development assistance, reduction of poverty and promotion of human rights' (para. 14). Positive and negative security assurances are also useful instruments, as they can serve both as an incentive to forgo the acquisition of WMD and as a deterrent. Although the strategy is not very specific, the EU will 'promote further consideration of security assurances' (para. 23).

As a last resort – if all other measures have failed, including political dialogue and diplomatic pressure – the EU is, for the first time, also prepared to consider the use of coercive means to enforce non-proliferation under Chapter VII of the UN Charter and international law (para. 25). These consist of sanctions, selective or global, interceptions of shipments and, as appropriate, the use of force. In this extreme form of action, 'the UN Security Council should play a central role' (ibid.). The role of the UN Security Council is further stressed and presented as 'the final arbiter on the consequence of non-compliance' (para. 17) and therefore 'needs to be effectively strengthened' (ibid.).[8]

The reference to the potential use of coercion, and above all the use of force, represents an important novelty in the traditional European approach, stretching the 'civilian power' model to its limits.[9] This evolution notwithstanding, the reference to the possible use of force should not be given undue weight and can alter the specificity of the EU approach to only a limited extent. This is evident in a comparison with the current US anti-proliferation doctrine and its focus on counter-proliferation, which emphasises the military option. Moreover, the EU generally disapproves of the US 'regime change by force' policy, preferring instead a 'coexistence' stance, in which regime change will result peacefully from a policy of 'constructive engagement', using diplomatic and economic means.

The final part of the document details a 'living action plan' (para. 30) to assure the effective implementation of the Strategy, which will be monitored constantly, subject to regular revision and updating every six months. To this end, the position of Personal Representative for non-proliferation of WMD of the High Representative for CFSP was created in 2003 to co-ordinate, help implement and further develop the Strategy, and to give sharper focus to these issues in dialogue with third countries.

As has been noted, the Strategy does not reflect any drastic departure in the way the EU acts on the global scene, but it is grounded in a EU international identity based on multilateralism, the rule of law, preference for political and economic diplomacy, focus on the 'root causes' of global issues, renunciation of the use of force, international co-operation and coexistence (Álvarez-Verdugo 2006: 418). The document was instrumental in making non-proliferation one of the main objectives of the EU's international involvement. It has – all things considered – helped make the EU collective policy against nuclear weapons increasingly robust, 'putting the EU into high gear with a flurry of new activities since 2003' (Tertrais 2005: 48). Another merit is that of containing 'some measures to ensure that the Union acts *accordingly*. Of particular importance is the fact that some systematic policy planning is envisaged, notably with the drafting of a detailed plan of diplomatic action – significantly, this constitutes the first measure for immediate action listed in the Action Plan' (Portela 2004: 29).

On the other hand, the EU's non-proliferation strategy retains a rather conservative profile due to its overemphasis on the revitalisation of the existing non-proliferation regime (Sauer 2004: 122). Moreover, despite the clarity of its definition of its objectives, the main question remains that of implementation, which must be resolved if the EU is to go beyond a declaratory diplomacy. On the way to this goal, Bruno Tertrais identifies five main interrelated hurdles:

1   The complexity of EU policies and institutional architecture, in a field that has to involve both the Commission and the Council.
2   The EU's cumbersome budgetary practice, which precludes it from responding appropriately to new international developments. Very limited resources are made available for non-proliferation.
3   The 'competition' that the EU faces from national efforts: individual member states also contribute, diplomatically and financially, to non-proliferation. Nuclear proliferation is seen by the two EU nuclear powers (France and the UK) as a key rationale for maintaining a nuclear deterrence posture.
4   The diversity of 'nuclear cultures' within the Union, ranging from countries which are members of the New Agenda Coalition (Sweden, Ireland) to the two European nuclear powers (France, the UK), with a mix of neutral or non-aligned countries, NATO members and NATO nuclear host countries in between.
5   The EU as an institution has had to overcome national preferences in a domain very closely associated with sovereignty and independence, in both the military and civilian spheres.

(Tertrais 2005: 53)

The Iranian nuclear controversy

The Iranian nuclear controversy and the critical diplomatic negotiations led by the EU to convince Iran to abandon its nuclear ambitions need to be contextualised in the greater Middle East region to be properly understood.[10]

The region is increasingly littered with WMD programmes, all of which are conducted clandestinely. Many states have a poor or utterly negative record in complying with the nuclear non-proliferation regime. The strategic landscape remains highly volatile, with several cases of ongoing, unsettled or potential conflicts: Arab–Israeli, India–Pakistan, Afghanistan, Iraq, Lebanon, the Caucasus. The entire area is of key strategic importance because it hosts about half the world's proven energy resources (oil and gas). In addition, the greater Middle East has experience of the actual use of WMD in warfare, the only instance since Hiroshima and Nagasaki (Russell 2005: 4–5). The 2003 military action by the US-led coalition against Iraq is the first example of a 'counterproliferation war'. As Kemp and Harkavy observe (1997: xiii): 'With the exception of North Korea virtually all of the world's concern about weapons proliferation focuses on countries in the greater Middle East, where rivalries are intense, distances short, and enemies contiguous'. Again, 'the power politics in the region is intense and fuels the demand for WMD among regional nation states. The weapons do not cause the rivalries, but rather are the symptom of the power struggles already underway' (Russell 2005: 5).[11]

Historically, the entire area has been at the centre of a 'great game' played by regional and global powers for influence and control of its strategic position and energy resources. The situation has been further complicated by 9/11 and the US-led war on terror, with its military operations in Afghanistan and Iraq. The latter in particular has considerably altered the Middle Eastern security landscape, where, 'traditionally, Iran and Iraq have balanced each other, preventing the emergence of a regional hegemony' (Bahgat 2007: 3). Bush's doctrine of preventive use of force as a tool of counterproliferation, his openly declared policy of 'regime change', and the massive presence of US military in the region (from Iraq to Afghanistan and Central Asia), have magnified Iran's traditional 'encirclement syndrome' and the fear of being – as a member of the 'axis of evil' – next in line for an armed attack (Russell 2006: 55).[12]

In this fluid geopolitical context, many states are competing for influence and hegemony in the region, and Iran has high ambitions to become the 'leader of the Islamic world'. Nuclear weapons are seen by Tehran as potentially a major military asset, with fundamental symbolic value, through which the regime would gain respect and recognition and improve its international standing.[13] The risk of nuclear terrorism – 'the ultimate preventable catastrophe', in the words of Graham Allison (2004) – is also high in the region.

Domestic politics considerations can also explain why states seek to acquire nuclear weapons. Focusing on the Iranian case, nationalism, prestige and cultural factors are seen as primary drivers for proliferation (Perkovich 2005). The 'nuclear card', combined with an 'external threat' strategy, is used by the ruling coalition as a 'rally round the flag' tactic to keep its grip on power, creating scapegoats to repress internal dissent and divert public attention from its failure to give political freedom and adequate living standards to its populace.

The Iranian controversy went up the international political agenda in 2002, when the National Council of Resistance of Iran (NCRI), an exiled Iranian opposition group, reported the government's clandestine nuclear fuel cycle programme, providing details about two undeclared nuclear facilities. The following year, the International Atomic Energy Agency (IAEA) issued a critical report on Iran, accusing the country of having failed to declare important nuclear activities and concealing important information, in contravention of its NPT-mandated full-scope safeguard agreement with the agency. Despite Iran's claims that its nuclear programme is exclusively of a civilian nature, there is widespread concern in the international community that the Persian state is in fact building facilities to produce fissile material for a clandestine nuclear weapons programme (Fitzpatrick 2008).[14]

The possible acquisition of nuclear weapons on the part of Iran could have serious consequences both at the global and European level. On the global level, a nuclear Iran will distress the entire greater Middle East region, risking the further destabilisation of an already unstable security landscape. Power relations will be altered by the hegemonic aspirations of a nuclear Iran. This will inevitably aggravate the security dilemmas in the region and possibly produce a nuclear domino effect, particularly in Saudi Arabia, Syria, Turkey and Egypt. Given the strategic importance of the area, the world's security will be affected. A nuclear drift in the Middle East could begin a global proliferation cascade with unimaginable costs for international peace and security. The net result would probably be the end of the non-proliferation regime. A nuclear Iran, it is feared, would also increase the risk of non-state actors acquiring non-conventional weapons, given Iran's known links with various terrorist organisations.[15] Due to Iran's enormous oil and gas resources and the country's strategic position on the maritime hydrocarbon routes through the Persian Gulf, the world's energy supplies could be compromised.

In this general context, several of the EU's interests are directly or indirectly threatened. First of all, a nuclear-armed Iran could pose a direct security threat to the continent of Europe. The Shahab III missile is capable of reaching parts of southern Europe and its successor is likely to have an even longer range. Some EU member states (i.e. France and the UK) have defence agreements and commitments in the Middle East (with Kuwait, Qatar, the United Arab Emirates) which might drag them into dangerous situations should the region flare up through an escalation of the Iranian crisis; European peacekeeping forces deployed in the region (particularly those in Lebanon) might also find themselves at risk of retaliation (Tertrais 2007).

Another threat to the EU's interests is economic. Besides relevant (but not vital) commercial opportunities for the EU,[16] the principal menace is to energy security, as the EU is largely dependent on oil and gas imports from the Persian Gulf. Iran is the world's fourth largest oil producer and, as already noted, it could seek control of (and easily sabotage) key routes passing through the Persian Gulf, potentially jeopardising the international energy supply.

Diplomatic and political EU interests are also at stake. The prime European concern is the possible collapse of the entire non-proliferation regime in the event of a breach by the Persian state. The cornerstone of the EU's non-proliferation policy is to support and internationalisation of the regime. EU involvement in the Iranian controversy is so great that its credibility as a non-proliferation actor would not survive Tehran's 'going nuclear'. Should the crisis become too prolonged or escalate further, EU internal cohesion and transatlantic relations might be stretched to breaking point, too, dealing a terrible blow to the young and still very fragile CFSP/ESDP.

The EU's efforts to engage with the post-revolutionary Iranian government date back to the early 1990s, when the Community decided to establish a 'critical dialogue' with Tehran.[17] The objective of the European initiative was to soften and open up the Islamic system, addressing four main areas of concern: terrorism, the Arab–Israeli conflict, human rights and weapons of mass destruction. This approach seemed to bear fruit, particularly after the unexpected victory of Khatami in the 1997 presidential elections with a more reformist political agenda and a more constructive international approach, in particular vis-à-vis the EU member states. These improved relations led the EU to begin a so-called 'constructive dialogue' with bi-annual high-level meetings to discuss a vast range of key political, security and economic issues. In 2001 the EU opened negotiations with Iran for closer co-operation, despite strong objections from the US. The signing of a far-reaching Trade and Co-operation Agreement (TCA), of great value to Iran to overcome its severe economic problems, was made contingent upon the holding of successful political dialogue, and positive developments on human rights, terrorism, non-proliferation and the peace process.

Unfortunately, progress was bound not to last. 'This European–Iranian honeymoon ended in two stages: first, with the evidence of Iran's decade-old violation of its NPT safeguard agreements with the IAEA, second, two years later, with the election of President Ahmadinedschad and the ensuing inflammatory rhetoric in foreign policy matters, notably on Israel' (Müller 2007: 184). While the EU inevitably became more critical of the Iranian government's intentions, it maintained its co-operative approach in an attempt to convince Tehran to: (1) sign the IAEA's Additional Protocol for more intrusive inspections; (2) answer all the Agency's objections satisfactorily; (3) make its entire nuclear programme transparent; and above all: (4) stop the enrichment of uranium. In exchange, the EU would recognise Iran's right to pursue the peaceful use of nuclear energy, offer easier access to modern technologies and a substantial package of economic incentives, while resisting US pressure to refer the issue to the UN Security Council and keeping the dialogue open.[18]

After the temporary success of the European initiatives and the signing of the 'Teheran Agreement' (October 2003) in which Iran agreed to 'suspend' uranium enrichment and to sign the Additional Protocol, the Islamic Republic opted for a 'stop and go' nuclear diplomacy, intermittently resuming and halting its nuclear activities. A small breakthrough was achieved with the signing of the November 2004 'Paris Agreement' between Iran and the E3/EU (EU-3 Ministers: France/Germany/Great Britain/High Representative of the CFSP), which essentially reproduced the clauses of the previous year's accord. But, again, Tehran broke its promises and in August 2005 informed the IAEA that it would resume enrichment activities in the Esfahan facilities. This move came as a 'shock' to the Europeans, convinced that two years of hard bargaining and intensive discussions had persuaded the Iranians that it was in their interests to forgo their nuclear ambitions (Posch 2006a: 106). Quite the contrary, a deep-seated lack of trust continued to characterise the European–Iranian dialogue (ibid.).

Despite several further attempts at finding a compromise, the rejection of the E3/EU's proposals by Iran and its intransigence in continuing its uranium enrichment programme brought the talks to deadlock. The negotiations were then extended to the other three non-European UN Security Council permanent members (China, Russia and the US), in the configuration EU3+3 or otherwise called P5+1 (Germany). After a new package deal of incentives was refused and a further critical report was issued by IAEA, the Agency's board of governors voted to refer Iran to the United Nations Security Council (UNSC), stating that the purpose of the Iranian nuclear programme was still uncertain. In December 2006 the UNSC imposed selective sanctions on the country for the first time, banning international trade in nuclear and missile technologies and freezing the foreign assets of twelve individuals and ten Iranian organisations.

From that point on events unfolded rapidly – but without any positive outcome – with new accord proposals from one side or the other, packaging and repackaging of deals, the adoption of new resolutions by the UNSC and the IAEA, and three new rounds of sanctions against Iran's non-compliance,[19] followed by a 'freeze for freeze' proposal in which it was promised that further sanctions would not be implemented if Iran froze the expansion of its nuclear activities.

Conclusion

Scholarly assessments of the EU's actions in non-proliferation vary from positive (Smeland 2004) to moderately positive (Sauer 2004; Tertrais 2005; Müller 2007), mixed and uneven (Álvarez-Verdugo 2006) to categorically negative in which the EU is 'still ineffective as a non-proliferation actor' (Portela 2004: 21).

Given the highly sensitive political nature of the sector, it is important to be aware of the improvements made by the EU in the non-proliferation field. Despite the lack of concrete results, the Iranian crisis has at least demonstrated the seriousness and proactiveness of the EU's attempt, and its resolve to emerge as a key player. According to Harald Müller (2007: 186), the member states kept 'their unity of purpose throughout the process despite occasionally different accents in the commentaries of the state of affairs, and did not deviate from their chosen line. Compared to their performance in nuclear crises before, this meant considerable progress'. In addition, 'by way of engagement, the EU has undeniably built up a body of institutional knowledge on Iranian affairs in member states' Ministries and EU bodies which is hard to match' (Posch 2006a: 112).

That said, the EU remains a junior player: it still has a long way to go in the process of acquiring a proper non-proliferation 'actorness'. The EU is handicapped by the same limits and difficulties it has in the wider field of foreign and security policy: it is not a unitary actor and is still characterised by the diversity of its member states' positions on major international issues.

The long-standing divide between Atlanticists and Europeanists represents the main cleavage and source of incomprehension among the member states.[20] The efficiency of the EU's international action is also compromised by the diversity of national histories, foreign policy interests, strategic cultures and military traditions within it. The EU includes 'big' and 'small' countries, 'haves' and 'have-nots' (in terms of military capabilities, nuclear weapons, membership of the UNSC, military industries), 'extroverts' and 'introverts', with different propensities to act on the global scene or to resort to the use of force. An additional divide is between EU proponents and opponents of peaceful nuclear energy. In short, in the field of non-proliferation, as in the general CFSP/ESDP, 'the crux of the matter is the prevalence of national idiosyncrasies and preferences over the norm of commonality. The latter has some impact, but is not yet capable of overruling perceived interests, even not precisely vital ones' (Müller 2007: 194).

Another major weakness of the EU is its inability to perform well when reacting to proliferation crises, or when controversies have grown acute. As Bruno Tertrais points out:

> The EU has three major assets in the fight against nuclear proliferation: its financial resources, its attractiveness as a trade and investment partner, and its preference for 'engagement'. However, it also lacks three significant non-proliferation instruments. One is the ability to extend a security guarantee to a country that feels threatened in order to persuade it not to embark on a nuclear programme. Another is the ability to dissuade, through missile defence, a country from investing in a ballistic programme – the inevitable companion of a nuclear programme. A third is the ability to threaten credibly the neutralization or destruction of a large nuclear programme by conventional means (more a lack of know-how, adequate planning and training than a lack of military assets).
>
> (Tertrais 2005: 54–5)

That clarified, it is important to recognise the importance of 'soft power' and the strengths of the EU approach of 'constructive engagement', which can be particularly effective in the medium to long term. 'The European Union possesses a unique suite of power, interest, facility, diplomatic connection, and credibility vis-à-vis Iran to bring about sufficient change in Tehran's policy' (Smeland 2004: 26). Given the history of extreme mistrust and enmity between the US and Iran, the EU can play a decisive role of mediation (Smeland 2004: 2).

In contrast to the US policy of banning all economic and political contacts, the EU's approach to engaging with the Islamic Republic, in an attempt to break its isolation and return it to the international community, could alter its leadership's nuclear logic and be instrumental to solving the problem. As Etel Solingen (2007) has convincingly explained, domestic models of political survival and their orientation to the global political economy have fundamental implications for nuclear trajectories. Hence:

> leaders of ruling coalitions advocating economic growth through integration in the global economy have incentives to avoid the costs of nuclearization, which impair domestic reforms favouring internationalization. By contrast, nuclearization implies fewer costs for inward-looking leaders and for constituencies less dependent on international markets, investment, technology, and institutions, who can rely on nuclear weapons programs to reinforce nationalist platforms of political survival.
>
> (Solingen 2007: 17)

If this is the right interpretation of the drivers behind Iranian nuclear aspirations, then the EU can play a significant role in helping the Iranians to recalculate their interests along more rational and less ideological lines. The right way to deal with the Iran nuclear programme is 'to modify Iran's decision making process regarding the utility of nuclear weapons, illustrate alternative ways for Iran to achieve its aims, and help orchestrate some degree of rapprochement between Tehran and Washington' (Smeland 2004: 14).

Yet it is impossible for the EU to achieve this objective without close cooperation with the US. Given the current intensification of the Iranian crisis – where issues of compliance and enforcement are predominant – a delicate combination of European 'soft' and US 'hard' power is required. To defuse the Iranian nuclear crisis both policies are necessary. They may not be sufficient, though. If Iran persists in going nuclear, nothing – short of military action, whose destructive consequences are hard to predict – can stop it. To a large extent, the ball is in the Iranian camp.

Notes

1 For a general analysis of the emerging role of the EU as an international actor see Foradori *et al.* (2007).
2 For an overview of the EU non-proliferation policy see Müller and van Dassen (1997), Grand (2000) and Portela (2004).

3 Indeed, the Strategy refers not only to the proliferation of nuclear weapons but to the entire range of WMD (nuclear, biological, chemical and radiological). This chapter focuses exclusively on the nuclear threat, which is the most powerful and dangerous of all non-conventional weapons. The analysis here proposed, however, could to a large extent apply to the more general issue of WMD.

4 Although the 9/11 terrorist attack did not involve WMD, its spectacularity and extreme destructiveness increased the fear of non-state actors utilising non-conventional weapons to cause destruction/disruption on a mass scale. In direct response to the event, the EU issued a 'targeted initiative' to tackle the terrorist threat in the field of non-proliferation and arms control (see European Council 2002).

5 The wording of the EU Security Strategy 'A secure Europe in a better world' of 2003 is even more clear-cut, describing proliferation as 'potentially the greatest threat to our security' (European Council 2003: 3).

6 The EU is also very much committed to strengthening national and internationally co-ordinated export control mechanisms and 'it will advocate adherence to effective export control criteria by countries outside the existing regimes and arrangements' (para. 19).

7 The term 'civilian power' was formulated first by François Duchêne (1973), who describes the EU – 'a civilian group of countries long on economic power and relatively short on armed force' (1973: 20) – as a novel type of actor, capable of exerting an impact on international affairs without conducting a traditional state-like foreign policy and above all without resorting to coercive means.

8 On the issue whether – given the rather ambiguous wording of the Strategy – EU military action against a would-be nuclear state requires an explicit authorisation by UN Security Council or not see Portela (2004: 27–8) and Sauer (2004: 127).

9 On the consequences of the 'militarisation' of EU external action on the 'civilian power' model see Foradori (2007).

10 The term 'greater Middle East' refers to the geopolitical area which encompasses the Middle East and South Asia (Kemp and Harkavy 1997).

11 For a general discussion of the motivations of states seeking to acquire (or abandon) nuclear weapons, see the seminal work of Sagan (1996/97) and Part One of Solingen (2007).

12 On Iran's security environment see Chubin (2001).

13 Tehran believes that nuclear weapons – the 'great equaliser' – can compensate for its shortcomings in conventional military and deterrent capabilities, especially vis-à-vis the US and Israel.

14 A full discussion of Iranian nuclear capabilities and intentions is beyond the scope of this chapter. The author's personal opinion is that Iran is indeed – for a complex mix of reasons and objectives, some of which are also discussed in the present paragraph – seeking to develop a nuclear programme with the intention of moving close to and perhaps crossing the nuclear weapons threshold. Taking advantage of the internal contradictions and tensions of the NPT on the universal right to acquire nuclear energy for peaceful purposes (which, technically speaking, includes the right to uranium enrichment and reprocessing, provided that they are open to IAEA inspections), it is reasonable to argue that Iran is at least seeking to acquire all weapons-related technologies, following the so-called 'Japan model' (Cirincione 2006). For an overview of Iranian WMD and missile capabilities see the country's chapter in Cirincione *et al.* (2005: 295–313). There

are also detailed accounts in Kile (2005), Russell (2005: chapters 5 and 6), Takeyh (2006), Bahgat (2007: 19–43), Solingen (2007: chapter 8). For a recent analysis of nuclear civilian programmes in the Middle East and the risk of their diversion to military uses see IISS (2008).

15 According to the EU European Security Strategy, 'The most frightening scenario is one in which terrorist groups acquire weapons of mass destruction' (European Council 2003: 4).

16 On the other hand, commercial ties with the EU are of primary importance to Iran, since the EU is its first trading partner with about 30 per cent of its trade exchanges.

17 A full account of the relations between the EU and Iran is beyond the scope of the chapter. For a more detailed analysis see Kile (2005) and Posch (2006b).

18 Negotiations since 2003 were initially carried out by the Foreign Ministries of the 'Big Three' (France, Germany and the UK), acting with little co-operation from the rest of the EU (format E-3). Javier Solana, the High Representative of CFSP, gradually became involved in the E-3's initiative, which was co-ordinated through the Council with the other member states (format EU-3). It was only in October 2005 that the EU Council officially recognised the EU's role in the EU-3 non-proliferation attempts.

19 Among the sanctions imposed by the EU in July 2008, the assets freeze on Iran's largest bank, Bank Melli, which was required to close its offices in Hamburg, London and Paris, is significant. Similar restrictions were placed on twelve other entities, primarily Iranian defence firms, plus asset freezes and travel bans on fourteen senior high-ranking Iranian officials of military organisations and of the Atomic Energy Organisation of Iran, which oversees Iran's nuclear programme.

20 For a general discussion of the differences that characterise the common foreign and security policies see Howorth (2000) and Heisbourg (2000).

References

Ahlström, C. (2005) 'The EU strategy against the proliferation of weapons of mass destruction', in S. N. Kile (ed.) *Europe and Iran: Perspectives on Non-proliferation*, Oxford: Oxford University Press.

Allison, G. (2004) *Nuclear Terrorism: the Ultimate Preventable Catastrophe*, New York: Times Books.

Álvarez-Verdugo, M. (2006) 'Mixing tools against proliferation: the EU's strategy for dealing with weapons of mass destruction', *European Foreign Affairs Review* 11: 417–38.

Bahgat, G. (2007) *Proliferation of Nuclear Weapons in the Middle East*, Gainesville, FL: University Press of Florida.

Bailes, A. J. K. (2005) 'The Role of the EU in Fighting Proliferation: an Assessment of the Iran Case and its Consequences', opening lecture of the second day in the international seminar for experts 'European Security and Defence Policy and the Transatlantic Relationship: How to Strike a New Balance?' organised by the Cicero Foundation in the series Great Debates, Paris, 8–9 December. Online. Available: www.cicerofoundation.org/pdf/lecture_bailes_dec05.pdf (accessed 4 October 2008).

Bowen, W. Q. (2006) 'Libya and Nuclear Proliferation: Stepping back from the Brink', Adelphi Paper 380, London: Routledge.

Chubin, S. (2001) 'Iran's strategic environment and nuclear weapons', in G. Kemp (ed.) *Iran's Nuclear Weapons Options: Issues and Analysis*, Washington, DC: Nixon Center.

Cirincione, J. (2006) 'The clock's ticking: stopping Iran before it's too late', *Arms Control Today*, November. Online. Available: www.armscontrol.org/act/2006_11/StopIran (accessed 13 September 2008).

Cirincione, J., Wolfsthal J. B. and Rajkumar, M. (2005) *Deadly Arsenals: Nuclear, Biological and Chemical Threats*, Washington, DC: Carnegie Endowment for International Peace.

Duchêne, F. (1973) 'The European Community and the uncertainties of interdependence', in M. Kohnstamm and W. Hager (eds) *A Nation Writ Large? Foreign Policy Problems before the European Community*, London: Macmillan.

European Council (2002), 'Conclusion of the 2421st Council meeting: General Affairs', 7705/02, Presse 91, Luxembourg, 15 April. Online. Available: http://europa.eu/rapid/pressReleasesAction.do?reference=PRES/02/91&format=PDF&aged=1&language=EN&guiLanguage=en (accessed 18 October 2008).

—— (2003) 'EU Strategy against Proliferation of Weapons of Mass Destruction', Brussels, 12 and 13 December 2003. Online. Available: http://ue.eu.int/uedocs/cmsUpload/st15708.en03.pdf (accessed 21 October 2008).

Fitzpatrick, M. (2008), 'The Iranian Nuclear Crisis: Avoiding Worst-case Outcomes', Adelphi Papers 398, London: Routledge.

Foradori, P. (2007) 'European citizens in arms: the EU's international identity and the militarization of a civilian power', in P. Foradori, S. Piattoni and R. Scartezzini (eds) *European Citizenship: Theories, Arenas, Levels*, Baden-Baden: Nomos.

Foradori, P., Rosa, P. and Scartezzini, R. (eds) (2007) *Managing a Multilevel Foreign Policy: the EU in International Affairs*, Lanham, MD: Lexington Books.

Grand, C. (2000) *The European Union and the Non-proliferation of Nuclear Weapons*, Chaillot Paper 37, Paris: EU Institute for Security Studies. Online. Available: http://aei.pitt.edu/494/03/chai37e.pdf (accessed 5 October 2008).

Heisbourg, F. (2000) *European Defence: Making it Work*, Chaillot Paper 42, Paris: European Union Institute of Security Studies. Online. Available: www.iss.europa.eu/uploads/media/cp042e.pdf (accessed 5 October 2008).

Howorth, H. (2000) *European Integration and Defence: the Ultimate Challenge*, Chaillot Paper 43, Paris: EU Institute of Security Studies. Online. Available: www.iss.europa.eu/uploads/media/cp043e.pdf (accessed 5 October 2008).

IISS (2008) *Nuclear Programmes in the Middle East: In the Shadow of Iran*, London: International Institute for Strategic Studies.

Kemp, G. and Harkavy, R. (1997) *Strategic Geography and the Changing Middle East*, Washington DC: Brookings Institution Press.

Kile, S. N. (ed.) (2005) *Europe and Iran: Perspectives on Non-proliferation*, Oxford: Oxford University Press.

Müller, H. (2007), 'Europe and the proliferation of weapons of mass destruction', in P. Foradori *et al.* (eds) *Managing a Multilevel Foreign Policy: the EU in International Affairs*, Lanham, MD: Lexington Books.

Müller, H. and van Dassen, L. (1997) 'From cacophony to joint action: successes and shortcomings of European nuclear non-proliferation policy', in M. Holland (ed.) *Common Foreign and Security Policy: the Record and Reforms*, London and Washington: Frances Pinter.

Perkovich, G. (2005) 'For Tehran, nuclear program is a matter of pride', *Yale Global*,

21 March. Online. Available: http://carnegieendowment.org/publications/index. cfm?fa=view&id=16694 (accessed 19 October 2008).

Portela, C. (2004) 'The Role of the EU in the Non-proliferation of Nuclear Weapons: the Way to Thessaloniki and Beyond', PRIF Report 65, Frankfurt: Peace Research Institute. Online. Available: http://se1.isn.ch/serviceengine/FileContent?serviceID= 47&fileid=4EF11EC8-F075-B981-50E7-8A7D00A81327&lng=en (accessed 15 October 2008).

Posch, W. (2006a) 'The EU and Iran: a tangled web of negotiations', in W. Posch (ed.) *Iranian Challenges*, Chaillot Paper 89, Paris: EU Institute of Security Studies, pp. 99-114. Online. Available: www.iss.europa.eu/uploads/media/cp089.pdf (accessed 19 October 2008).

—— (2006b) (ed.) *Iranian Challenges*, Chaillot Paper, 89, Paris: EU Institute of Security Studies. www.iss.europa.eu/uploads/media/cp089.pdf (accessed 19 October 2008).

Russell, J. A. (2006) *Proliferation of Weapons of Mass Destruction in the Middle East*, London: Palgrave Macmillan.

Russell, R. L. (2005) *Weapons Proliferation and War in the Greater Middle East: Strategic Contest*, New York: Routledge.

Sagan, S. D. (1996/97) 'Why do states build nuclear weapons? Three models in search of a bomb', *International Security* 21 (3): 54-86.

Sauer, T. (2004) 'The "Americanization" of EU nuclear non-proliferation policy', *Defence and Security Analysis* 20 (2): 113-31.

Smeland (2004) 'Countering Iranian nukes: a European strategy', *Non-proliferation Review* 11 (1): 40-72.

Solingen, E. (2007) *Nuclear Logics: Contrasting Paths in East Asia and the Middle East*, Princeton, NJ: Princeton University Press.

Takeyh, R. (2006) 'Iran at the strategic crossroads', in J. A. Russell (ed.) *Proliferation of Weapons of Mass Destruction in the Middle East*, London: Palgrave Macmillan.

Tertrais, B. (2005) 'The European Union and nuclear non-proliferation: does soft power work?', *International Spectator* 40 (3): 45-58.

—— (2007) 'Deterring a nuclear Iran: what role for Europe?' in P. Clawson and M. Eisenstadt (eds) *Deterring the Ayatollahs: Complications in Applying Cold War Strategy to Iran*, Washington Institute for Near East Policy, *Policy Focus* 72 (July): 16-20. Online. Available: www.washingtoninstitute.org/pubPDFs/PolicyFocus-72FinalWeb.pdf (accessed 2 October 2008).

United Nations (1945) 'Charter of the United Nations', UN Press. Online. Available: www.un.org/aboutun/charter/ (accessed 23 October 2008).

12 India and the European Union

Anton Pelinka

India and the European Union (EU) have many things in common: (sub)continental size, political systems based on a liberal understanding of plural democracy, an underdeveloped international potential and especially a variety of ethnic, linguistic, religious and other cultural diversities. But the parallels have to be seen in combination with the differences: India is a federation, acting as one sovereign state. The EU, on the other hand, is an unfinished federation whose members still see themselves as sovereign states. And, of course: despite impressive economic growth rates for almost two decades, India has still to be considered a rather poor subcontinent – while the EU belongs to the group of the most prosperous societies.

The following article discusses to what extent the parallels and differences can be used as a sound basis for improving the ties between India and the EU. But the article's main focus is in the possibility for the EU to learn from India's experience – and vice versa. For that reason, the chapter is to be seen first and foremost in the field of comparative politics. but it does include aspects of international relations as well.

Parallels and differences

India is the second most populous country in the world. Its population is about 1.1 billion, and according to some extrapolations, India will overtake China in three or four decades to become the No. 1. India's size (3.3 million km^2) makes it No. 7 among the United Nations (UN) members, and among the states with a bigger size than India (Russia, Canada, the US, China, Brazil, Australia) none has the population density India has: 333 persons per km^2.

The EU, not considered to be a state, has (after its enlargement of 2007) almost 500 million inhabitants and a size of 4.3 million km^2. This would make the EU – if seen as a state – No. 3 regarding population and No. 7 regarding geographical size. India as a state and the EU as an unfinished state are both playing in the league of global giants.

Both – India and the EU – are too big and too diverse to be seen as traditional nation states, especially not in the European tradition. Both are transgressing the traditional criteria states like France or Poland are defined by. India and the EU are examples for post-national, especially for post-ethnic politics. The EU does not have a national and ethnic 'majority' – it is an ensemble of minorities. The situation is the same in India: with the exception of the religious Hindu majority, it makes no sense to speak of India by referring to (national, ethnic, linguistic) majorities or minorities – because there is no majority.

These parallels are counterbalanced by the differences – especially concerning the nature of the EU as an entity with a very special status, something of a hybrid between a federation and a confederation and certainly not a state; and concerning the economic disparities: the EU, consisting of three members of the G-7, the loose organisation of the biggest industrialised democracies, belongs to the rich sectors of the global economy, despite a rather significant internal economic imbalance, especially after the last round of enlargement (Aslund and Dabrowski 2007: 1–5). India, on the other hand, is still defined by its status as a developing society with a significantly less developed economy.

After the last waves of enlargement, the economic and social diversity within the EU has become significantly greater. Nevertheless, the economic gap between the enlarged EU and India is still dramatic: In 2006 the Human Development Index (according the UN Development Programme) gave India rank No. 126; the lowest ranking EU member, Romania, was No. 60 (*Fischer Weltalmanach* 2007: 538–41).

Indian and European federalism

Nevertheless parallels concerning the political structure are obvious. This begins with federalism: India is a federation, according to its constitution and its political system. Political power is divided between the central level – the republic – and the states. The EU is a federation in the making. Elements of a confederation – not interfering with the sovereign status of the members – and elements of a federation are coexisting. And although nobody can predict whether the process of European integration will produce, at its very end, at its final stage, a federation: the EU's 'deepening' is strengthening, step by step, the federal elements.

Concerning federal structures, there are other differences to be considered: The Indian states are founded and shaped by the central state, by the Union. Modern India started in 1947 by declaring independence as a centralised state. Step by step, India's central authority established – by devolution – the states, making India a federation comparable to the United States (US) and Switzerland, the two traditional models of a federal state. The big difference: the US as well as Switzerland is the product of a consensus of already existing states (in Switzerland, cantons) to merge and to form a federation. The US and Switzerland became federations as a result of a bottom–up process. In India the process was top–down.

The EU – as an unfinished federation – is following the US and the Swiss example by defining its semi-federal structures bottom–up. The EU is the product of the consensus of already existing sovereign states to renounce some segments of their national sovereignty – as expressed especially in the EU's 'First Pillar' and the 'Common Policies' (Van Oudenaren 2005: 147–69). But this consensus includes also the agreement that the power not explicitly given to the Community by consensual agreement constitutes the still existing national sovereignty.

Unfinished as it is, the EU's federal structure already resembles in many respects the Indian federal structure. There is a directly elected federal parliament, following the rules any democratic parliament enjoys and respects – beginning with the fairness of the elections and ending with the parliament's ability to control and to censure the executive. The Indian Lok Sabha's majority controls indirectly but efficiently the Prime Minister's appointment; the European Parliament has to legitimate by majority decision the European Commission's president and the Commission itself. A simple Lok Sabha majority can end a Prime Minister's tenure by declaring the parliament's non-confidence in his (her) performance. A qualified (two-thirds) majority of the European Parliament can vote the Commission out of power – also by declaring its non-confidence in the EU's executive body.

Of course, significant differences have to be acknowledged. The office of the Indian Prime Minister, following the design of Britain's Westminster democracy, is the undisputed centre of executive power. The office of the European Commission's president does not enjoy the same kind of central power: the Commission's president – due to his (her) dependence on the national governments (which have to nominate him) and especially due to the very existence and the weight of the EU's Council (the European Council as well as the Council of Ministers) – is just one but not the decisive factor in the EU's (sometimes frustratingly) complex decision-making process.

Despite this difference, any kind of extrapolation of the EU's integration process – as defined by the Union's 'deepening' – will lead to a stronger federal character of the EU. The Constitutional Treaty, not ratified as a consequence of the French and the Dutch referenda in 2005, and the Reform Treaty have to be seen as a (rather small) step in the direction of a European Federation. The strengthening of the European Parliament, an ongoing development since 1979, and the shifting within the Council of Ministers from unanimity to more majority decisions are indicators of the federalising process within the EU (Van Oudenaren 2005: 71–97).

Of course, the decisive factor which makes all the difference between India's fully developed and the EU's unfinished federal structure is the existence of the Council. There is no equivalent in the Indian political system. The Indian state governments have been strengthened as a result of the decline of the – in the first three decades undisputed – dominance of the Congress Party. As soon as the states developed their own specific party systems the state governments became a countervailing power. But even as the Indian political system is characterised by an increase in state power – at the cost of the central government, the state governments are not a bloc able to play on the same level the central government controls. The Indian states have no instrument like the EU's Council which channels national interests very efficiently – mostly in the form of veto power – into the EU's decision-making process.

The EU's unfinished federalism is becoming, very slowly, stronger – meaning that the power is shifting from the member states to the Union. The Indian political system is defined by just the opposite trend – the states are winning in the ongoing power game with the central government. But there is no possibility to see in the next future that the Indian states will become as strong as the EU member states still are – as there is no chance in the foreseeable future that the EU's Parliament and Commission will become as strong as the Indian Parliament and the Indian Prime Minister (plus Cabinet) still are. It is possible to argue that there is a convergence going on – making Indian federalism more European and the EU's federalism more like the Indian. But the differences are still too strong to overlook the EU's lack of a final design, the absence of a clear understanding of the EU's final status.

Democratic values, democratic realities

The parallels between the Indian kind of federalism and the EU's develop-ment of a very special mix of federal and confederal elements are counterbal-anced by significant differences due to the unfinished status of the EU's federal structure. But a much stronger parallel is the democratic quality both – India as well as the EU – are exemplifying. India is a liberal democracy in the sense that political power has to be legitimised by free and fair elections. The Indian government as well as the state governments is dependent on electoral results. The fairness of this procedure can be measured by the ability to change governments peacefully. In India this has happened regu-larly since 1977, when Indira Gandhi's defeat ended the undisputed (but democratically legitimate) period of Congress dominance.

The same understanding of democracy does exist within the EU. The EU itself guarantees the standards of free and fair elections when it comes to the European Parliament. Even more significant, the Copenhagen Criteria, formulated in 1993 to define the standards the EU expects from future members, are based on this understanding of democracy: a competitive party system plus guarantees for basic human rights (especially concerning minorities) and the rule of law. No state which does not live up to this standard of democracy will be accepted as member (Van Oudenaren 2005: 342–5).

At the heart of the model of democracy India and the EU are bound to respect there is the principle of a multi-party system. In India this quality was given from the very beginning but with particular Indian elements:

1 The dominance of the Indian National Congress, the party based on the tradition of India's fight for independence under the guidance of Mahatma Gandhi and led after independence by India's first three Prime Ministers, Pandit Nehru, Lal Bahadur Shastri and Indira Gandhi, created an unbalanced party system. India's party system became only operational with 1977 and, especially after the Congress Party's second electoral defeat, in 1989, a balanced one.

2 Despite a concentration of the party system during the last years, favouring two major parties – Congress and the BJP (Bharatiya Janata Party, Indian People's Party), the party system is extremely fragmented. The existence of various regional parties, speaking for regional interests, and caste parties makes it necessary to form complex alliances within the Lok Sabha. Usually, one of the two major parties seems to dominate these fragile coalitions – like the BJP between 1998 and 2004 and like Congress since then. But the special interest parties prevent a traditional, Westminster-style two party system (Pelinka 2003: 157–81).

The EU's party system is not so different from the Indian situation. The European parties, built along the lines defined by the party groups in the European Parliament (like Conservatives, Socialists, Liberals and Greens) are rather loose alliances of national parties which in doubt follow national and not European interests. Because national parties control the European party system, and because national parties are directed by their primary interest to win national elections, the European party system is fragmented not so much along the traditional cleavages (like left versus right or materialism versus. post-materialism); it is *de facto* lacking coherence as a result of the dominance of national over European interests. It is based on the necessity to organise party groups within the European Parliament, but it still is secondary to the national party systems (Kreppel 2002: 30–51).

Unity out of diversity?

Any visit to the European Parliament in Strasbourg or Brussels helps to understand the challenge the EU faces by the multitude of official language: The speeches have to be translated simultaneously in all (now more than twenty) official languages; and all materials have to be translated and printed in more than twenty languages: from English to Maltese, from French to Estonian. Any visit to the Indian Parliament underlines the parallels between the Indian and the European diversity: There is no Indian language – there are Indian languages. But in India, differently from the EU, the fiction that all officially recognised languages are equal does not exist: Only Hindi and English enjoy the special status of pan-Indian languages. Seventeen other languages are recognised as state languages: each of them dominates in one of the states. And in the Indian Parliament you can use actively other officially recognised languages – but it will be translated simultaneously only into Hindi and English.

India deals with linguistic diversity by defining the state borders – outside the Hindi-speaking belt in the north – according to linguistic borders. This principle makes language the defining criterion for the state level. But for the federal level – in politics, in the economy, at universities – Hindi and/or English are necessary prerequisites.

David Laitin (Laitin 1997: 282–6) has compared the consequences of Indian and of European linguistic diversity. By observing social trends, he concludes that, in India, the formula 'three plus one minus one' defines not the official policy but the social reality. In Europe, Laitin thinks, the formula will be 'two plus one minus one'. In India, everybody interested in a national career in politics or business has to be fluent in Hindi and in English; and of course, he/she is fluent in his/her mother tongue, which for more than 60 per cent of Indians is neither Hindi nor English; that makes three languages. If he/she speaks a mother tongue which – as a minority language – is not the official language of the state he/she is coming from, the number of spoken languages is four, because the state language has to be mastered too. But if he/she has Hindi as mother tongue and is from a Hindi-speaking state, no other language than English has to be learned, that makes two.

In Europe, Laitin argues, the trend favours English and English alone as the continent's 'lingua franca'. That means any person interested in a European career has to be fluent in his/her mother tongue plus English. If his/her mother tongue is a minority language (like Catalan in Spain or Hungarian in Romania), the state language (Spanish, Romanian) has to be added. But if he/she speaks English as the mother tongue and lives in the UK or in Ireland, no other language is required.

When the European Communities were established by the treaties of 1951 (European Coal and Steel Community Treaty) and 1957 (Rome Treaty) it was obvious that – besides the clear anti-Soviet agenda – the basic philosophy of building a future Europe should be to overcome the nationalistic obsession European history had been defined by. When India was founded in 1947 it decided not to become Hindustan – not the Hindu answer to Islamic Pakistan, but a secular state giving a high degree of autonomy to different linguistic and religious groups. More than any other benchmark, the EU's success in overcoming European nationalisms defines the outcome of European integration; and more than other possible results, India's ability to deal with the explosive religious diversity defines whether India can survive as a democratic and secular state.

Both, the EU and India, are trying to separate religion and politics. In India, this is marked by the term 'secular'. The government has to abstain from any attitude which could be seen as partisan, favouring one denomination over the others. Within the EU, the pattern is much less unified – because the different member states follow different traditions: From the strict separation between state and church in France to the existence of the Church of England, linking state (England) and church; from the Irish and

Polish tradition of giving the Catholic Church a special position in fields like education to the contemporary Spanish developments of dissolving the links between Catholicism and state: the legal and social aspects of the relationship between politics and religion are much more diverse in Europe than they are in India.

But even the multitude of regulations within the EU is based on one principal rule: the freedom of any individual to decide about his or her creed must be guaranteed, including the freedom not to believe in any of the offered denominations. In that respect, secularism is the EU's doctrine also.

In India, the ongoing debate is how to define secularism. As the BJP's roots include Hindu fundamentalist tendencies, the period of BJP-led governments from 1998 to 2004 was an interesting experiment in the extent which the Congress-defined secularism would be redefined. There have been attempts to strengthen official recognition of Hinduism as the dominant religion and cultural tradition of India, but as the BJP depended on a complex coalition agreement with other parties not at all interested in shifting the balance within the general concept of secularism, the impact of the BJP rule on the federal level can be called secondary (Pelinka 2003: 213–19).

The impact is more felt on the state level. The extreme violent riots in Gujarat in 2002 have to be seen as the consequence of the BJP governing that state. The victims were mostly Muslims, and the responsibility of the state government – at least for not responding effectively to the violence – cannot be disputed. Gujarat 2002 has been a warning signal as to what kind of violence can erupt if a government does not implement efficiently the secular doctrine (Shani 2007: 135–55).

The European situation is very different – and not so different at all. The EU has to deal and will have even to deal in the future with two major challenges regarding religious diversity:

1 How to reconcile the French position of strict separation with the tendencies especially in new member states to give the church (in Poland, the Catholic Church; in some of the other countries, the national Orthodox churches) a prominent, rather official position?
2 How to come to terms with the rise of Euro-Islam, the result of migration from North Africa, the Middle East and South Asia – but also the result of bringing countries with Muslim majorities (Albania) or pluralities (Bosnia-Herzegovina) into the EU's realm?

The EU is part of the history of Christian or Judaeo-Christian civilisation. But the increasing impact of non-Christian elements – agnosticism and atheism, but even more of non-Christian denominations, especially of Islam – makes it necessary to debate the way the EU will possibly rethink and reconstruct its position regarding religious diversity.

Pluralism versus fundamentalism

The key term for what India and the EU have to face is fundamentalism. Fundamentalism has many faces. Considering the existing diversity, fundamentalism today exists in two major variations: religious and national fundamentalism.

Fundamentalism in principle has to be regarded as the antithesis of universal rights: especially the right of any person to choose his/her religious beliefs; and to the right of any person to participate in society and politics independently of his/her ethnic or national identity. Other rights are also challenged by fundamentalist trends: gender equality as well as the right of everybody to define personally his/her sexual orientation without political or social consequences.

In India as well as in the EU, the clash between pluralism and fundamentalism is a double one:

1   There is the contradiction between different kinds of fundamentalism. In India, this can be observed in the violent conflicts between Muslim fundamentalists, more or less backed by circles in Pakistan, and Hindu fundamentalists, more or less linked to the BJP. This contradiction may be less visible in Europe. But the influx of Islam and the sometimes violent response by non-Muslim Europeans – who consider Islam not acceptable in Europe – may create a more explosive climate that some political parties may feel tempted to exploit, and some fundamentalist tendencies within Islam may try to use for their own purposes.

2   There is the contradiction between the secular thesis and religious or national beliefs. This can be seen in India regarding the debate over conversion: to what extent is it legitimate to promote a certain creed (e.g. Christianity)? This can be seen especially in the conflicts between national majorities and minorities in Europe – from Northern Ireland to Bulgaria, from Romania to Spain. In India, especially the conflicts in India's north-east has similar roots: has a traditional national majority the obligation not only to tolerate but to promote the rights of ethnic (linguistic, national) minorities, e.g. in the form of regional autonomy?

The EU and India are built upon secularism and pluralism. As soon as the authorities cannot be considered to be impartial – regarding religious, regarding national conflicts, the basic philosophy of both entities is in danger. For that reason, India is more or less compelled not to allow Kashmir to leave India. If a specific religion is entitled to define the future of one part of India, India as such may fall apart. For the same reason, any wave of strong nationalisms endangers the very existence of the EU. It is nationalism of any kind (German or British, Polish or Slovak, French or Hungarian) which tends to oppose not only specific policies the EU is following, but the Union. This is an opposition for the right reason: as the process of European integration is motivated by the interest to tame nationalism, the different nationalisms have all the reasons to be against European integration.

The different waves of 'Euro-scepticism' are expressing this contradiction. Any emphasis on national sovereignty – e.g. in response to the EU's rule regarding minority rights – is especially rooted in national fundamentalism (Harmsen and Spiering 2004: 13–35). There may be various reasons for opposing European integration. But the most coherent and probably strongest one is the emphasis on national sovereignty. By putting 'the nation' above anything else, nationalism becomes fundamentalism – and this is exactly what the European integration is bound to overcome.

Common interests

Alliances and friendships are based on common interests. There is no alliance in the formal sense between India and the EU. But there are enough common interests to permit increasing co-operation and a relationship designed as friendship.

The first reason is the economy. India is one of the fastest-growing economies worldwide. In 2005 India's gross national product (GNP) grew 9.2 per cent (*Fischer Weltalmanach* 2007: 218). As literacy, life expectancy and other indicators of human development are growing also, India's position is shifting from the group of the very poor to the group of fast developing countries. In that respect, India is not so different from China – economically, about a decade delayed; and, of course, under the auspices of a democratic political system, while China is still a one party-system.

For the EU, India must be an interesting partner: the argument of systematic violations of human rights, overshadowing the relations between China and the EU – as it does in the case of Tibet, does not have this significance concerning the EU–India relationship. India's nuclear potential has already forced the US to rethink US–Indian relations (Mohan 2006: 257–84). The EU has not reacted – yet – in the same way, because the EU does not have a common policy regarding nuclear armament – yet. This policy is still exclusively a British and a French one. The absence of integration of aspects so important for security and defence prevents the EU from playing any visible role.

Two rivalries

India's nuclear armament is not only and not so much the consequence of the ongoing conflict with Pakistan. India went nuclear first and foremost as an answer to China. When China became a nuclear power, shortly after routing the Indian troops in Ladakh, 1962, and when the Chinese pro-Pakistan policy became obvious, India reacted by developing its nuclear programme. The Neruvian assumptions and belief in friendship with China had been replaced by a policy of distrust and confrontation (Cohen 2001: 256–65).

India's relations with China have improved in recent years. Some conflicts – like the border disputes in the Himalayas – have not been solved, but China and India have agreed to disagree and to postpone solutions. This has helped to cool the rivalry between the two Asian giants. But India is still developing a global policy China has already designed. Africa is an example: the Chinese presence in Africa is so much stronger than India's African role. This gives China leverage India is missing. India has not many partners it can call dependable friends because India has still not translated fully its potential into a coherent international policy beyond the mantra of 'non-interference in internal affairs'.

India's inability to get a permanent seat in the UN Security Council underlines the comparative weakness of India in world politics. Of course, the failure of the UN reform has many reasons. But India was unable to overcome the different interests blocking a reform which would have given India a prominent and highly visible role in world affairs.

There is the parallel to the EU: the debate about reform of the Security Council, from the European viewpoint, was a debate about a permanent German seat. The intrinsic logic of the EU – officially bound to have a 'Common Foreign and Security Policy' – would have implied that the EU itself would claim permanent membership in the Security Council. But this was never seriously discussed because it would have challenged a general principle and a special privilege: the general principle that EU member states (and not the EU) are entitled to UN membership; and the special privilege of the UK and France as permanent members of the Security Council.

The US, officially backing Germany's bid for a permanent seat on the Security Council, has no interest in replacing the present status of the different EU members within the UN. This highlights the American hesitation regarding the possibility of an internationally stronger EU. Of course, the uneasiness the US is demonstrating regarding the EU is not a rivalry like the Chinese–Indian relationship. But a rivalry it is, nevertheless, even if it is also a partnership (Van Oudenaren 2005: 365–92).

The US and Europe don't have the same interests in many important matters. Russia is a good example. The European attitude towards the Russian Federation is influenced by geopolitics and by the economy: Russia has already a long common border with the EU, and Russia is extremely important for Europe's energy imports. The US geographic as well as economic situation is very different. But the EU has no coherence in its Russian policy. This can be seen in the agreements between the US and two EU members, Poland and the Czech Republic, regarding radar and missile installations – agreements the EU has not been consulted about and which Russia defines as a provocation. The differences between US and EU interests are not translated into negotiations between allies on the basis of equality – because the EU can easily be divided into different actors.

The US has a certain and understandable interest in preventing Europe from becoming a single actor. As long as Europe can be easily divided – e.g.

into 'old' and 'new' Europe – the transatlantic relationship is not a balanced one: Europe is too weak to balance the American superpower; and Europe is too weak because it is politically not integrated enough.

On the eve of the 2003 Iraq war, Robert Kagan put the European dilemma that way:

> So what is to be done? The obvious answer is that Europe should [...] build up its military capabilities. [...] There is not much ground for hope that this will happen. But, then, who knows? Maybe concern about America's overweening power really will create some energy in Europe.
>
> (Kagan 2003: 101)

Kagan should be corrected: it is not so much about a military build-up – it is about the integration of different and contradicting national foreign and security policies. It is the lack of a really common foreign and security policy (CFSP) which guarantees the US dominance in the transatlantic relationship. And it is not the US that can be expected to become interested in a Europe that develops into a power the US would have to deal with on an equal footing.

Towards a multipolar international order?

India and the EU have a common interest: an interest in a multipolar order replacing instability, the product of an unbalanced and therefore unpredictable global situation, which has been the main quality of international affairs since the end of the rather balanced and predictable East–West conflict. This common interest is not necessarily a Chinese and an American interest: China seems to cherish its privilege as one among only five veto powers in the UN – why should China welcome any change diminishing its leverage in such a very small club? And China especially is opposed to any understanding of 'order' that would create policy benchmarks justifying interventions – like the need of humanitarian interventions if basic human rights are violated in a genocide-like disaster?

Two African cases are examples of the implications of an international order which is more than the rule of an undisputed national sovereignty: the case of Ruanda as an example of supreme tragedy and crime; and the case of Darfur as an example how the principle of non-intervention prevents any efficient international solidarity. China has made it clear that it opposes human intervention even in such cases because intervention contradicts the principle of non-interference in internal affairs.

The US, on the other hand, is especially hesitant to accept any kind of global governance limiting the American role as the dominant global actor. The American non-acceptance of the Kyoto Protocol and of the International Criminal Court are just some of the examples that the world's only superpower sees global governance structures as a contradiction to American interests.

Of course, India is – to say the least – also quite ambivalent about any kind of rules, of order, that could impose norms on sovereign states. But India's hesitant attitude is not so much the product of a systematic interest as the result of feeling excluded from international norms like the Non-proliferation Treaty. And India is still also affected by an anti-colonial reflex because an order that includes the possibility of intervention can be seen as based on 'neocolonial' thinking.

In the long run, India and the EU – perhaps in collaboration with Japan – could become the vanguard of an international order that could be able to combine stability with principles based on a common understanding of universal human rights. But, as any order has to be built on interests, the question is still open whose interests can be used as the basis of such an order.

Immediately after the end of the Cold War, Henry Kissinger predicted that the result of the implosion of the Soviet Union and the end of the Eastern political, economic and military system would not be an American century but a return to the traditional rule of international affairs: a multipolar order. The bipolar system of the decades dominated by the East–West conflict will not and cannot be replaced by a unipolar order dictated and controlled by the US. Joseph S. Nye, Jr – coming from a rather different school of thinking – agrees: 'The US is unable to provide stability by acting alone. The US needs partners' (Nye 2008: 61–9).

A multipolar order needs a balance between a certain number of actors. This balance cannot be provided by a Europe divided – and neither by an India still shying away from a coherently defined global role. But the EU and India cannot be interested in the creation of such an order defined only by the US and China, Russia and Japan. The European and the Indian interests have a common ground: an order defined also by a Europe able to overcome its national divisions; and by an India accepting global responsibility.

Conclusion

The EU has been compared in its (unfinished) federal dimension especially with the US (Nicolaidis and Howse 2001). The parallels are manifold: the starting of the federation building from the level of already existing states (bottom–up) and the ongoing discourse about the separation between powers reserved for the states and the powers of the Union. The term 'United States of Europe', used by Winston Churchill and many others, underlines these parallels.

The case of India tells a different story. The federation was built top–down, and despite some conflicts between states and union, the federalism discourse in India is much less vibrant than in the US and the EU. In India, this debate is overshadowed by the discourse about other aspects of diversity – like religion and caste. But India has to be and is already part of the academic discourse about the ability to use federal structures for bridging social conflicts and contradictions. In the book *Forging Unity out of Diversity*

(Goldwin *et al.* 1989), published in 1989, India is part of the comparative analysis together with the US, Belgium, Canada, Switzerland, Spain, Malaysia and Yugoslavia.

The missing link in this concert of comparisons is the comparison between the EU and India. As in all cases, comparing different systems has to consider parallels and differences. But the existence of differences – and there are very significant differences between India and the EU – does not prevent the necessity to compare; and to look for dynamics that could strengthen the differences and/or the parallels.

The dynamics seem to be quite clear. As European integration goes on, any step in the process of 'deepening' the EU brings the Union a little bit nearer to the status of a federation – and strengthens the parallels wirth India. Any process that integrates step by step the European foreign and defence policies into a 'Common Foreign and Security Policy' makes the EU able to speak more often with one voice – transforming more of its economic potential into the ability of an emerging global power: in that respect, European integration strengthens per se the parallels with the other emerging global power, with India (Dannreuther 2004: 1–11).

As European integration goes on, the need to implement the concept of the CFSP, even at the cost of national policies, will increase. This would enable the EU to act in the same league as the US, Russia, China, Japan – and India. This would fill the gap between the as yet unused potential the EU has in international politics and the reality defined by the absence of a coherent EU policy in most of the cases – from Iraq to Iran, from the reform of the UN Security Council to the conflict between Israel and the Palestinians.

In that respect, the EU and India are more or less in the same situation, in the same boat. Both are international giants, hesitant – for different reasons – to fulfil the role of major actors. Both are actors with unfulfilled promise. Both are – in all probability – pillars of any future global order.

The concept of European integration is based on the ability to convert ideas into interests. First, there was the idea of a post-national Europe able to prevent any return of the murderous European nationalisms of the past: the First World War, the Second World War and the Holocaust. This idea was used to shape economic interests and direct them into lifting national borders – the common market, the single market, the Monetary Union, the Schengen agreement (Parsons 2003: 231–42).

The Indian situation is different, but not too different. Indian independence had been based on the concept of Indian exceptionalism: Following Mahatma Gandhi's teaching, implemented more or less by the first Congress governments, India perceived its role not as an ordinary global actor like the others but as a moralising teacher the others should learn from. This 'idealistic' approach had to change – as a result of international isolation as experienced in the military defeat by China; and as a result of economic failure. The India of the 1990s and of the twenty-first century's first decade is an

India which has accepted that it cannot be the world's guru; it has to be one actor among others (Pelinka 2003: 265–83).

The EU and India are on a path towards normalisation: India by abandoning the Gandhian and Neruvian role of the teacher of all other nations; the EU by becoming more of a federal state, due to the integration of some – not all – national policies. As India and the EU are entering more and more the rough world of global politics, global politics will have to learn to live with two new global actors.

References

Aslund, A. and Dabrowski, M. (eds) (2007) *Europe after Enlargement*, Cambridge: Cambridge University Press.

Cohen, S. (2001) *India. Emerging Power*, Washington, DC: Brookings Institution Press.

Dannreuther, R. (2004) *European Union Foreign and Security Policy: Towards a Neighbourhood Strategy*, London: Routledge.

Fischer Weltalmanach (2007) *Der Fischer Weltalmanach 2008. Zahlen, Daten, Fakten*, Frankfurt am Main: Fischer.

Goldwin, R., Kaufman, A. and Schambra, W. (eds) (1989) *Forging Unity out of Diversity: The Approaches of Eight Nations*, Washington, DC: American Enterprise Institute.

Harmsen, R. and Spiering, M. (eds) (2004) *Euroscepticism: Party Politics, National Identity and European Integration*, European Studies 20, Amsterdam: Rodopi.

Kagan, R. (2003) *Of Paradise and Power: America and Europe in the New World Order*, New York: Alfred A. Knopf.

Kissinger, H. (1994) *Diplomacy*, New York: Simon & Schuster.

Kreppel, A. (2002) *The European Parliament and Supranational Party System: a Study in Institutional Development*, Cambridge: Cambridge University Press.

Laitin, D. (1997) 'The cultural identities of a European state', *Politics and Society* 25 (3): 277–302.

Mohan, R. (2006) *Impossible Allies: Nuclear India, United States and the Global Order*, New Delhi: India Research Press.

Nicolaidis, K. and Howse, R. (eds) (2001) *The Federal Vision: Legitimacy and Levels of Governance in the United States and the European Union*, Oxford: Oxford University Press.

Nye, J. (2008) *The Powers to Lead*, Oxford: Oxford University Press.

Parsons, C. (2003) *A Certain Idea of Europe*, Ithaca, NY: Cornell University Press.

Pelinka, A. (2003) *Democracy Indian Style: Subhas Chandra Bose and the Creation of India's Political Culture*, New Brunswick, NJ: Transaction.

Shani, O. (2007) *Communalism, Caste and Hindu Nationalism: The Violence in Gujarat*, Cambridge: Cambridge University Press.

Van Oudenaren, J. (2005) *An Introduction to the European Union*, 2nd edn, Lanham, MD: Rowman & Littlefield.

13 Civility meets realism

The prospects of a strategic partnership between the European Union and China

Liselotte Odgaard

The European Union and China as strategic partners?

In the second half of the 1990s, China was just starting to experiment with multilateral security co-operation; prior to that time, China refused to participate in such initiatives, preferring to base its security on its armed forces and bilateral strategic partnerships rather than alliances and permanent security institutions. China's participation in multilateral security institutions in Central Asia and in South East Asia became a testing ground for China to see if the neighbouring states would take Chinese interests into account to an extent that made it worth while for China to begin emphasising multilateralism as a central element in its post-Cold War foreign policy. Chinese security co-operation with Russia, Central Asia and the South East Asian countries was a fruitful experience for China that encouraged Beijing to play a more proactive role in multilateral security institutions outside Asia. This chapter asks the question if China has come to see multilateral security co-operation as essential to the successful pursuit of its national interests, and if so, what the consequences are for strategic co-operation between China and the European Union (EU).

In contrast to China, the EU is inherently multilateral. The EU has state-like characteristics such as for example a well functioning common market, a Parliament, and a European Court of Justice. This makes the EU the most integrated institutional structure among forms of regional integration in contemporary international relations. The EU is also able to forge a large measure of solidarity in extra-regional affairs, manifested in agreement on common principles of state conduct. One of the EU's weakest points is the issue of a common foreign and defence policy, as implied by the fact that the EU does not have a common army, and that the popularity of the proponents of an integrated European defence policy has been greatly reduced. Nevertheless, the EU has forged agreement on a European Security Strategy that lists physical security or 'freedom from fear', political participation, the rule of law and respect for human rights and fundamental freedoms, an open and inclusive economic order that provides for the wealth of everyone or 'freedom from want', and social well-being in all its aspects such as access to health services, to education, to a clean and hazard-free environment, etc. The security strategy involves the EU's commitment to multilateral security instruments, to a multipolar international system that allows weaker states to have a say in global security governance, and to the importance of civic and social rights protection for the preservation of international peace and stability (Biscop 2005). The second question addressed here is if China's recent commitment to multilateralism provides the EU and China with sufficient common ground that a strategic partnership can be forged.

The prospects of a strategic partnership between the EU and China are slim. China is walking on two legs in its relations with the outside world, prioritising multilateral foreign policy elements as well as a unilateral build-up of its domestic economic, military and political resources. The multilateral elements appear in China's support for the extensive expansion of the breadth and depth of dialogue fora within as well as outside the field of traditional strategic issues. However, the unilateral elements in Chinese policies continue to give cause for concern because they repeatedly emerge as impediments to the establishment of substantial strategic co-operation between the EU and China, for example due to opposing policies on Taiwan and China's unsuccessful attempts at convincing the EU that it should lift its arms embargo against China. Beijing has been quite successful in highlighting the attractive multilateral elements of its foreign policy and concealing the more dubious unilateral aspects in its dealings with the EU. Thereby, China has succeeded in driving wedges between the EU and the US, with which the majority of EU member states are allied. Beijing's ability to constrain Washington's ability to pursue its security interests is the result of successfully presenting Chinese interests as the common interests of states and therefore also as contributions to international peace and stability. This policy allows Beijing to obtain widespread support for its insistence that permanent security institutions of global and regional reach used for the management of international peace and stability remain firmly embedded in the old United Nations (UN) system. In addition, this policy is compatible with the EU's support for maintaining the UN system at the centre of global and regional security management.

On the other hand, at the end of the day the EU supports the US role as the global security guarantor of the last resort and US efforts to revise the UN system so as to allow civil and human rights as fundamental a role as the principles of absolute sovereignty and non-intervention. Therefore, a strategic partnership involving extensive policy co-ordination and co-operation between the EU and China is not on the cards.

Multilateral and unilateral elements in Chinese foreign policy

China is located in a neighbourhood with no stable alliance partners. The legitimacy of Communist Party rule is increasingly called into question, and although China experiences surging economic growth rates, it also has growing problems with socio-economic inequality which constitutes a threat to the survival of the current regime. China is a *status quo* power in the sense that it is imperative for China to maintain peace and stability in its neighbourhood, since it still struggles with vast economic and social problems (Odgaard 2007b).

China's concept of co-operative security is about building trust, confidence and multilateral co-operation with the purpose of removing the risk of armed conflict. Co-operative security is to engender peaceful coexistence at the international level, allowing China to concentrate on its internal economic and social development. It involves the use of diplomatic means to test whether the surroundings are willing to take into account Chinese demands and interests (Yahuda 2003). Co-operative security requires that moderation permeates foreign policy behaviour in general so as to allow peaceful security interaction to dominate international politics. Peaceful interaction implies multilateral security dialogue and institutionalised security governance on the basis of the Cold War UN system and its principles of absolute sovereignty and non-intervention that allows the preservation of heterogenous political systems. China's domestic economic and military resources are far too modest to pursue a policy of imposition. The bias towards reliance on diplomatic instruments inherent in the policy of co-operative security is well suited to China's modest economic and military resources compared with the US (Odgaard 2007b). Co-operative security is also well suited to Beijing's long-standing aversion to alliance commitments, which has allowed Beijing to swiftly adjust its foreign policy goals and intentions to changing circumstances.

The Chinese concept of multipolarity implies building strategic partnerships with secondary powers. These partnerships form the basis for warding off US dominance by poaching on US alliances and partnerships. The Chinese concept of multipolarity does not imply traditional power balancing through alliances, but through the looser concept of strategic partnerships. China increasingly focuses on the forging of compromises with states that are at least partially supportive of Chinese demands for respect for the absolute sovereignty of states, acceptance of political authorities with a proven record of control over geographically delimited territories and people, and institutionalised security arrangements founded in the UN system of the Cold War (Odgaard 2007a: 114–15).

China hence also supports the preservation of the old UN system and its principles of absolute sovereignty, effective territorial control as a basis for regime recognition, and the authority of the UN Security Council in global security management (Gill 2007: 135–6). China uses its institutional affiliations to confirm its image as a responsible power committed to proactively protecting the common interests not only of states, but also of mankind, at least if these do not threaten the survival of the states system. China's contribution of personnel to UN peacekeeping operations is an example of this policy (Odgaard 2007c: 213). China's contribution to UN peacekeeping operations in terms of peacekeepers has grown from approximately fifty in 1996 to approximately 1,500 in 2006 (Stähle 2008: 655). More significantly, China's affiliation with UN-based institutions is used to manifest its commitment to maintaining the old political framework for international security in co-operation with other states (Odgaard 2007a: 191–214).

Beijing has been able to cash in on the reservations regarding the US alliance system by invoking the old interpretation of the UN system, allowing much less flexibility on this issue than on other aspects of its post-Cold War security diplomacy. Many secondary powers and entities such as the EU agree with Beijing that the UN system should be preserved, in order to prevent the US from using the alliance system as a basis for promoting US hegemony. China has actively pursued the preservation of the UN system, by buying into existing institutions committed to the old principles of state conduct, such as ASEAN's institutional network in South East Asia and the South Asian Association for Regional Co-operation (SAARC), and by promoting the establishment of new UN-based institutions, such as the Shanghai Co-operation Organisation (SCO) in Central Asia. Seen from the perspective of secondary powers and entities such as the EU, partial co-operation with the US and China on consolidating both the alliance system and the UN system serves their interest in promoting neither a US-dominated nor a China-dominated order, but instead an order that combines elements from both, in a way that maximises their influence on Asia-Pacific security.

The international order advanced by China is non-intrusive in the sense that it is not designed to foster extensive co-operation or the rearrangement of existing political structures according to the values of major powers. It allows for a diversity of political systems and security institutions combined with a multi-level system of dialogue aiming at conflict prevention. This type of system provides secondary and minor powers with more influence than would be possible under a regional order solely defined by Washington. The Chinese version of order is conducive to a diversity of political systems that insulates regional states from US demands to implement liberal concepts of human rights and democracy and to base their national security solely on the US alliance system and it is therefore attractive to secondary and minor powers such as the EU member states (Odgaard 2007b).

There are, however, also worrying aspects of Chinese foreign policy. These are the Chinese military build-up and China's lack of a positively defined concept of political legitimacy. China's military spending continues to increase. In 2006 the official budget increased by 14.7 per cent to US$35.1 billion (Xinhua, 5 March 2006). China's defence modernisation priorities include reforms driven by the US-led Revolution in Military Affairs, having fewer but better troops, and stepping up its military posture across the Taiwan Strait (State Council Information Office, 27 December 2004). Substantial amounts of the People's Liberation Army's (PLA) budget allocated to the procurement of weaponry are used to buy defensive and offensive arms such as fighter aircraft, amphibious assault ships, reconnaissance aircraft, missile destroyers and submarines. China also spends heavily on military communication satellites, and in 2007 it demonstrated that it was able to construct anti-satellite missiles, expanding its space capacity. So far, China's military pretensions depend on access to Russian arms and know-how, but its military modernisation programmes are making headway in decreasing its dependence on external sources of arms and technology. China uses considerable resources on transforming its armed forces from self-sufficiency in manpower to self-sufficiency in military technology (Ross 2006: 369–71). These changes are intended to enable China to adopt swift and flexible defence responses. China has also expanded its military presence in one form or another across North East, South East, Central and South Asia. For example, during later years a troop build-up has taken place along the Chinese–North Korean border, and China has assisted Myanmar in building a deep-sea port near Mergui on the Andaman Sea. It has also won permission to operate a naval observation facility in the Cocos Islands at the top of the Andaman chain, which helps China to become a naval power in the Indian Ocean (Velloor, 26 October 2004). Chinese military co-operation with Russia and Central Asia was institutionalised by treaty in 2001, legalising the projection of Chinese troops into the area (*People's Daily*, 17 July 2001). In Pakistan, Beijing has agreed to fund, construct and develop a deep-sea port and naval base in Gwadar, which will allow China to monitor US–Indian naval activities in the Arabian Sea (Ramachandran, 21 January 2006).

The problem with the military build-up, growing defence expenditure and the gradual extension of China's strategic reach is that they potentially contradict Beijing's alleged commitment to co-operative security and to the non-use of force. The extension of Beijing's strategic reach and the nature of its defence modernisation process are not merely designed to protect China's territorial borders, but also to consolidate China's position as a major power. Examples are China's military co-operation with Pakistan and traditional Indian dependants on the subcontinent such as Bangladesh that can be used by China to access the Bay of Bengal and the Indian Ocean. Also, Chinese occupations in the Spratlys in the maritime heartland of South East Asia have sparked decade-long concerns about China's long-term intentions. Another problem is the continued lack of defence transparency. The defence budget is really just five pages of overall plans for defence spending and as such not comparable to the detailed defence budgets of the West (interview with Chinese professor, 7 October 2006). Beijing leaves the impression that, despite the numerous strategic dialogues China is engaged in, it continues to withhold essential information necessary to establish a political framework to preserve international peace and stability rather than mere paper tigers.

China's lack of a positively defined concept of political legitimacy is equally disconcerting (Odgaard 2007a: 197–9). The same concerns apply to this policy as to Beijing's defence modernisation. What is the long-term purpose? Is it to preserve a plurality of political systems and promote multipolarity and international co-operation, or has this policy been born out of necessity, suggesting that China's numerous affiliations with regional and global institutions might in future be used to promote a Sinocentric order, the contents of which are unknown? China does not admit having intentions of promoting an international order based on Chinese interests in public, and yet it seems unlikely that China would refrain from doing so; China's unwillingness to talk about the possible contents of such an order only serves to enhance suspicions about future Chinese activities.

Joint initiatives and disagreements in EU–China relations

Both the EU and China have vowed enhanced co-operation based on a strategic partnership. At the abstract level, China looks favourably upon the economic and social goals promoted by the EU. China's inclination to emulate EU policies can be detected in its domestic reform policies dealing with the issue of poverty in general and the flow of wealth from rural to urban areas in particular, which is seen as a major threat to Chinese unity and continued Communist Party rule. To sustain economic growth, China is pleading for additional development aid and is keen to enhance technological co-operation with the EU. China's mounting energy supply and environmental problems have urged Beijing to look to the EU for ideas on energy efficiency and environmental legislation (Odgaard and Biscop 2007: 70).

China continues to encourage co-operation with the EU in the areas of service trade, investments, and science and technology, due to its concerns about sustaining economic growth. China is the EU's second biggest trading partner, and the EU is China's first trading partner. Although EU–China political relations have grown considerably, economic relations are the cornerstone of EU–China relations, calling for enhanced policy adjustments and co-operation. A major obstacle for these plans is EU concern about the trade imbalance with China (interview with European Commission official, 10 July 2006). Chinese exports to Europe are seen to crowd out European manufacturing and labour and give rise to trade disputes due to the widening trade imbalance, which was around €106 billion in 2005 (European Commission, October 2006). In the EU's view, China needs to meet its obligations as a member of the WTO, whereas the EU needs to focus on becoming more competitive. According to EU Trade Commissioner Peter Mandelson, the EU cannot continue to silence calls for greater protection from China in Europe unless China complies with internationally recognised trade standards such as those for intellectual property rights (European Commission, 7 July 2006). Serious obstacles to economic co-operation between the EU and China thus remain, which calls for adjustments. Most important, China–EU relations need to be changed from the assumption that China is a developing country in need of EU assistance to a balanced relationship of equal partnership (interview with European Commission official, 10 July 2006).

The EU and China share many commonalities as regards their strategic and security outlook. The EU does support parts of China's demands for a global order, namely the elements of a co-operative foreign policy and multipolarity. They also agree that the UN should be at the centre of global security management, and the EU supports China's demand for the preservation of the UN Security Council as the principal forum for the management of global security issues. The two powers agree that persuasion and dialogue are preferable to resort to force. Foreign and security policy form an integral part of the political dialogue, and global governance issues now routinely figure on the agenda of bilateral meetings. However, for a true strategic partnership to be established, more actual joint EU–China policy initiatives leading to policy adjustments and practical co-operation must be undertaken on the basis of the political dialogue (Odgaard and Biscop 2007: 71–2).

Despite the potential for co-operation, vast differences prevail in the EU's and China's strategic outlook, notably on issues of human rights and democracy. The EU agrees with the US that the UN principles of state conduct should be revised so as to list democracy and human rights as fundamental, on a par with absolute sovereignty and non-intervention in the domestic affairs of other states. Serious concerns remain on the human rights situation in China itself, and on the prospects of democratic development in China. Both facts are reflected in China's foreign policy. For example, China is usually not in favour of conditionality and is generally reluctant to mandate intervention, even when grave human rights violations have taken place (Odgaard 2007a: 233).

One area where the seriousness of EU–China differences on human rights and democracy issues has emerged is China's entrance as an economic and political player on the African continent. Access to raw materials such as oil and minerals has been the main motive for China to get a foothold on the African continent. Initially, China's presence was mainly in the form of businessmen who established themselves for economic reasons and without much central planning or control. However, the Chinese government also approached African governments to make agreements allowing China to import raw materials such as oil, gas and minerals in return for economic assistance. China's growing economic presence was increasingly criticised by the EU because China did not make political demands on African governments a condition for providing economic assistance. China's offers of economic aid in return for access to buy raw materials were often a much better deal for African governments compared with existing agreements with Western countries. Western aid policies are usually at odds with the policies of African governments. By contrast, China's adherence to the principles of absolute sovereignty and non-interference in the domestic affairs of other countries implies that political conditionality is not part of China's aid policy, leaving recipient countries to define their domestic political model without interference from Beijing.

Despite the alleged apolitical Chinese presence in Africa, China and African countries such as Angola, Sierra Leone, Liberia, Zambia, Zimbabwe and Sudan share the determination to preserve absolute sovereignty and the right of governments to determine the domestic political set-up of their jurisdiction as the fundamental principles of international relations. Chinese backing has therefore allowed African governments to resist outside pressure for domestic political change, such as demands for the Zimbabwean government to open dialogue with the opposition and for the Sudanese government to halt the genocide in Darfur (Kurlantzick 2006: 5).

EU concerns that China's presence in Africa undermines its aid policy are probably exaggerated, in part because the Chinese presence is likely to remain modest compared with that of European countries, in part because China is not likely to risk severing its steadily expanding ties with the EU to defend its modest interests in Africa except in cases such as Darfur in Sudan where China's core global interest in defending the old UN system is challenged. In line with this pattern, Zimbabwean President Mugabe failed to secure a bail-out from the Beijing government from US and EU sanctions (Tull 2006: 473). In turn, the EU does not attempt to raise the issue of good governance in the intra-Chinese context, demanding the implementation of political reforms in return for economic and technological assistance. Instead, the EU's approach to China is that continuous dialogue and co-operation engender higher living standards and gradual political reform. China's insistence that the UN should not undertake military intervention in Sudan has, however, driven the point home that when African issues impact on issues of global order, then China is disinclined to compromise. China's economic presence in Africa hence quickly, and unexpectedly, turned out to have unavoidable political implications that encouraged Beijing to develop some kind of standard for the Chinese regional presence. That may be seen as a kind of good governance policy Chinese-style that challenges Western good governance policies, in addition to the mentioned difficulties in establishing a genuine strategic partnership between the EU and China. One indication that this process is already taking place is that China is seen as a development model by many African countries because China combines market economic principles with authoritarian political structures in a way that appears to promote economic growth, social stability and growing global influence. A similar process is happening in the Middle East, where numerous countries are keen to base their development on a model that brings them into the group of developed countries without having to adopt the liberal political ideas of the West (interview with Chinese professor, 6 November 2007). The differences between China and the EU on human rights issues are hence likely to grow stronger despite China's intention to strengthen its strategic partnership with the EU.

China as yet does not seem to agree with all the rules which the EU puts forward in the context of effective multilateralism as a way of promoting multipolarity. Multilateralism in the sense of effective constraints on the pursuit of national interests is different from mere balancing of the US, which seems to be the definition often used by Beijing. The promotion of democracy, human rights and the rule of law in China itself remains very difficult. The EU may not agree on the means the US sometimes uses to promote democracy, human rights and the rule of law. However, Brussels and Washington agree that these principles of domestic conduct should be given the status of fundamental rules of state conduct in the UN system on a par with absolute sovereignty and effective territorial control. Chinese experiments with top–down controlled village democracy does not alter the fact that Beijing, by contrast, is firmly committed not to compromise on the principles of absolute sovereignty and effective territorial control (Odgaard and Biscop 2007: 74).

The incentives to create a genuine strategic partnership are further diminished by the fact that the EU does not have much influence in the Asia-Pacific. One reason is that the EU's weakest point is the issue of a common foreign and defence policy, and another that the US has no great desire to enlist the EU's involvement in Asia-Pacific affairs. Moreover, although China is aware that a strategic partnership with the EU benefits China's modernisation process and contributes to international peace and stability and to its image as a great power embedded in multilateral international structures, it is not willing to abandon its demands for international order to extract these benefits. These demands include the rise of China as a military great power with legitimate claims to the territory that it defines as the Chinese motherland and the continued authority of the UN Security Council as the principal forum for managing international order. The alliance relations between the majority of EU member states and the US imply that the EU cannot accommodate essential Chinese security goals.

Prevailing differences between the EU and China on political and security issues promoted by the EU and the EU's still developing foreign and security policy, which prevents it from carrying much weight as a strategic actor in Asia, indicate that the EU remains much closer to US visions of global order than those models advocated by China. Like the US, the EU is doubtful about the intentions and consequences of China's continuous military build-up. Both the EU and China may be keen to avoid proliferation of weapons of mass destruction. However, at the end of the day the opportunities for practical co-operation are circumscribed by the fact that they are on different sides of the fence (Odgaard and Biscop 2007: 76).

A major limitation to EU–China co-operation is that Beijing's co-operative foreign policy and its prioritisation of diplomacy remain experimental. By contrast, the EU is predominantly a civilian power relying heavily on economic and diplomatic means for international influence. Beijing sees a strong national defence and continued authoritarian rule as a necessity to maintain domestic stability and to protect China against future aggression from foreign powers such as the US and Japan, should they prove unwilling to accommodate Chinese demands and interests in a future global order. EU diplomacy and co-operative foreign policy are one of its defining characteristics, which allow it to present itself as the prototype of how economic and political power may appeal to contemporary China because it helps Beijing to convince the surrounding countries that China has no interest in promoting a Sinocentric order, but that China's rise will be accompanied by a continued focus on the common interest of states in international peace and stability. However, in view of US efforts to strengthen its alliance system and revise the UN system, China's commitment to co-operation and diplomacy remains experimental and is therefore not, as of yet, a reliable basis for long-term EU policy planning towards China (Odgaard 2007a: 233–4).

China's half-hearted commitment to co-operative security and multipolarity comes to the fore in its relations with several international actors. One indicator is the lack of permanent politico-strategic dialogue and co-operation mechanisms between China and Japan (Yahuda 2006). In South Asia, China seems to use co-operative security and multipolarity as rhetorical devices of appeasement rather than to settle agreements and to establish co-operation. Japan and India are both likely challengers to China's position as a major Asia-Pacific power, encouraging Beijing to focus on curbing the growing influence of Tokyo and New Delhi in the Asia-Pacific and to strengthen its strategic relations with Russia (Odgaard 2007a: 98–107).

Another inherent problem of an EU–China strategic partnership is China's policy on political legitimacy. Fundamental disagreement prevails between the two international actors on the standard by which governments obtain legitimacy in the long term. Their mutual commitment to a common understanding of the principle of non-interference is therefore questionable. The EU and China may be able to agree that a narrow interpretation of legitimacy is acceptable in the short to medium term, focusing on the common goal of effective control over territory and citizens within existing states, rather than the promotion of divergent ideas of political authority. However, China has reservations about the narrow interpretation of legitimacy, as indicated by its long-term commitment to the reunification of the Chinese motherland as defined by Beijing and including Taiwan (Kang 2003). The EU prefers US ideas on political authority to China's historical understanding of sovereignty and what is perceived as Beijing's creeping promotion of a Sinocentric order based on Chinese superiority through the pursuit of a large-scale military build-up while claiming to be committed to co-operative security and a multipolar international system (Odgaard 2007a: 139–63). Beijing's subtle promotion of Sino-centric political authority by means of sovereignty claims and economic, political and strategic dominance in areas such as Taiwan, the Korean peninsula and the Russian Far East threaten to alienate China from the EU as well as numerous other states in the West and in Asia. For this reason, China adopts a pragmatic approach to the promotion of civilisational elements of a Sinocentric order beyond these border areas, advocating stability rather than immediate reunification of the motherland and equality rather than hierarchy in international relations (interview with professor in Beijing, 13 November 2004). Nevertheless, Beijing's inclination towards Sinocentrism comes to the fore in its international relations. For example, in its home region Japan is seen as a pariah state,

North Korea as a tributary state, and Taiwan as part of Chinese civilisation. By contrast, the EU would emphasise that Japan and Taiwan are democracies and tend to see North Korea as a pariah state.

The EU is aware of the uncertainty as regards China's future foreign policy priorities and therefore continues to gravitate towards support for the US and its demands for a post-Cold War global order. The US is currently in the process of parting company with the old UN system, pursuing hegemony by using the US alliance system to demand compliance with US interests such as participation in the war on terror and preventive measures against the spread of WMD-related material. Being the weaker power, Beijing has presented its UN-based alternative as a democratisation of Asia-Pacific politics that is not intended to enhance China's regional influence, but instead to allow small and secondary powers an equal say on regional security issues (interview with professor in Beijing, 13 November 2004). However, in so far as China starts using its network of institutional affiliations to promote a Sinocentric order, the EU is likely to retreat from its current co-operative politics with regard to China, relying on US security guarantees to prevent the emergence of a Sinocentric order.

Conclusion: China's foreign policy and the European Union

The chapter has looked at how China's two-sided strategy of multilateralism and unilateralism affects the prospects of creating a strategic partnership between the EU and China characterised by institutionalised policy co-ordination and substantial co-operation rather than a mere proliferation in dialogue fora. I have argued that the prospects of such a genuine partnership are not promising in view of the uncertainty surrounding China's commitment to the multilateral elements of its foreign policy. As is the case with most international powers, if forced to choose between multilateral and unilateral strategies, Beijing would opt for unilateralism, including stepping up its economic and military build-up and its efforts to redesign the political foundations of regime legitimacy to prevent the demise of Communist Party rule. The problem with China's current two-sided foreign policy is that it is inherently expensive to prioritise both the multilateral elements of co-operative security, multipolarity and the UN system at the same time as China is heavily engaged in building up its domestic resources. The risk of overextending its resources due to the extensive reach of China's foreign policy, both in terms of policy instruments and in terms of its global reach, is a growing problem. One example is the 2002 US–Democratic People's Republic of Korea (DPRK) nuclear stand-off. As a central actor during the crisis, China made considerable efforts to establish itself as the convenor of negotiations that brought the contenders into contact without choosing sides. Although Beijing was fairly successful in positioning itself as a convenor, it could not escape the expectation that China was capable of ensuring

North Korea's compliance with international demands for denuclearisation on a par with the political influence of a great power dominating its smaller neighbour. Another example is the challenge China's growing economic presence in African countries is said to pose to the good governance policies of the EU, which entail the demand for political and socio-economic reforms in return for development aid. Even if China intended to be only an economic actor on the African continent, it cannot escape the responsibilities accompanying its status as a political great power that challenges the principles of state conduct adhered to by Western countries. However, should the risk of over-extension of China's resources become too much of a reality, China is likely to disengage from many of its overseas activities to concentrate on the expansion of its domestic resource base.

The EU is a different type of actor, as it is inherently multilateral, an approach that has proved viable as a strategy for making Europe a voice to be reckoned with in international politics, as is evident from China's numerous relations with the EU alongside its contacts with individual member states of the Union. The limitations of the civilian power of the EU have, however, also come to the fore in its dealings with China. For example, the EU's decision not to lift its arms embargo against China despite its inefficiency and following pressures from Washington to maintain the embargo demonstrated that the EU is far from being an independent actor on strategic and security issues despite their continued centrality to exercising global political influence. The EU's negligible influence on the security agenda of the Asia-Pacific is no doubt to a large extent caused by its inability to act as a political-strategic unit. Again, the EU's failure to be heard during the 2002 US–DPRK nuclear stand-off is one example of the relative weakness of the EU's political-strategic influence in China's home region. This does not mean that China neglects the EU as a partner. On the contrary, China is keen to establish co-operation with any states and international entities that are at least partially supportive of Chinese strategic goals. But Europe's closeness to Washington and its inability to manifest itself as a global strategic actor does imply that China does not see the EU as a reliable and trustworthy partner on strategic issues that it can co-operate with in preventing the consolidation of US hegemony. The strategic partnership between the EU and China is therefore likely to remain predominantly a talking club rather than a platform for joint political-strategic operations and initiatives. China's foreign policy is thus suitable for accommodating the EU as a strategic partner in words, but not in practice.

References

Biscop, S. (2005) *The European Security Strategy: a Global Agenda for Positive Power*, Aldershot: Ashgate.

European Commission (7 July 2006) 'EU Trade and Investment with China: Changes, Challenges and Choices', speech by P. Mandelson at the EU–China Conference, Brussels. Online. Available: http://ec.europa.eu/commission_barroso/mandelson/speeches_articles/sppm109_en.htm (accessed 23 June 2008).

European Commission (October 2006) 'Bilateral Trade Relations: China', Trade Issues. Online. Available: http://ec.europa.eu/comm/trade/issues/bilateral/countries/china/index_en.htm (accessed 23 June 2008).

Gill, B. (2007) *Rising Star: China's New Security Diplomacy*, Washington, DC: Brookings Institution Press.

Interview with Professor Niu Jun (13 November 2004), School of International Studies, Peking University, Beijing.

Interview with Chinese professor (7 October 2006), Beijing.

Interview with Chinese professor (6 November 2007), Beijing.

Interview with European Commission official (10 July 2006), Brussels.

Kang, D. C. (2003) 'Getting Asia wrong: the need for new analytical frameworks', *International Security* 27 (4): 57–85.

Kurlantzick, J. (2006) 'Beijing's Safari: China's Move into Africa and its Implications for Aid, Development, and Governance', Policy Outlook: China Program 29, Washington, DC: Carnegie Endowment for International Peace. Online. Available: www.carnegieendowment.org/publications/index.cfm?fa=view&id=18833&prog=zch (accessed 9 June 2008) and http://doc.cerium.ca/serv1/kurlantzick_outlook_africa2.pdf (accessed 21 September 2008).

Odgaard, L. (2007a) *The Balance of Power in Asia-Pacific Security: US–China Policies on Regional Order*, London: Routledge.

—— (2007b) 'China's Premature Rise to Great Power', Audit of the Conventional Wisdom, Cambridge, MA: Massachusetts Institute of Technology.

—— (2007c) 'China: Security co-operation with reservations', in E. Kirchner and J. Sperling (eds) *Global Security Governance: Competing Perceptions of Security in the Twenty-firstst Century*, London: Routledge.

Odgaard, L. and Biscop, S. (2007) 'The EU and China: partners in effective multilateralism?' in D. Kerr and L. Fei (eds) *The International Politics of EU–China Relations*, Oxford: Oxford University Press.

People's Daily (17 July 2001) 'China–Russia sign Good-neighborly Friendship, Co-operation Treaty'. Online. Available: http://english.people.com.cn/english/200107/16/eng20010716_75105.html (accessed 15 March 2008).

Ramachandran, S. (21 January 2006) 'China's pearl loses its luster', *Asia Times*. Online. Available: www.atimes.com/atimes/South_Asia/HA21Df03.html (accessed 24 January 2006) and http://intellibriefs.blogspot.com/2006/01/chinas-pearl-loses-its-luster.html (accessed 20 November 2008).

Ross, R. S. (July–September 2006) 'Balance of power politics and the rise of China: accommodation and balancing in East Asia', *Security Studies* 15 (3): 355–95.

Stähle, S. (September 2008) 'China's shifting attitude towards United Nations peacekeeping operations', *China Quarterly* 195: 631–55.

State Council Information Office (27 December 2004) 'China's National Defence in 2004', White Paper 2004. Online. Available: www.fas.org/nuke/guide/china/doctrine/natdef2004.htmlwww.fas.org/nuke/guide/china/doctrine/natdef2004.htm (accessed 23 November 2007).

Tull, D. M. (2006) 'China's engagement in Africa: scope, significance and consequences', *Journal of Modern African Studies* 14 (3): 459–79.

Velloor, R. (26 October 2004) 'India welcomes Myanmar ruler', *Straits Times*.

Xinhua (5 March 2006) 'China's defence budget to increase 14.7% in 2006', *People's*

Daily Online. Online. Available: http://english.peopledaily.com.cn/200603/05/ eng20060305_247883.html (accessed 15 January 2008).

Yahuda, M. (2003) 'Chinese dilemmas in thinking about regional security architecture', *Pacific Review* 16 (2): 189–206.

—— (2006) 'The limits of economic interdependence: Sino-Japanese relations', in A. I. Johnston and R. S. Ross (eds) *New Directions in the Study of China's Foreign Policy*, Stanford, CA: Stanford University Press.

14 The European Union as an important (low-profile) actor in the Israeli–Palestinian conflict

Michael Schulz

The European Union (EU) has increasingly become involved in the Israeli–Palestinian conflict since its initial first formal involvement in 1971. Despite this, it continuously has been seen as a marginal actor, compared not least with the US. However, the EU is by far the most important economic player for both Israel and the Palestinian self-rule areas in the West Bank and in the Gaza Strip, i.e. the Palestinian Authority. At the same time, the parties of the conflict have expressed a desire to have close linkage and healthy relations with the EU. Despite close linkages with the US, Israel's biggest trade partner is the EU, while the weak Palestinian economy has almost developed a dependence relation with the EU. The framework of the European neighbourhood policy that was initiated in early 2002 was aimed at securing that friendly associated neighbours would surround EU's new members.

Long before the EU's Security Strategy Paper of 2003, the EU's main strategy vis-à-vis the latter has mainly been to stimulate regional projects in their neighbourhood area, such as the Mediterranean, North Africa, the Middle East and the Caucasus. This in turn was built upon the EU Common Foreign and Security Policy (CFSP) from 1993. The Israeli–Palestinian conflict has had its security ramification beyond the Middle East region for a long time. Hence the EU saw the Barcelona process, that was launched in 1995, as to support and push the peace process between Israel and the Palestinians forward, but also develop closer relations with the Mediterranean neighbours (Tocci 2005; Gomez 2003). The EU has also paid more than half the money that was invested in the Oslo peace process between 1993 and 2000. Since the quartet of the UN, the US, Russia and the EU promoted the so-called 'road map', a stepwise plan for implementing a two-state solution, the EU has also increasingly become involved in hard security issues.

At the same time, the EU, due to its resource dependence on oil in particular has to consider the wider perspectives. On the one hand it needs to find a way to approach the Arab and North African world, as well as Turkey and Iran (in which its security and economic links are made functionally available). On the other, the EU also needs to find an approach vis-à-vis other external actors, not least the strategic partner US and the much less influential Japan, but also giant 'newcomers' like China and India which increasingly – due to their economic and developmental global expansion – have a resource need for oil.

Hence, in this chapter an evaluation of the EU's role in the Israeli–Palestinian conflict will follow, by investigating the EU's political visions, ambitions and strategies. More specifically the chapter dwells on both how EU actions can be linked to political consideration within the greater Middle East, and challengers from outside the region, as well as its direct actions vis-à-vis the conflict parties themselves.

One could argue that the EU, during the years 1987 to 2008, had three different periods to work with within a context in which the Israeli–Palestinian conflict has changed in pattern, scope and content on several occasions:

1   The first Palestinian uprising, *intifada*, 1987–93 (December 1990)
2   The Oslo Peace Process, 1993 (13 September) – 2000 (28 September)
3   The second Al-Aqsa *intifada*, 2000 (29 September) – 2008 (present)

Previous research

Previous studies of the EU's role in the Israeli–Palestinian conflict emphasise the weakness it has if compared with the US (Dachs and Peters 2005; Hollis 2004; Kemp 2003; Miller 2006; Tocci 2007). In line with these studies, it is the US that has the capacity to influence the parties. However, far less emphasis has been placed on analysing the EU's motives, strategies and concerns to be involved in the Israeli–Palestinian conflict. In contrast to the US, the Middle East is a close neighbour to Europe and therefore for the latter it has a different strategic position. EU actions in relation to the Israeli–Palestinian conflict have to be understood inside the framework of its political and economical ties with the Arab world, including Turkey and Iran. Furthermore, since China has become a global player, not least in Africa and to an increasing extent also in the Middle East, the EU feels challenged. The EU is usually seen as a soft player taking a strong normative position on human rights and democracy (Telò 2007: 297–326). The EU has been claimed to play, at best, an economic role by firstly supporting the peace process, and secondly by enlarging its economic co-operation with the Mediterranean and Middle Eastern neighbours, via the European Neighbourhood Policy (ENP) Action Plan, the Barcelona process, and so on (see Keukeleire and MacNaughton 2008; Telò 2007). It also has a number of free-trade agreements with individual Arab states, as well as with Israel (which is close to being a EU member state without being one).

Hence there is a research gap in understanding the EU's action towards the Israeli–Palestinian conflict and what implications it has for its relations in their neighbourhood regions, as well as towards global players within the greater Middle East.

The European Union's neighbourhood considerations

The EU action towards the Israeli–Palestinian conflict also has to be linked with the European Strategic Security Paper (ESS) of 2003, seen as an outcome of the post-11 September terror attacks on the US. The ESS emphasises three aspects; strengthening of a multilateral world order and international law, conflict prevention and civil co-operation, as well as inserting political pressure and the use of robust military intervention. However, an implementation strategy, as well as the interlink between the three aspects have, so far, been relatively vague (Faust and Messner 2005: 425).

Also, when applied to the Middle East, it becomes evident that these three aspects have no equal importance. When it comes to the military intervention aspect, the EU's military credibility has, so far, been low despite its involvement in the peacekeeping forces in the aftermath of the Hezbollah–Israel war. The EU's members' different strategies with respect to the US war on Iraq, as well as the violent aftermath of the American presence in the region, has further weakened the EU's military credibility, not least in the eyes of the Middle East and North African states. In addition, despite the US setback in Iraq and the wider Middle East, as well as in Afghanistan, the EU has very much adopted the same *Weltanschauung* (world view), as the US in its 'war on terror' (Joffé 2007: 266). Hence this further weakens the potential to intervene in the Israeli–Palestinian with, for instance, security forces that historically and categorically has been rejected by Israel when proposed as an option (mostly by the Palestinians and/or the Arab states).

Not only the parties themselves, but the Middle Easterners as well, perceive the US and the EU as strategic partners, despite the occasionally different views on how to handle the difficult security situations in Iraq and Afghanistan. Hence, on the one hand, the EU can see the transatlantic partnership as a division of labour, in which the US role is linked to its military presence in the Middle East, while the EU emphasises economic and cultural ties. On the other hand, the EU needs to develop healthy relations with the Middle Eastern partners, which means to offer as close relations as possible, in the spheres of economy, political and cultural co-operation, without making them full members (Biscop 2005).

The strategy that the EU has adopted is to push for a world regional order, built upon its link with international law. Hence, despite the setbacks of the Barcelona process, which was heavily linked to (the lack of) progress of the Israeli–Palestinian peace process, several more initiatives have been launched since then. The ENP has included Israel and the Palestinian Authority (PA) since 2004. At the same time the Mediterranean partnership plans have been challenged by Arab initiatives, exemplified by the Greater Arab Free Trade Area (GAFTA) (1997) and Agadir agreement, also called Mediterranean Arab Free Trade Area (MAFTA) (2004), as counterbalancing negative effects of free trade with the EU. Also, the US has come up with its plans to promote democracy and co-operation between the Arab states. They launched the Greater Middle East Initiative (GMEI) at the G-8 meeting in May 2008. It should be seen as Bush's forward 'strategy of freedom', but builds upon co-operation with the G-8 members.

Hence the EU cannot solely rely on its economic capacity and offers to the regional players in order to improve its role without considering the Middle Eastern needs as well. In a situation where US actions are seen with great scepticism, which strengthens negative images of the US, the EU has a challenging position. Further, the historical Arab world's persistent support for the Palestinian state-building ambitions forces the EU to carefully balance between the US's and Arab states' diverging positions. What further weakens a coherent EU CFSP implementation is the fact that the single EU member states are split in their position vis-à-vis the parties to the Israeli–Palestinian conflict, as well as in relation to the wider Middle Eastern context. However, there is increasing awareness that the solution of the Israeli–Palestinian conflict would have positive ramifications for the entire region, and the EU's possibility of securing its need of healthy neighbour relations.

On a closer look, historical records show that the EU has been firm in its position, at least at its rhetorical level. It has constantly given criticism of the lack of democratic capacity of the Palestinian Authority (PA), not least the underdeveloped judiciary. At the same time it underlines the need to establish a democratic Palestinian state. The EU – particularly during the al-Aqsa *intifada* requested the PA to do what it can in order to combat terrorism – requested it to halt missile launching on Israel from PA areas. Since Israel occupied the West Bank and the Gaza Strip, the EU has questioned Israeli settlement activities in the occupied territories, and the way Israel fought its 'war on terror' in the PA areas. The EU also criticised Israel's violation of international law, human rights and IHL, as well as its collective punishment of Palestinians by closing the PA areas, and its extra juridical assassination of Islamic militants (Tocci 2007: 102).

A further consideration is the increasing interest in the Middle East from new economic giants such as China and India. For instance, China's galloping oil dependence has led it to open up ties with both Iran and other less friendly Western-oriented regimes in the region, as well as in the African context. The dilemma the EU faces is how to continue to link much of its co-operation with the Middle East, as well as with other world regions, to human rights and democracy promotion issues in a situation when India, and to a much lesser extent China, request no conditionalities of the partners. Not surprisingly, the EU has been careful not to push these conditionalities in Asia, as seen for instance in its negotiations with ASEAN within the ASEM platform (Gaens 2008). At the same time, the Arab world, and even more so the Palestinians, who frame the Israeli–Palestinian conflict in justice terminology, perceive the EU's own flexible approach as double standards, increasing the EU's risk of eroding its third-party credibility.

The EU also has to convince Middle Eastern partners of becoming successful in their capacity to work with the second aspect of the CFSP linked to conflict prevention and civil co-operation. Moreover its reputation as third party in the Israeli–Palestinian conflict, as well as its credibility in the broader Middle East, is partly dependent on success in involvement in various ongoing missions also in other parts of the Islamic world. Operations that are part of the Transitional Government built up in Somalia, that was initiated in 2002, with a mediation mission with the Islamic courts could be a test case for EU involvement in so-called failed states. Success for EU mediation would improve its standing in the Islamic world, and more specifically in the Arab world (Raffaelli 2007: 121–7). One successful example is the Aceh–Indonesia case that can improve the EU stand in the Middle East as a different partner from the US (Braud and Grevi 2005). However, so far, the EU has not changed its strategies in the Israeli–Palestinian conflict. EU sticks to the so-called road map for peace, but has been relatively passive in direct interactions with the Israeli and Palestinian parties.

The European Union's direct involvement in the Israeli–Palestinian conflict

The EU has gradually stepped up its involvement as a third-party actor in the conflict since its formation. Before the Oslo Accord was signed in 1993 the EU was a passive actor, but during the Oslo peace process period, until September 2000, increased its involvement with building the Palestinian Authority, with particular emphasis on civil society. Since 2000 EU has emphasised that it needs to be involved also at the top-level scene, and it has even become directly involved in the so-called hard security issues, exemplified when the EU sent 7,000 troops under the UN umbrella to oversee the fragile cease-fire after the 2006 Hezbollah–Israel war. In 2005, through the EU Co-ordinating Office for Palestinian Policing Support (COPPS), also upgraded through a European Security and Defence Policy (ESDP), resulted in EU support to Palestinian police, as well as assisted with ESDP support at the Gaza Strip's entry at Rafah next to the Egyptian border (Tocci 2007: 114).

Historically, the EU was among the first to push for a compromise solution of the conflict. Already, in 1980, the Venice declaration of the nine members in the EC proposed a two-state solution, twenty-one years before a US President officially declared a similar solution, and twenty-two years before the Security Council adopted the principle. This principle has become a firm EU position, and particularly the Palestinian right to self-determination has been emphasised, not least in the important European Council meeting in Berlin 1999. The EU has since the 1990s placed much emphasis on becoming an important political player in the Israeli–Palestinian conflict. However, until the road map of 2002–03 was formulated, the EU was forced – due to the EU's clearer pro-Palestinian position, particularly in the eyes of the Israelis (Dachs and Peters 2005: 1–20; Dieckhoff 2005: 52–62), and the US's unwillingness to let the EU play an important role – to find alternative ways to become a player, or at least be allowed to participate in the process. Hence, despite the EU's historically sidelined role compared with the US, one can identify that the EU played an immensely important role, not least due to its economic contribution, but also its political and mediating role between Israeli and Palestinians, between the Arab states and Israel, as well as a diplomatic force balancing the US.

At Madrid in 1991, when a conference on Israel and its neighbours – co-sponsored by the US and USSR – started, the EU was very much sidelined and marginalised. In practice, the process became an American 'high politics' affair in the different bilateral tracks,[1] in which the EU only was allowed to participate in the multilateral track (dealing with economics, the environment, refugees, arms control and water), and this due to its experience on economic integration. Hence the idea was to let the EU spur regional integration ideas among the Middle Eastern parties.

When Israel and the Palestine Liberation Organisation (PLO) signed the Norwegian-brokered Declaration of Principle in September 1993, the EU immediately came to the fore as an economic provider for the forthcoming Palestinian Authority (PA) that was established in July 1994. More then 50 percent of the international community's assistance came from the EU and Norway, and the EU gave grants and loans up to €3.47 billion during the period 1994–2001 (Dieckhoff 2005: 55).

During the entire Oslo peace process, that finally collapsed with the eruption of violence in September 2000, when the so-called al-Aqsa *intifada* started, the EU made several attempts to play a more important role as mediator between the parties. EU's special envoy, Miguel Moratinos, made several attempts to influence the Israeli government under Benyamin Nethanyahu, in which the idea was to improve Palestinian access to external markets, unblocking the Israeli restriction on free movement, as well as promoting new border-based industrial projects (Gomez 2003: 138).

Similarly, the EU's attempts to press Israel to halt its efforts to build new settlements in the Jaba Abu Ghneim/Har Homa area outside Jerusalem was in line with a strategy to find new EU diplomatic initiatives. However, the EU could not bring Israel to change its policy, not least due to US backing of Israeli positions. The EU position became more clear by underlining the need to go along with a two-state solution based on the UN Security Council resolutions 242 and 338. Hence, the EU could be seen as taking a pre-diplomatic role, thereby many times preparing the political ground, which the US or the parties themselves were able to launch. Hence the EU, despite its low-profile role, has had an immensely important role in the long-run developments of the conflict (resolution) developments.

Indeed, in accordance with previous positions from 1980, in 2003 the EU, along with Russia, the UN and the US, proposed the so-called road map for peace, suggesting the implementation of a stepwise schedule towards a two-state solution. This is still the formal proposal that the Bush administration had as the basic platform, and also from which the Annapolis negotiations started at the end of 2007, aiming at an overall final peace agreement in December 2008. However, few believed that this was a realistic timetable, not least due to several setbacks in the negotiations, as well as due to political rivalry and challenges from oppositions among the parties themselves.

Again, the EU could be seen as serving a role to balance the American position vis-à-vis the parties. Its economic ties with the parties, as well as with many other players in the Middle East region, can, in the long run, serve the EU. However, despite the ambition to create a larger momentum, via the 1995 Barcelona process, and the various following Mediterranean Partnership strategies from the beginning of the twenty-first century, the soured political relations between Israelis and Palestinians clearly showed how these initiatives came to a halt. Hence the EU has, so far, not successfully played a diplomatic political role that can shift the positions of the parties towards a more viable peace process, in which the parties search for a compromise solution. So far, too obviously, the US has much more room for manoeuvre in relation to both Israelis and Palestinians.

The stalemate between the Hamas and the Fateh movements in the Palestinian Authority (PA) has, however, created a difficult diplomatic situation. The EU boycott of Hamas, in which Hamas since 2003 is considered as a terrorist organisation, has given few possibilities for the EU to act. With Hamas's election victory the EU could have played an important mediating role between the polarised Israel–US positions and the Hamas position. In line with Israel and the US, the EU requested that Hamas recognise Israel's right to exist, renounce all use of violence against Israel, and accept the previous agreements of the PLO/PA and Israel. Without downplaying the responsibility of Hamas's slow political, and often contradictory vocal actions during the spring of 2006, one can argue that several attempts to approach these requests were made, but not considered by the EU (Tamimi 2007; Gunning 2008). Instead, the EU quickly left the option of direct talks with Hamas, and sided with the Israeli/US boycott, thereby also risking to push Hamas away from compromise solutions. Further, the EU missed an opportunity to play a mediating role after Fateh and Hamas signed the 'Mecca Agreement' of 9 February 2007 (Mecca Agreement 2007). In this agreement, the parties stipulated the division of power and government seats between Fateh, Hamas and the other political factions. However, Hamas declared its readiness to *respect* the previous agreements between PLO/PA and Israel. De facto, a cease-fire was held by Hamas since 2005, and was ready to prolong this cease-fire for several years ahead. Furthermore, in its documents from 2005, Hamas had the intention to join the PLO itself, which furthermore would indicate its readiness to accept the two-state formula (Schulz 2007; Hroub 2006).

The EU also saw its chance to get involved in the Oslo process by constituting one of the most important donors to the majority of the Palestinian

NGOs. The EU had a rather passive role in relation to the Palestinian NGO sector but did vocally encourage NGOs that systematically allowed and promoted an Israeli–Palestinian dialogue as a way to move the peace process forward. The EU had such a low profile during this period and could hence avoid becoming subject to criticism by hardliners on either side. Also, the EU did not become involved with the Hamas and Islamic Jihad civil society sector, with which it had no relations during the entire peace process between 1993 and 2000, or after.

The EU did not know where to place the Islamic movements in terms of civil society. Despite the often taken-for-granted perception that Islam is incompatible with democracy, and basically the counter-structure of a civil society, such is not necessarily the case. The form of social infrastructure and networking established by Islamist organisations might themselves serve as a catalyst for more participatory politics. Islamic institution-building and networking in the form of schools, mosques, health clinics, kindergartens, charities, sports clubs, choirs, computer centres, etc., are a form of mobilisation from below, although there are also instrumental reasons behind them. With these kinds of networks, a sort of parallel institution-building has taken place in Palestinian society.

Before Hamas won the elections in 2006, instead of acting as an independent, autonomous sphere side by side with the state-in-the-making, the PA, Islamist institution-building aspired to establish a space in order to challenge the Arafat-led PA. However, the kind of social work and grass-roots mobilisation that is provided by this kind of organisation should be included in the perceptions of civil society. EU's non-contact with the Islamist NGO sector has created a situation in which it becomes difficult to build peace from below, where many EU supported (and 'secular' donor-driven) NGO organisations failed to meet the needs of the weakest part of the Palestinian society.

Many have argued that the first uprising, the *intifada*, breaking out in December 1987, implied a breakthrough in the conflict. The media coverage (including media from Europe) of the Palestinian uprising implied a great political impact both on the domestic and international arenas. In 1986 an Israeli law had been passed that prohibited any Israeli citizen to engage in talks with the PLO. In the Palestinian society, the first *intifada* was seen as support for the PLO, a public resistance against the Israeli occupation and a struggle to gain Palestinian national recognition. There were thus no discussions at official level. There were, however, a number of track-two initiatives. The *intifada*, a mass-based uprising, implied new self-esteem and political pride among the Palestinians. To the Israeli Labour Party, the uprising proved the impossibility of continued occupation, and there was a growing sentiment in Israeli society that the status quo could not be maintained. After the Iraq–Kuwait war in 1991 the first official negotiations between Israel and all its bordering Arab neighbours, including the Palestinians, took place at the Madrid conference. Many of the Palestinians that participated in these official talks (although as members of a joint Jordanian–Palestinian delegation) had previously engaged in civil society meetings between Israelis and Palestinians. Many of these meetings took place in various places in Europe. Hence, during that period, the EU took the role as being a 'host' for (often secret) unofficial, so-called Track 2 initiatives. Civil society, as well as individuals, began to discuss ways how Israelis and Palestinians could meet and engage in discussions on future solutions. These unofficial (meaning associated people to the top leaders) or citizen diplomacy (meaning grass-roots initiatives between conflicting parties) efforts were relatively few but increased in number.

The signing of the Declaration of Principle – the result of secret negotiations in Oslo – signified the starting point of a new era. The peace process implied a new role for civil society. A 'peace industry' mushroomed in which the EU played a major role. The Oslo peace process was seen, primarily by the donor community, as a post-conflict phase where social reconstruction of Palestinian society and Israeli–Palestinian relations should be emphasised. Political interests of the international community in participating in the Palestinian Israeli peace process basically invaded the area and the local NGO sector. Among other initiatives, 'people-to-people' programmes were an attempt to strengthen co-operation between Israeli and Palestinian organisations through international aid. Also, think-tank constructs became replicated and the NGOs that were involved with the major conflicting issues (Jerusalem, Palestinian refugees, final status, Israeli settlement, etc.) produced similar output. In fact, donors developed a contributing role while the NGOs focused on fund-raising strategies. Hence little attention was paid to co-ordination between donors and NGOs. Identifying the real need as well as following up, evaluating and monitoring became less of a priority.

Many NGO activities came to an abrupt end with the eruption of the al-Aqsa *intifada*. The collapse of NGO initiatives for peace had to do with the impact of the overall conflict, the issue of normalisation, the withdrawal of funding of many NGO activities, the inability of the donor communities to find functional ways in the conflict zones, as well as the unpreparedness of the NGOs to cope with the changes on the ground.

Atieh *et al.* (2005) gave five reasons for the failure of the people-to-people programmes. (1) The programmes focused on the individual and did not affect the perceptions that participants held of the others nation. (2) The programmes failed to reach important sections of society. (3) They ignored the socio-economic disparities between Israelis and Palestinians. (4) They placed too much focus on joint activities rather than inter-communal dialogue. (5) The programmes implied an overly static view, with little reflection about the future or the painful past.

Supporting these arguments is the fact that many of these programmes were not based on long-term interaction between the participants. Meetings of short duration and with limited space available for the airing of issues related to the past and the future are difficult to assess and evaluate in terms of long-term impact and sustainability. Similarly, Abu Nimer found – in six different Israeli Jewish–Israeli Arab contact programmes – that 'for most participants this remained a "fun" experience that did not reach beyond spending "good" time with friends' (Abu-Nimer 1999: 127). The EU made an external evaluation of these activities and came to the conclusion that the programmes were inefficient and therefore should not be supported any longer. However, due to the breakdown of peace initiatives, particularly in Track 1 and Track 2, paradoxically, there was an even more acute need for citizen diplomacy and NGO initiatives than before. The withdrawal of the EU from these activities not only missed an opportunity to continue to build peace capacities with the civil society sectors, but also contributed to the collapse of important peace initiatives from below. Instead of asking how one could cope with the problems identified above as causes to the collapsed initiatives, the EU simply saw these activities as dysfunctional and not useful, and stopped spending money on them. The entire peace camp became paralysed, on both sides, as well as marginalised, making it thorny for the remaining NGOs that were working with peace issues.

The negative changes on the ground had also an impact on public opinion. Until now (May 2008) the EU has not used or developed an opinion-building strategy vis-à-vis the public in Israeli and Palestinian societies. The Israeli and Palestinian publics have quit divergent opinions about the EU role in the conflict. Although occasionally they agree to the fact that the EU is a weak diplomatic player and could do more, it is always a judgement in relation to their own situation, and not to the overall situation. Hence Israelis have been increasingly worried about the EU barometers that show that Europeans are reluctant to see Israel's actions, such as extra-juridical killings of Islamist leaders (Hamas, Islamic Jihad), air strikes in positions in Gaza, or military incursions into the West Bank, as justified. Particularly concern came with the November 2003 Euro-barometer that indicates that Europeans considered Israel to be the greatest threat to world peace. Europeans are seen as pro-Palestinian as well as pro-Arab in their attitude to the conflict. Paradoxically, a year later, a majority of Israelis claimed their readiness to become part of the EU (Tocci 2007: 115), which indicates that the EU still has a strong standing in Israel despite its favourable position vis-à-vis the Palestinian position. Despite its verbal criticism of Israeli actions against the PA and Hamas during the al-Aqsa *intifada* the EU has never used any boycott pressure on Israel. No real protest over the destruction of EU-funded PA institutions, buildings and infrastructure was followed up by trade boycotts (Tocci 2007).

The Palestinians regard the Europeans as weak, unwilling to challenge Israel and the US. They claim that the EU, with its strong economic ties with Israel, could do much better. Although they recognise that several single players within the EU are sympathetic they still are to weak in order to make a difference. With the boycott of the democratically elected Hamas government many Palestinians consider the Europeans to apply double standards. Palestinians, generally, feel that the EU follows the US and Israeli line despite vocally supporting the Palestinian position.

Conclusion

In line with previous research one could claim that, historically, the EU has been a weak second-range player in the Israeli–Palestinian conflict. The US still is the most important actor vis-à-vis the Israelis and the Palestinians. However, it is also true that the EU has counterbalanced the American position, seen as pro-Israeli, by putting forward also the needs of the Palestinians. The Israeli leadership as well as Palestinian leadership also accepts the road map for peace, which is the political platform for how the EU, the US, the UN and the Russians jointly are working towards the implementation of a two-state solution. Hence the EU has played an important role, not least at the grass-roots level and NGO sectors, as balancing positions, as well as preparing the ground for a shift in positions.

Due to its oil dependence, its need to avoid increased terror from organisations such as al-Qaida, the EU has to reconsider its position within the broader Middle East. Due to the US's decreasing reputation as an honest broker, not least due to its action in Iraq, the strategic alliance with the US has to be carefully balanced vis-à-vis Arab needs, since most parties in the Arab world support the Palestinian position. Hence EU upgrading of its role in the Israeli–Palestinian conflict is likely to follow.

In conclusion, the EU could play a very important role in the conflict developments by taking a more active diplomatic mediating role, as well as use its economic power if needed. This requires also a more united CFSP among its members. Finally, the EU could restart a more careful but important support to civil society, and the grass-roots levels. In comparison with the US, the EU is much better equipped for that role, and could thereby contribute to gradually build the much needed compromise willingness among both Israelis and Palestinians.

Note

1 The bilateral tracks at Madrid consisted of one Israeli–Lebanese, one Israeli–Syrian and one Israeli–Jordanian. The Palestinian representatives were included in the Jordanian delegation; however, in practice an Israeli–Palestinian track soon evolved as well.

References

Abu-Nimer, M. (1999) *Dialogue, Conflict Resolution, and Change: Arab–Jewish Encounters in Israel*, Albany, NY: State University of New York Press.

Aoun, E. (2003) 'European foreign policy and the Arab–Israeli dispute: much ado about nothing?' *European Foreign Affairs Review* 8: 289–312.

Asmu, R. D. and Jackson, B. P. (2005) 'Does Israel belong in the EU and NATO?' *Policy Review*, February–March, pp. 47–56.

Atieh, A., Ben-Nun, G., El Shahed, G., Taha, R. and Tulliu, S. (2005) 'Peace in the Middle East: P2P and the Israeli–Palestinian Conflict', UNIDIR/2004/33, Geneva: United Nations.

Biscop, S. (2005), 'The European Security Strategy and the Neighbourhood Policy: a new Starting Point for a Euro-Mediterranean Security Partnership', conference paper presented at EUSA IX Biennial International Conference, Austin, TX, 31 March–2 April. Online. Available: http://aei.pitt.edu/2984/02/Paper_EUSA_ESS-EMP.doc (accessed 15 September 2008).

Braud, P. A. and Grevi, G. (2005) 'The EU mission in Aceh', Occasional Paper 61, Paris: EU Institute of Security Studies. Online. Available: http://aei.pitt.edu/5735/01/occ61.pdf (accessed 15 September 2008).

Dachs, G. and Peters, J. (2005) 'Israel and Europe, the Troubled Relationship: between Perception and Reality', paper presented at the Centre for the Study of European Politics and Society. Online. Available: http://hsf.bgu.ac.il/europe/index.aspx?pgid=pg_1277842633616617872 (accessed 15 August 2008).

Del Sarto, R. A. (2007) 'Wording and meaning(s): EU–Israel political co-operation according to the ENP action plan', *Mediterranean Politics* 12 (1): 59–75.

Dieckhoff, A. (2005) 'The European Union and the Israeli–Palestinian conflict', *Journal Inroads* 16: 52–62. Online. Available: http://iab.sagepub.com/cgi/pdf_extract/57/1/94 (accessed 10 August 2008).

Eurobarometer: Online. Available: http://ec.europa.eu/public_opinion/index_en.htm (accessed 26 October 2008).

European Community (1980) 'The Venice Declaration of 1980'. Online. Available: domino.un.org/unispal.NSF/d80185e9f0c69a7b85256cbf005afeac/fef015e8b1a1e5a685256d810059d922!OpenDocument (accessed 26 October 2008).

Faust, J. and Messner, D. (2005) 'Europe's new security strategy: challenges for development policy', *European Journal of Development Research* 17 (3): 423–36. Online. Available: www.ingentaconnect.com/content/routledg/edr/2005/00000017/00000003/art00006 (accessed 27 November 2008).

Gaens, B. (ed.) (2008) *Europe–Asia Interregional Relations: a Decade of ASEM*, Aldershot: Ashgate.

Gertz, B. (17 January 2005) 'China builds up strategic sea lanes', *Washington Times.*

Gomez, R. (2003) *Negotiating the Euro-Mediterranean Partnership: Strategic Action in EU Foreign Policy?* Aldershot: Ashgate.

Gunning, J. (2008) *Hamas in Politics: Democracy, Religion and Violence*, New York: Columbia University Press.

Hollis, R. (2004) 'The Israeli–Palestinian road block: can Europeans make a difference?' *International Affairs* 2 (2004): 191–201.

Hroub, K. (2006) 'A "New Hamas" through its new documents', *Journal of Palestine Studies* 35 (4): 6–27.

Joffé, G. H. (2007) 'The EU and the Mediterranean: open regionalism and peripheral dependence?' in M. Telò (ed.) *European Union and New Regionalism: Regional Actor and Global Governance in a Post-hegemonic Era*, Aldershot: Ashgate.

Kemp, G. (2003) 'Europe's Middle East Challenges', *Washington Quarterly* 27 (1): 163–177.

Keukeleire, S. and MacNaughtan, J. (2008) *The Foreign Policy of the European Union*, Basingstoke: Palgrave/Macmillan.

'Mecca Agreement' (2007). Online. Available: www.khaleejtimes.com/DisplayArticleNew.asp?xfile=data/middleeast/2007/February/middleeast_February141.xml&section=middleeast&col (accessed 21 November 2008).

Miall, H., Ramsbotham, O. and Woodhouse, T. (1999) *Contemporary Conflict Resolution*, Cambridge: Polity Press.

Miller, R. (2006) 'Troubled neighbours: the EU and Israel', *Israel Affairs* 12 (4): 642–64.

Mohamed, R. (1992) 'The US–PLO Dialogue: the Swedish connection', *Journal of Palestine Studies* 21 (4): 54–66. Palestinian Center for Policy and Survey Research. Online. Available: www.pcpsr.org/survey/polls/2007 (accessed 26 October 2008).

Raffaelli, M. (2007) 'The EU in Somalia: furthering peacemaking and reconciliation', *International Spectator* 42 (1): 121–7.

Schulz, M. (2007) 'Hamas between Sharia rule and democracy', in S. Ashok, R. Amer and J. Öjendal (eds) *Globalization and Challenges to Building Peace*, London: Anthem Press.

Shlaim, A. (2005) 'Europe and the Israeli–Palestinian Conflict', Oxford Research Group, Occasional Paper, February. Online. Available: www.oxfordresearchgroup. org.uk/publications/briefing_papers/online/israel-palestineonline.php (accessed 26 October 2008).

Smith, K. E. (2007) 'Promoting peace in the backyard?' *International Spectator* 42 (4): 594–6.

Tamimi, A. (2007) *Hamas: Unwritten Chapters*, London: Hurst.

Telò, M. (ed.) (2007) *European Union and New Regionalism: Regional Actors and Global Governance in a Post-hegemonic Era*, Aldershot: Ashgate.

Tocci, N. (2005) 'Conflict resolution in the neighbourhood: comparing EU involvement in Turkey's Kurdish question and in the Israeli–Palestinian conflict', *Mediterranean Politics* 10 (2): 25–146.

—— (2007) *The EU and Conflict Resolution: Promoting Peace in the Backyard*, London and New York: Routledge.

Conclusion
From a global security triangle to a normative international society?

Valeria Bello and Belachew Gebrewold

The present situation

The Global Security Triangle, as the interaction between Europe, Asia and Africa has been called, is a complex governance system of external relations, including different and sometimes contradictory elements, confronted by many exigencies, but, nevertheless, a system of global governance which is indeed emerging within international relations. As it is a complex situation, one needs to schematise it in order to understand its peculiarities, and we will do so by distinguishing the strategies of the most important actors.

As far as the EU is concerned, its normative approach in external relations is confirmed; the EU suggests common rules and uses formal agreements, preferring multilateral and particularly regional co-operation. However, when it has to deal with difficult situations, mainly when it intervenes in hostile situations, the EU proves to be firstly minded to maintain peace and stability, avoiding dangers for its main partnerships. In general, the EU is inclined to the use of soft power, and this is apparent even when conceiving appropriate responses to threats (see Chapter 2).

Africa and the Asian regions are shown to be willing to follow the EU in its attempts to address global challenges normatively, despite the fact that sometimes this proves to be difficult, for different reasons. In general, Africa's confidence in the EU is still undermined by the legacy of colonialism (see Chapter 7) and this feeling has been exacerbated by the EU's double standards, especially when discussing tariff and non-tariff barriers, particularly in the agricultural sector.

Africa–EU relations have indeed suffered from the legacy of colonialism and the resulting prejudices on both sides. The EU has long treated the AU as a minor and immature partner, at least until the new joint EU–Africa Strategy, while African countries still consider the EU's position to be quite ambivalent, due largely to the fact that the EU did not work towards a positive end to the Doha round, despite its declarations that it would do all it could to help Africa's development. Africa is particularly dissatisfied about non-tariff barriers, which it considers to be purely a product of the EU's intention to protect its economic interests, above all in the agricultural sector. In fact, non-tariff barriers serve the EU's wish to protect political and social rights, and the environment (not only within its own territory) as well as its economic interests. As mentioned in Chapter 3, these barriers are the result of the EU's attempts to protect its own identity. However, this is a critical point in its relations with Africa.

Nevertheless, Africa has been able to increase its role at the international level, partly due to the growing involvement of China in the region (see Chapters 3, 7 and 13), but also as a result of EU support for its regional integration process, which has made significant progress in recent years. This has definitely impressed African countries positively.

While it was thought that Asia's collaboration would be difficult to obtain, particularly in relation to the social and environmental clauses and political conditionality (especially on the human rights issue), it has proved to be much easier than expected for the EU, because Asia is generally keen to imitate Europe, and because of the importance of the EU market for China and most other Asian countries.

Asia considers the EU to be a successful integration model, thus it is willing to follow Europe and collaborate in global governance. Less predictably, China appears to be willing to work in partnership with Europe and to collaborate in multilateral activities. However (as shown in Chapters 1, 4, 5, 7, 9 and 13), China is not completely reliable on this point; whenever it feels its interests are threatened it acts unilaterally.

The Chinese case shows us that the EU is far from being an independent actor on considerable strategic and security issues; in the Democratic Republic of Congo, even though the EU has intervened extensively both military and economically, as Belachew Gebrewold illustrates in Chapter 5, it has not played a decisive role, because of the inconsistency and incoherence of its member states, which have not been able to put aside their shortsighted national interests.

The inconsistency and incoherence of EU member states is also a problem when speaking about human rights issues and other fundamental freedoms, as pointed out in Bello's Chapter 3. This decreases the EU's credibility vis-à-vis its normative approach to international relations. If the EU talks to the AU and ASEAN about security and terrorism, using phrases like 'mutual recognition of cultures' and 'respect for diversity', how can these words be trusted, and how can the EU be effective in its search for security, when member states undermine its discourse through their actions? The EU must first obtain respect for its values and principles on the part of its members if it wants to be considered seriously in the international arena as an advocate of these issues.

The same can be said about the EU's energy and immigration policies. Both issues should be addressed seriously; immigration policies of EU member states should be in line with European common ethical principles and by including migration policy in the community pillar (see Chapter 6); and energy through the diversification of energy sources, with an increase in the development and use of renewable energy. The EU Commission outlined this necessity in 2007 (see Chapter 10). Unfortunately, European member states have not taken this assessment into due consideration. In general 'the EU is handicapped by the same limits and difficulties it has in the wider field of foreign and security policy: it is not a unitary actor and is still characterised by the diversity of its member states' positions on major international issues' (Chapter 11).

These problems excepted, the EU regional integration model is successful in African and Asian eyes (see Chapters 1 and 9); both areas appear to be willing to follow its example and seem to prefer global governance to anarchic relations. And there are reasons to believe that China will do the same, if doing so proves beneficial to its interests. China will never take part in a regional integration process, because of its size, but will use multilateralism rather than unilateralism, whenever it considers this will serve its purposes (Chapter 13). This means that China is actually following the EU's example. Several case studies in this volume have demonstrated that 'the EU attempted to act on the basis of ideals without setting aside the most essential rule of *Realpolitik*. It brought normative pressure to bear and at the same time felt obliged to maintain the regional power balance that promised to secure political stability' (Chapter 8: 146). 'As the Iranian case shows, despite some important assets at its disposal and the undoubted value of its "comprehensive engagement" approach, Europe as a "civilian power" has to overcome major constraints which significantly restrict its capacity to play a major role' (Chapter 11: 186). In any case, as Pelinka outlines:

> the need to implement the concept of the CFSP [...] will increase. This would enable the EU to act in the same league as the US, Russia, China, Japan – and India. This would fill the gap between the as yet unused potential the EU has in international politics and the reality defined by the absence of a coherent EU policy in most of the cases – from Iraq to Iran, from the reform of the UN Security Council to the conflict between Israel and the Palestinians.
>
> (Chapter 12: 213)

So, what can we predict from these analyses? Is it possible to depict future scenarios? We think so.

Future scenarios

Strangely, it is not Africa or China menacing European values and interests, but Europe itself. If the EU member states – and the EU itself – do not proclaim, clearly and unequivocally, that the European social model is still alive and still makes sense, it will not be possible to explain its motives for the imposition of political and social clauses in its international agreements. If member states do not respect human rights within their own boundaries, whether of their own or of foreign citizens, the request for similar respect in other regions appears illusory. Furthermore, the role of civil society should be extended in co-operation agreements, and should be a necessary requirement, like the social and political clauses. The EU has not always recognised – or has underestimated – the important role which civil society has played in difficult situations (see Chapter 14 on the Middle East). Encouraging the involvement of civil society could well work in the EU's favour; civil society and citizens are much better disposed to the EU than politicians, as noted by Kohnert, and not only in Africa (see Chapter 3). Therefore, an increasing involvement of civil society could pave the way to the establishment of a normative international society. Two scenarios are thus possible, considering current interactions.

The first scenario is one in which the EU continues to be noncommittal with member states, and shy in promoting its values when discussing economic and social models internationally. In this scenario, if the EU does not intervene firmly, those European member states which have already proved to be only weakly committed to the norms and democratic ideals of the EU will be the first to abandon the European social model. The EU has the opportunity to affirm its values and insist on their being respected because European member states have no chance alone in a globalised world run by great powers (and we should never forget that, in the past, this impossible search for power led weakly democratic European countries to commit great atrocities). If the EU started to assert itself and its values the second scenario might actually be realised.

This second scenario is the development of a normative international society, a new era for international relations. The EU, as pacesetter, with Africa and Asia, and the US – considering President Obama's intention to change the course of US policy – can together transform the anarchic international arena – where states compete – into a global *agora*, where problems are solved and not created.

Index

www.ingramcontent.com/pod-product-compliance
Ingram Content Group UK Ltd.
Pitfield, Milton Keynes, MK11 3LW, UK
UKHW020859280225
455677UK00006B/97